SCIENCE
DICTIONARY

SEYMOUR SIMON

DOVER PUBLICATIONS, INC.
MINEOLA, NEW YORK

To my grandchild,
Joel Fauteux Simon,
and all other grandchildren to come,
both mine and others,
I dedicate this book with joy.

Bibliographical Note

This Dover edition, first published in 2012, is an updated
and expanded version of the edition originally published by
HarperCollins Publishers, New York, in 1994.

International Standard Book Number

ISBN-13: 978-0-486-48865-3
ISBN-10: 0-486-48865-9

Manufactured in the United States by Courier Corporation
48865901
www.doverpublications.com

Contents

Acknowledgments

I want to thank my collaborator and editor Liz Nealon for the enormous task she undertook of organizing the entries in the book, identifying which new words needed entries, which entries needed updating and revision, and which entries needed to be eliminated or combined. She is also the person responsible for doing the photo research and selection. Without her wonderful work and efforts, the new edition of this book would not have been possible.

I want to also thank Jason Schneider and Suzanne E. Johnson who worked professionally and with great care on the new edition of this book.

The writing, checking, editing, illustrating, and production of the original publication of this book by HarperCollins required the help and cooperation of a great number of people. Their efforts were prodigious, thoughtful, and caring. I want to thank them all. The good results I share with them; the errors are all mine. I want especially to thank Linda Zuckerman, my first editor on this book at HarperCollins. Without her efforts, this book never would have seen the light of day. I also especially want to thank Kathy Zoehfeld, at that time an editor at HarperCollins, who took over the enormous job of seeing the book to completion. Katherine Tegen, my senior editor at HarperCollins at that time, also was responsible for the supervision of this book.

My friends, Dr. Sheldon Aronson, former Professor of Biology, Queens College, CUNY, and Dr. Alfred B. Bortz, formerly at the College of Education, Duquesne University, checked every definition in the book. Two other people contributed greatly to the book: Joel Honig, my etymologist, and my copyeditor, Renee Cafiero. Thank you all. I also want to thank the people at Oxprint and Oxford Illustrators Ltd. They were very patient and understanding. Finally, on a personal note, I want to thank my late agent, Claire M. Smith of Harold Ober Associates and my current agent Wendy Schmalz.

Introduction

Your life is filled with science. The sun comes up in the morning; the weather is cloudy or bright, rainy or snowy; you eat breakfast and your body digests what you eat; you walk to school or take a bus; you work with a computer; you play a game with a ball that bounces in a certain way; the sun goes down at night and the stars come out; you watch television or listen to music from a tape or disk; and you set your alarm and go to sleep. Almost you do can be understood and explained by science.

Science is one way of knowing about the world and the universe—even when it doesn't seem to make sense. Think about it. Does it make sense that blue and yellow paint mixed together turns green? That we live on a round planet that is spinning quickly, but that to us, the earth looks flat and doesn't seem to be moving? And that people don't even fall off the other side? Does it make sense that a magnet attracts some metals but not others? That there are as many stars in the Milky Way galaxy as there are grains of sand on an ocean beach? That the nearest star beyond the sun is so far away that traveling at the speed of a jet plane it would still take a million years to get there?

There are too many things to make sense of all at once, so scientists try to examine and understand small pieces of our surroundings one at a time. Geologists study mountains and valleys, minerals and rocks. Biologists study animals and plants, people and their surroundings. Chemists study atoms and molecules, and the ways they group together. Physicists study matter and energy, motion and what makes things move.

Each of these major sciences can be broken down into hundreds or even thousands of specialized fields, such as anatomy, astronomy, botany, meteorology, paleontology, and zoology. In many advanced scientific studies, specialized words and symbols and the language of mathematics are often used. These are not easy to understand by people who are not in that scientific field. But like any foreign language, science can be translated into ideas and concepts that use simple

English words. And when we understand these words and concepts, the beauty and magnificence of science can be shared by everyone.

That's what this science dictionary is all about. We have tried to use simple, everyday words in our definitions and explanations. Each word was chosen because it is used in one or more of today's sciences. If the word has both a scientific and an everyday meaning, we have included only the scientific meaning. We have also included the names of many important scientists and explained their discoveries. Science is finally and always about discovery. Sir Isaac Newton, one of the greatest scientists who ever lived, explained it this way:

"I do not know what I may appear to the world, but to myself I seem to have been only a boy playing on the sea-shore, and diverting myself in now and then finding a smoother pebble or a prettier shell than ordinary, whilst the great ocean of truth lay all undiscovered before me."

—SEYMOUR SIMON

SCIENCE
DICTIONARY

abacus A frame with sliding beads used as a counting device. The use of the abacus dates back to early Greek and Roman times. The abacus is still used in Eastern countries such as China and Japan. [*Abacus* is a Latin word that comes from a Greek word meaning "board."]

abdomen 1. ANATOMY. The part of a human or animal body that contains the stomach and the intestines. 2. ZOOLOGY. The last of three sections of the bodies of most insects and other jointed-leg animals.

absolute zero A temperature so cold that it can only be approached, never reached. Absolute zero is –273.16° C or –459.69° F. At absolute zero, molecular motion nearly stops. Scientists have been able to lower the temperature of an object to within a few millionths of a degree of absolute zero.

absorb To take in or soak up something. [*Absorb* comes from a Latin word meaning "to swallow up."]

acceleration Any change in the speed or direction of a moving object. Also, the rate of change of velocity (speed with direction) of an object. The acceleration of a falling body due to the pull of the Earth's gravity is about 32 feet per second for each second it falls. An accelerometer is a device used to measure acceleration.

[*Acceleration* comes from a Latin word meaning "to speed up."]

Achilles tendon The tendon that connects the calf muscle of the leg to the heel bone. Achilles was the hero of *The Iliad*, a poem written by the early Greek poet Homer. Achilles was unprotected only in the heel. An "Achilles' heel" has come to mean a small but important weakness.

achromatic lens A compound lens used in telescopes and cameras that gives a clear image without fuzzy color fringes around the edges. [*Achromatic* comes from a Greek word meaning "colorless."]

acid A substance that produces hydrogen ions (H+) when dissolved in water. Acids turn a specially treated paper called litmus from blue to red. A strong acid, such as sulfuric or nitric acid, can burn the skin and can eat away the strongest metals. Other acids, such as citric acid in oranges and lemons and acetic acid in vinegar are harmless. Still others, such as ascorbic acid (vitamin C), are used by the body.

acid rain A form of pollution caused by the large-scale burning of nitrogen- and sulfur-rich fuels such as coal, gasoline, and diesel oil. The weak acids that form in rainwater as a result can cause death to many kinds of water plants and animals.

acne   An inflammation of the oil glands in the skin causing pus pimples, mostly on the face.

acoustics   The science of sound. Also, the qualities of a room, microphone, or speaker that affect the sound you hear.

activate   To start or speed up a reaction by different methods such as heating or adding a chemical called a catalyst.

Adam's apple   A bulge at the front of a person's neck formed by a protrusion in the cartilage tube in the throat. The Adam's apple moves when swallowing.

Adapt   To change in ways that help a living thing to better survive in its surroundings. [*Adapt* comes from a Latin word meaning "to fit."]

adaptation   The change that takes place over a number of generations in an animal or a plant which increases its chances of survival. A seal's thick fur is an example of an adaptation to a cold environment.

adhesion   The force that attracts molecules of unlike substances to each other. When you write with pencil on paper, graphite particles stick to the paper because of adhesion between the molecules of graphite and paper.

adolescence   In humans, the time of life between childhood and maturity. [*Adolescence* comes from a Latin word meaning "growing up."]

adrenal glands   In animals with backbones, the two endocrine glands, one above each kidney. The adrenal glands produce the hormone adrenaline together with a smaller amount of noradrenaline. The two hormones are chemically similar. The outer wall of the adrenals also produces cortisone and other hormones.

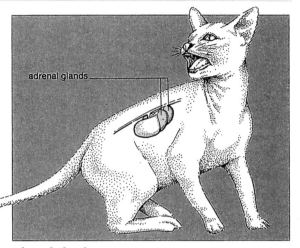

adrenal glands

adrenaline   A hormone produced by the adrenal glands. It speeds up the pumping of the heart and increases the flow of blood to the muscles and brain. In humans, adrenaline is present in large amounts in times of fear or pain and during exercise.

adult   An animal or plant that is mature and fully grown. An adult human female is called a woman; an adult human male is called a man. [*Adult* comes from a Latin word meaning "mature" or "grown-up."]

aerate   To pump or force air or gas into a solid or a liquid

aerobic   Living in an oxygen environment. Most animals and plants are aerobic.

aerodynamics   The science that deals with the flow of air or other gases around an object in motion. Aerodynamics is useful for scientists and engineers who design streamlined aircraft and automobiles. [*Aerodynamics* comes from Greek words meaning "air" and "power."]

aeronautics   The science of building aircraft. [*Aeronautics* comes from Greek words meaning "air" and "sailor."]

aerosol   A fine spray or mist of liquid or solid particles suspended in a gas. Examples of aerosols are smoke (solid particles in air), and fog and clouds (liquid particles in air). Commercial aerosol cans contain a substance such as paint or cosmetics and a propellant gas under high pressure. When you push the button on top of the can, a valve opens up and the pressure forces the propellant and the substance to spray out from a fine nozzle.

aerospace   All space beyond Earth's surface, including the atmosphere and outer space.

agar *or* **agar-agar**   A jellylike substance made from seaweed that is used in laboratories to grow bacteria.

agent   A substance that produces a change or reaction. Soap is a cleaning agent. [*Agent* comes from a Latin word meaning "to act" or "to do."]

agriculture   The science or industry of farming and the raising of livestock for food.

AIDS   *Acquired Immune Deficiency Syndrome.* A disease transmitted from people carrying the HIV virus through the exchange of bodily fluids such as blood and semen from infected people. AIDS cannot be contracted through casual contact such as touching ill people or being in the same room with them. Many doctors and other scientists are working on finding ways to treat AIDS and prevent its spread.

ailerons   The movable flaps on aircraft wings

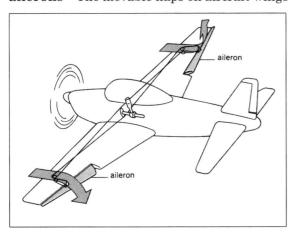

ailerons

used to bank or roll the plane from side to side.

air   A colorless mixture of nitrogen, oxygen, water vapor, and small amounts of other gases. The air that surrounds our planet Earth is called the atmosphere.

air mass   A large body of air that has about the same temperature and humidity at any altitude. An air mass can be cool or warm, moist or dry. The movements of air masses cause changes in the weather.

air pollution   Substances in the air that cause harm to humans and the environment. Air pollutants can be in the form of solid particles, liquid droplets, or gases. They can be natural or man-made. Some of the main pollutants produced by human activities include sulfur and nitrogen oxides, carbon monoxide, ammonia, and particles given off by burning of oil and coal in vehicles, power plants, and industrial factories. Natural sources of air pollutants include dust, methane, smoke from wildfires, and volcanoes.

air pressure   The force or weight of the atmosphere on a unit of area. At sea level, air pressure is about 14.7 pounds per square inch (1,013 millibars).

aircraft   Any flying machine or device such as an airplane, a blimp, a helicopter, a glider, or a paper airplane.

airplane   Any aircraft that has wings and is heavier than air. Airplanes are held up by air moving across the wings and are driven forward by propellers or jet engines.

albino   An animal or a plant that lacks ordinary coloring in its skin, hair, and eyes. Albino animals such as white rabbits have white skin, white fur, and pink eyes. [*Albino* comes from a Portuguese word meaning "white."]

alchemist   A chemist who lived during the Middle Ages (the fifth to the fifteenth centuries). Many alchemists tried without success to turn iron or lead into gold. They called their science alchemy.

algae Simple green water plants without stems, leaves, or roots. Algae are the plants that may turn pond water green during summers.

alimentary canal The tube in the body of humans and animals through which food passes and is digested. The alimentary canal includes the esophagus, the stomach, and the intestines. [*Alimentary* comes from a Latin word meaning "to nourish" or "to feed."]

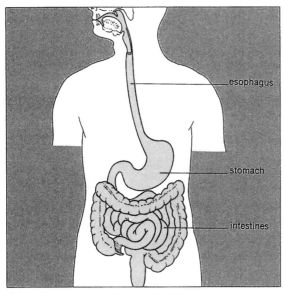

alimentary canal

alkali A substance that releases a large amount of hydroxyl ions (OH–) when dissolved in water. An alkali has a bitter taste and turns a specially treated paper called litmus from red to blue. An alkali can be used to neutralize or counteract an acid. Sodium carbonate (washing soda) is a common alkali used to soften water and make soap and glass. Sodium hydroxide (caustic soda) is used for making soap and paper and for bleaching. Caustic alkalis can cause severe burns if accidentally touched or swallowed.

allergy An unusual sensitivity to certain foods, pollen, dust, or animals. Hay fever is a common allergy.

alloy A mixture of metal with another metal or with a nonmetal such as carbon. Brass is an alloy of copper and zinc; steel is an alloy of iron and small amounts of carbon and other substances. Alloys are useful because their properties, such as hardness or the ability to be drawn into wires, are often quite different from the pure metals from which they are made. [*Alloy* comes from a Latin word meaning "to bind."]

almanac A yearly calendar of days, weeks, and months that contains weather forecasts, sunrise and sunset times, and other tables of useful information. [*Almanac* probably comes from Arabic words meaning "the calendar."]

alpha particle A positively charged particle given off by radioactive substances. A stream of these particles is called an alpha ray. [*Alpha* is the first letter of the Greek alphabet.]

alternating current An electric current that reverses direction in a regular cycle many times a second. Most countries in the world use alternating current in homes and factories. The abbreviation is AC (or ac).

alternator An electric generator that produces alternating current. Most modern automobiles have alternators.

altimeter An instrument that shows altitude. Aircraft use altimeters to show the height at which they are flying.

altitude Height above sea level. Mount Everest is the highest land mountain in the world with an altitude of about 29,035 feet (8,850 meters).

aluminum A lightweight, silvery-white metal, aluminum is the most common metallic element found in the earth's crust. Because aluminum is strong when alloyed and is a good conductor of heat, it is often used in the construction of aircraft and cooking utensils. It is also a good conductor of electricity and is used to make overhead electric cables where light weight is important. Aluminum has an atomic number of 13 and an atomic weight of 26.982. Its chemical symbol is Al.

alveoli   Tiny, thin-walled air sacs surrounded by small blood vessels found in lungs of mammals. A single air sac is called an alveolus. [*Alveoli* is a Latin word meaning "little cavities."]

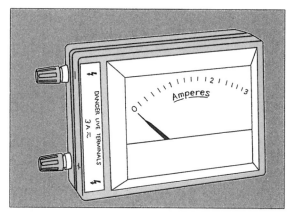
ammeter

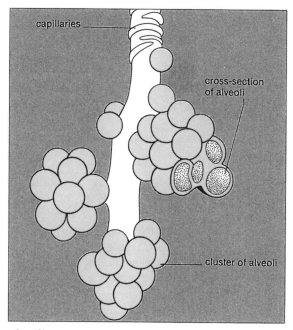

capillaries

cross-section of alveoli

cluster of alveoli

alveoli

amino acids   The basic parts of the proteins in body cells. The body gets amino acids by breaking down the proteins in food during digestion. Then the amino acids are reformed as protein to make new cells to replace old cells and for new growth.

ammeter   An instrument used to measure the strength of an electric current.

ammonia   A colorless strong-smelling gas. Ammonia is a base. A solution of ammonia dissolved in water contains ammonium hydroxide and is used in homes as a cleaning fluid and as a bleach. In other forms it is used in drugs, dyes, and plastics, and as a fertilizer. [*Ammonia* comes from Latin words meaning "Ammon's salt," a substance from which gas was once obtained.]

amoeba   A microscopic, one-celled organism. An amoeba has a jellylike body that moves by changing shape. [*Amoeba* comes from a Greek word meaning "change."]

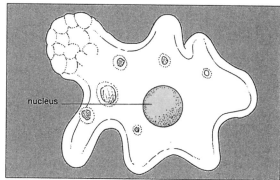

nucleus

amoeba

ampere   A unit used to measure the strength of an electric current. It is named after André Ampère (1775–1836). A French scientist who investigated the relationship between electricity and magnetism. The electric current used by a 100-watt light bulb is about one ampere. The abbreviation is amp.

amphibian   Amphibians are animals that are cold-blooded, have a three-chambered heart, and live part of their life in water and part on land. Amphibians have moist, smooth skin without hair, scales, or feathers. They absorb water directly through their skin. Many kinds hatch and develop in the water, getting oxygen from the water by the use of gills. They later develop lungs, breathe air, and spend part of their adult life on land. But they must return to the water to lay their eggs. Amphibians were one of the earliest groups of animals to emerge on land, appearing nearly 400 million years ago. Frogs, toads, and salamanders are amphibians.

anaerobic   Able to live without oxygen. Many kinds of bacteria are anaerobic.

analog   In electronics, an analog signal is used in its original form called an analog wave. In digital technology the analog wave is sampled and then turned into numbers that are used to represent the analog wave.

analyze   To find out what a substance is made of by breaking it down into its parts or elements and identifying each of them. [*Analyze* comes from a Greek word meaning "to loosen" or to "undo."]

anatomy   The science of the structure of animals and plants. Also, the structure of an animal or a plant or any of its parts is called its anatomy.

anemia   A medical condition in which the blood lacks enough red blood or hemoglobin cells to carry needed oxygen to the cells of the body. People with anemia may appear pale. They often feel weak, tired, and breathless, and have a rapid heartbeat.

anemometer   An instrument used to measure wind speed. The most common kind is one that measures wind speed from the spinning of cups mounted on a shaft.

aneroid barometer   An instrument used to measure air pressure. It is made by removing some of the air from a sealed metal container and attaching a pointer to the container. As air pressure squeezes the container together, the pointer moves to show the pressure on a nearby scale. In the barograph, another kind of aneroid barometer, the pointer is used to draw a line on a slowly moving drum, providing a continuous record of the atmospheric pressure. The aneroid is also used in aircraft altimeters, which show altitude (height above sea level).

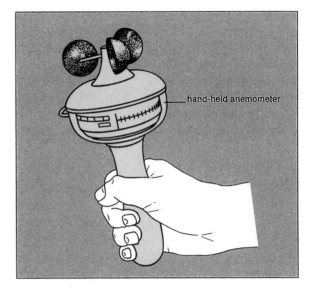

hand-held anemometer

anemometer

anesthetic   A substance used in medicine that blocks pain impulses from the nerves, or makes a person unconscious. Ether and chloroform are two anesthetics used during surgery since the middle of the nineteenth century. Anesthetics, such as novocaine, are also used in the practice of dentistry.

animal   Any of a group of living things that usually moves around by itself, takes in other animals or plants as food and is sensitive to its surroundings. An animal is unlike a plant in that its cells do not contain chlorophyll and it is not able to make its own food by photosynthesis. A snail, an earthworm, an ant, a shark, a frog, an alligator, an eagle, and a tiger are all animals. There are hundreds of thousands of different kinds of animals known on Earth, and thousands of new kinds are discovered every year. [*Animal* comes from a Latin word meaning "to have the breath of life."]

annual   Something that happens every year. Some animals travel to a distant place every year and then return; that is, they migrate annually. A plant that goes through a complete cycle from seeds to flowers every year is called an annual.

anode   1. The positive electrode of a battery

or electron tube. 2. The negative terminal of a battery that is producing electricity.

antenna 1. ZOOLOGY. A moveable, hairlike feeler found on an insect's head and on the head of some shelled animals such as shrimp and lobsters. These feelers are usually found in pairs and are called antennas or antennae. 2. ENGINEERING. A device used to send or receive radio or television signals. A sending antenna changes electrical energy into electromagnetic radiation such as radio or television signals. A receiving antenna does the reverse. [*Antenna* comes from Greek words meaning "to stretch up."]

anthropoid ape An ape that is similar to humans in appearance and in its skeleton, skull, teeth, and so on. Anthropoids include gorillas, chimpanzees, and gibbons.

anthropology The study of the customs and characteristics of different groups of people. Scientists who study anthropology are called anthropologists.

antibiotic A substance that can destroy or stop the growth of certain kinds of microbes. A doctor prescribes an antibiotic to help fight an infection. Penicillin, tetracycline, and streptomycin are commonly used antibiotics. [*Antibiotic* comes from Greek words meaning "against life."]

antibody A substance produced in the body that protects it against outside substances called antigens. A specific antibody is produced by the white blood cells for each antigen. A vaccine can make the white blood cells produce antibodies against a specific disease. For example, the polio vaccine stimulates the body to produce antibodies against polio.

anticyclone A large, high-pressure air mass from which winds blow outward. The winds in an anticyclone blow clockwise in the Northern Hemisphere and counterclockwise in the Southern. An anticyclone usually brings fair weather to the area it covers.

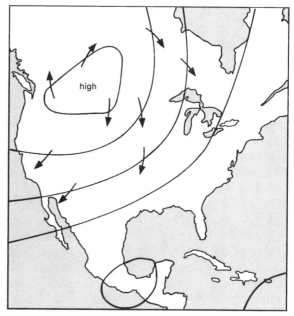

anticyclone

antidote A substance that acts against the effects of a poison. A poisonous snakebite requires a particular antidote depending on the kind of snake.

antigen A foreign substance that causes the body to produce a counteracting substance called an antibody. Antigens include viruses, bacteria, other blood cells, and poisons.

antiseptic A substance used in medicine that kills or stops the growth of microbes that cause infection. Tincture of iodine is a common antiseptic.

anus The opening at the end of the large intestine through which solid wastes and undigested foods leave the body.

aorta The largest artery in the body. It carries blood from the left side of the heart to smaller branch arteries and then to all parts of the body except the lungs. [*Aorta* comes from a Greek word meaning "to raise" or "to lift."]

ape A large monkey without a tail that can stand and walk in an almost upright position.

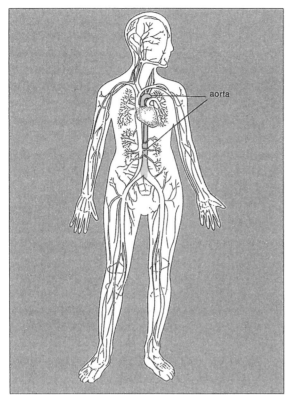

aorta

aperture The opening at the front of a camera or a telescope through which light enters.

aphelion The part of a planet's or a comet's orbit that is farthest from the sun. Halley's comet reaches its aphelion when it is 3 billion miles (about 4,800 million kilometers) from the sun, far beyond the orbit of Neptune.

apogee The part of a moon's or a satellite's orbit that is farthest from Earth. At apogee, the moon is 252,667 miles (406,610 kilometers) from Earth.

Apollo Space Program The United States' effort in the 1960s to reach the moon with a manned spacecraft. *Apollo* astronaut Neil Armstrong became the first person to step on the moon on July 20, 1969.

app An abbreviation for an application or program running on a computer, a mobile device, or other digital device (for example a cell phone or a tablet). An app is really any stand-alone program of software.

apparatus Any equipment or tool used for a special purpose, such as a microscope (to look at tiny objects) or a telescope (to look at distant objects). [*Apparatus* comes from a Latin word meaning "to get ready" or "to prepare."]

appendix A small, finger-sized pouch attached to the beginning of the large intestine in humans. It has no known function. Sometimes it becomes infected and inflamed in a condition called appendicitis and is then usually removed in an operation called an appendectomy.

aquarium A bowl, jar, or tank where water animals and plants are kept and studied. Also a place where aquatic life is kept for research and public viewing.

aquatic Describing animals or plants that live in the water.

archaea A group of single-celled microscopic living things that have no cell nucleus. Some kinds of archaea live in harsh environments such as hot springs and salt lakes but they also live in oceans where they are part of the plankton.

archaeology The study of past cultures and civilizations. Archaeologists examine the physical remains that humans left behind, such as decaying ruins and buried objects.

Archimedes (287–212 B.C.) A Greek mathematician and scientist. In science he is best known for Archimedes' principle, which states that an object in a fluid, such as water, becomes lighter by as much weight as the weight of the fluid it displaces. The story is told that Archimedes discovered this while stepping into a bath and noticing how the water overflowed. He is supposed to have shouted "Eureka!" (I have found it!), and raced out into the street, forgetting to put on his clothes. Archimedes also invented Archimedes' screw, a device for bringing up water from wells. Archimedes' screw is still used to irrigate fields in some Mideastern countries.

Archimedes

arctic The North Pole or the north polar regions.

argon An element that is an odorless, colorless gas that makes up about 1% of the air. It is used to fill incandescent electric light bulbs because it is chemically inactive, which prevents the filament in a bulb from burning out quickly. Fluorescent light bulbs contain a mixture of argon and mercury vapor. [*Argon* comes from a Greek word meaning "lazy" or "idle."]

Aristarchus (310–230 B.C.) An early Greek astronomer who was the first to maintain that the sun is larger than Earth and that Earth orbits around a motionless sun

Aristotle (384–322 B.C.) An early Greek thinker and scientist who proposed important methods of classifying animals by comparing

Aristotle

the ways in which their bodies were similar and different. He also proposed some (mistaken) theories about the nature of matter and of the universe. For example, he maintained that all matter was composed of four elements—earth, air, fire, and water. For more than fifteen hundred years, most people accepted both his correct and incorrect views without question.

artery Any main blood vessel through which blood moves away from the heart. You can feel the pulse of blood in an artery in your wrist.

arthropod An animal that has a hard outer covering and jointed legs. Arthropods include shrimps, crabs, and lobsters that live in water, as well as insects and spiders that live on land.

artificial intelligence The science of making computers do things that usually require human intelligence. Scientists working in AI hope to imitate or duplicate human intelligence in computers and robots.

artificial organs Human-made mechanical devices such as an artificial heart or an artificial kidney. These machines can carry out the functions of body organs for a length of time until replaced by a donor organ.

asbestos A grayish-white fibrous material that does not burn. Asbestos is used to weave fireproof fabrics for protective clothing for fire fighters and for safety curtains in theaters. It is also used in industry to make brake linings and electrical insulators. Asbestos must be used carefully because the fibers may cause lung diseases and cancers if inhaled over long periods of time. [*Asbestos* is a Greek word meaning "something that cannot be extinguished."]

asteroid One of several hundred thousand small, oddly-shaped, minor planets. Thousands more are discovered every year. Most of the asteroids travel around the sun in irregular orbits between Mars and Jupiter. The largest asteroid by far is Ceres, about 605 miles (975 kilometers) across. Ceres contains about one-quarter the mass of all the asteroids combined.

asthma A lung illness that causes wheezing and difficulty in breathing due to the accumulation of mucus in the lungs and spasms in the bronchial tubes.

astigmatism A visual defect caused by irregular curves in the lens of the eye, which prevent light rays from an object from meeting at a single focal point, thereby causing blurred images. [*Astigmatism* comes from Greek words meaning "without a point or a spot."]

astrology A nonscientific method of using the time and date of a person's birth and the position of the celestial bodies to predict the future and to tell about the person's character. The science of the stars is called astronomy. Astrology and astronomy are not the same. Astrology uses some of the information gathered in astronomy, but its predictions are not based on known facts.

astronaut A person who has studied astronautics, the science of space flight, and has been especially trained to fly in space. [*Astronaut* comes from Greek words meaning "star sailor."]

astronomy The science that deals with the solar system, the stars, and the universe. A scientist who studies these things is called an astronomer.

atmosphere The gases that surround Earth or other planets. Aside from water vapor, Earth's atmosphere is about 78% nitrogen, 20% oxygen, 0.9% argon, 0.03% carbon dioxide, and traces of many other gases. The amount of water vapor (humidity) varies from place to place and from time to time. Beyond Earth's atmosphere lies outer space.

atoll A narrow, round coral island that encircles a lagoon.

atom The smallest part of an element that still has the chemical properties of that element. Atoms are made up of even smaller particles such as protons, neutrons, and electrons.

[*Atom* comes from a Greek word meaning "something that cannot be cut up or divided."]

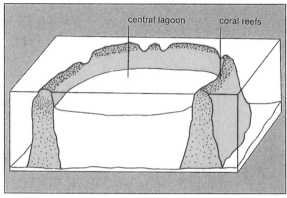

atoll

atomic energy The huge amounts of power that are released when atoms are split, as with atomic fission, or combined, as with atomic fusion. Atomic energy can be used to generate electricity. Since these processes actually take place with the nuclei of atoms, this is more properly called nuclear energy.

atomic number The number of protons found in the nucleus of an atom. This is different for every element. The element hydrogen has an atomic number of 1; oxygen, an atomic number of 8; and uranium, an atomic number of 92.

atomic weight The number representing the weight or mass of an atom compared with the weight or mass of an atom of carbon, which is defined as exactly 12. The atomic weight of hydrogen is 1; the atomic weight of oxygen is 16; and the atomic weight of uranium is 238.

attraction A force that draws objects together, such as magnetism or static electricity.

audible Able to be heard. High-pitched sounds are usually more audible to young people than to older people. Some animals (such as dogs and bats) can hear very high-pitched sounds that are not audible to people at all.

auricle Either of the two upper chambers of the heart that receives blood from the veins.

Another name for auricle is atrium. Humans, other mammals, and birds have two auricles. Auricle also refers to the external ear, the part of the ear that can be seen projecting from the head. [*Auricle* comes from a Latin word meaning "little ear."]

aurora Flickering, colored lights in the atmosphere that are caused by electrons trapped in Earth's magnetic field. The aurora borealis, also called the northern lights, are seen over arctic regions; the aurora australis, also called the southern lights, are seen over Antarctic regions. [*Aurora* is the Latin word for "dawn" and also the name of the Roman goddess who brought the morning sun into the sky.]

automation The use of machines—computers as well as mechanical ones—to do jobs that were once done by humans.

autonomic nervous system The part of the body's nervous system that controls breathing, heartbeat, and digestion.

autopsy An examination of a dead body to find out the cause of death. [*Autopsy* comes from Greek words meaning "to see for yourself" or "to be an eyewitness."]

autotroph An organism that makes food from water and simple salts. Algae, grass, cacti, and certain bacteria are autotrophs.

autumn The three-month-long season between the autumnal equinox and the winter solstice.

avalanche A great mass of snow and ice or of dirt and rock that suddenly plunges down a mountainside. Avalanches are usually caused by loud noises or other shock waves acting on melting snow.

avatar In computing, an avatar is a person's representation of himself/herself in the form of a model (used in computer games) or an icon or picture (used in Internet communities). The term can also refer to the kind of person connected with a screen name, or handle, when used on the Internet.

axis A straight line that passes through an object and around which the object spins. An axis can be real or imaginary. Earth's axis is an imaginary line that passes through the North and South poles.

axon The long, thin part of a nerve cell that carries impulses away from the main cell body.

B

bacillus A group of rod-shaped bacteria. One kind of bacillus causes diphtheria. [*Bacillus* comes from a Latin word meaning "little rod."]

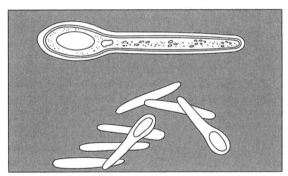

bacillus

backbone A column of small bones called vertebrae that run down the middle of the back. Also called the spine. The backbone serves as the main support for the body in humans and other mammals, birds, reptiles, amphibians, and fish. Animals belonging to these groups are called vertebrates.

Bacon, Roger (1214–1292?) An Englishman who studied many branches of science, sometimes considered the first modern scientist. He is said to have predicted the inventions of the microscope, the telescope, and aircraft centuries before they were actually designed.

bacteria Microscopic, one-celled organisms that live almost everywhere on Earth including in and on the human body. There are thousands of different kinds of bacteria. Under a microscope, some are round, others are rod-like, and still others look like spirals. Some kinds of bacteria cause diseases and infections. Other kinds break down and help in the decay of dead animal and plant materials and thus enrich the soil. Within our bodies, bacteria help in the digestion of food. They also are used to produce dairy products such as cheese and yogurt. [*Bacteria* comes from a Greek word meaning "little rods."]

bacteriology The science that deals with bacteria. A scientist who studies bacteria is called a bacteriologist.

balance A kind of scale used to measure the weight of an object. A balance works by comparing an object whose weight is unknown with a known weight. [*Balance* comes from Latin words meaning "two flat plates," like those used on this type of scale.]

balance of nature An interdependence between the plants and animals in a particular area, which is sometimes called a natural equilibrium. In fact, the balance of nature is often very unsteady because factors such as violent weather or pollution may cause great changes in animal or plant populations.

ball bearings Small metal balls that roll easily and are used to cut down sliding friction in some machines. Ball bearings can be found in bicycle wheels and roller skates.

ballistics The science that deals with the movement of bullets, shells, and other missiles. (*Ballistics* is based on a Latin word for an ancient weapon that hurled rocks and large objects.)

balloon A large bag of thin, lightweight material filled with hot air or lighter-than-air gas. Weather balloons carry instruments to study winds and upper air currents. Some balloons have compartments for passengers attached to them. The first manned hot air balloon was launched by the Montgolfier brothers in 1783 in France.

ballpoint pen A writing tool that has a small metal ball in a socket at one end. When the pen is used, the ball rotates and ink is drawn out onto the writing surface.

bark The outer layer of wood on a tree or woody plant. Bark is tough and waterproof and protects the more delicate parts of the plant within. Old bark cracks and peels off as new wood grows underneath.

barograph An instrument that keeps a record of changes in air pressure. Also called a recording barometer. [*Barograph* is based on Greek words meaning "weight" (in the sense of pressure) and "writing."]

barometer An instrument used to measure air pressure. There are two kinds of barometers in common use—the aneroid and the mercury. A barometer helps to predict weather changes. Rising air pressure usually means fair weather to come, while falling air pressure usually means rain or snow is in the forecast. [*Barometer* is based on Greek words meaning "weight" (in the sense of pressure) and "measure."]

barrier reef A coral reef that lies roughly

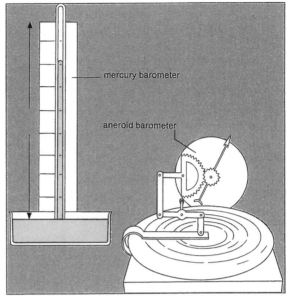

barometer

parallel to the shoreline. One of the most famous is the Great Barrier Reef of Australia.

basalt A hard, dark-grey to black, igneous rock. It is formed by the cooling and hardening of molten lava from a volcano. Volcanic islands, such as Hawaii and Iceland, are mostly basalt.

base A bitter liquid that turns litmus paper blue. The chemical formula for bases contains OH (hydroxide). A base reacts with an acid to neutralize it and form a salt. Ammonia dissolved in water (ammonium hydroxide) is a common base.

BASIC The word stands for *B*eginner's *A*ll-purpose *S*ymbolic *I*nstruction *C*ode. A computer language often used by beginners.

bathyscaphe A deep-sea research vessel used to explore the ocean depths. It was invented by Auguste Piccard and dived for the first time in 1948. A bathyscaphe has an oval flotation tank with a small, pressurized passenger cabin attached beneath. It is not attached to a ship but uses electric motors to move about on the floor of the ocean. The bathyscaphe has dived to nearly seven miles (about eleven kilometers) below the surface. [*Bathyscaphe* comes from Greek words meaning "deep" and "boat."]

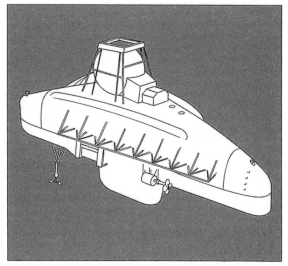

bathyscaphe

bathysphere An airtight, diving steel ball scientists first used in 1930 to explore the oceans. A bathysphere is lowered by a cable from a ship on the surface and remains attached to the ship. [*Bathysphere* comes from Greek words meaning "deep" and "ball."]

battery A device that produces electricity from a chemical reaction. Some kinds of batteries, such as those used in transistor radios and flashlights, give only a certain amount of electricity before the chemical reaction is completed. Other kinds of batteries, such as those used in automobiles, are called storage batteries or accumulators. They can be recharged and reused.

bauxite The main ore from which aluminum is taken. [*Bauxite* comes from Les Baux, France, where it was discovered in 1821.]

bay A part of the shoreline that makes a wide curve into the land.

beach A stretch of sand, rocks, or other materials along the shoreline of a lake, river, or sea.

beak The hard, outer part of a bird's or turtle's mouth. A bird's beak is often called its bill.

[*Beak* may be related to a Gaelic or Irish word meaning "hook."]

beaker A glass or plastic container, shaped like a cup with a lip, often used in laboratories to pour liquids.

beam A ray of light or radiation, such as a laser beam.

bearing A part of a machine that reduces friction and allows a moving part to turn or slide more easily. Roller bearings and ball bearings are often used to help wheels turn.

Beaufort wind scale A method of measuring the force of the wind on a scale ranging from 0 to 12. It measures wind speeds of less that 1 mile per hour (calm) to 73 miles (117 kilometers) per hour or more (hurricane).

Becquerel, Antoine-Henri (1852–1908) A French physicist who discovered that the element uranium was naturally radioactive. In 1903 he shared the Nobel Prize with Marie and Pierre Curie.

bedrock The solid rock of the earth's crust that usually lies beneath a layer of sand, soil, or pieces of rock. Bedrock is sometimes exposed at the earth's surface.

behavior The ways in which an animal acts. Behavior is often a response to changes in an animal's surroundings. Scientists sometimes study animal behavior in order to better understand human behavior.

Bell, Alexander Graham (1847–1922) A Scottish-American scientist and educator who invented the telephone and founded the Bell Telephone Company. Bell also invented the wax cylinder phonograph. In 1872, he opened a school in Boston for training teachers of deaf children.

bends, the Sharp pains in the arms, legs, and body of a deep-sea diver. The bends result from a too-rapid ascent from underwater. The

Bell, Alexander Graham

rapid decrease in pressure creates nitrogen bubbles in a diver's blood, which causes pain and sometimes injury and even death.

Bernoulli, Daniel (1700–1782) A Swiss scientist who proposed that when a gas or liquid moves over a surface, the pressure against the surface is reduced at right angles to the line of motion. This is now called Bernoulli's principle. Bernoulli's principle explains how an airplane gets most of its lift from air moving across its wings.

berry A small fruit that usually has many seeds, such as a strawberry or a blackberry.

Berzelius, Jöns Jakob (1779–1848) A Swedish chemist who determined the atomic weights of nearly forty elements and discovered three new elements: cerium, selenium, and thorium.

beta particle A very tiny particle given off by a radioactive substance such as radium. Beta particles are high-speed electrons. A stream of beta particles is called a beta ray. [*Beta* is the second letter of the Greek alphabet.]

biceps A large muscle in the front of the upper arm that is attached to the shoulder blade. Biceps divide in the upper arm to form a Y-shape. Also, a similar muscle in the back of the thigh. [*Biceps* comes from Latin words meaning "two-headed."]

biennial A plant that blooms and produces seeds in its second year of growth. Biennials such as carrots and cabbages store food in their leaves and roots the first year for use in the second year when the seeds are produced.

bile A bitter, yellow-green liquid produced by the liver and stored in the gall bladder. Bile helps the body to digest fats in foods.

bill The hard beak or mouth part of a bird. Birds have bills of different shapes, suited to the way they feed.

binary system A number system that uses two digits, 0 and 1, instead of 10 digits, as in the decimal system. Binary numbers are used in computers. For example, 25 in the decimal system (two 10s and one 5) is represented as 11001 (one 16, one 8, zero 4s, zero 2s, and one 1) in the binary system.

biochemistry The study of the materials that make up living animals and plants. The main materials of living matter are water, carbohydrates, proteins, and lipids (fats and other substances). A scientist who studies the materials of living matter is called a biochemist.

biodegradable The ability to be broken down or decayed by bacteria. Things made from plants and animals, such as wood products, are biodegradable, plastic is not.

biological clock An internal rhythm in plants and animals that caused them to behave in certain ways on a regular basis. For example, many plants open their leaves during the day and close them at night. Fiddler crabs become active at the times of low tide and quiet at the times of high tides. These activities continue regardless of the surrounding of the plant or animal.

biological control To kill or reduce the amount of undesirable plants or animals by using other plants or animals that are hostile to them. Ladybugs were introduced in California in 1888 to reduce the number of insect pests.

biology The science that studies living

things. There are two main branches of biology: the study of animals called zoology, and the study of plants, called botany. Nowadays, there are dozens of biosciences that specialize in one particular subject, such as mammals or reptiles, or cover both branches, such as marine biology or microbiology. A scientist who studies living things is called a biologist.

bioluminescence The light without heat displayed by living things such as fireflies, many marine animals, and some kinds of plants. The female firefly's stomach is bioluminescent.

bionics The science of designing and engineering a system that has the characteristics of a living organism. A robot arm that can move objects, in imitation of an animal, is a bionic design. Bionics can apply a principle observed in nature, such as echolocation in bats, which resulted in the concept for radar and sonar.

biosphere The parts of the land, sea, and air in which the living things are found.

biota The total of living things in a geographic region such as North America or a time period such as the Jurassic. The biota of planet Earth is called the biosphere. Humans are not usually counted as biota.

biped Any two-footed animal, such as a human or a bird.

bird A class of animals that has feathers, is warm-blooded, lays eggs, and has wings. Most birds can fly, though some, such as the penguin, cannot. Birds have hollow, lightweight bones and strong breast muscles for moving their wings. There are about 8,000 different kinds of living birds. They range in size from the ostrich, which can weigh over 300 lbs (136 kilograms) to the hummingbird, which weighs about as much as a paperclip.

birth The time when a human or an animal separates from its mother and comes into the world on its own. Also, birth is the act of being born.

bit A computing term standing for *binary digit.* A bit is the smallest unit of information a computer handles—either 1 (on) or 0 (off).

black box An electronic instrument on an airplane that automatically records details of the flight.

black hole In space, the densely packed remains of a star that has collapsed in on itself. A black hole's force of gravity is so great that not even light rays can escape; thus a black hole is invisible. Black holes can only be detected by their gravitational effect on nearby stars and by the radiation released by matter that falls into them.

bladder The hollow sac in the body of many animals in which liquid wastes, also called urine, are stored.

blast-off The moment when a rocket is launched into space.

bleed To lose blood from a cut or damaged blood vessel.

blind spot The area of the retina of each eye where the optic nerve and blood vessels enter. It has no light-sensitive nerve endings. The blind spot is usually not noticeable because it covers a different part of the image in each of our eyes.

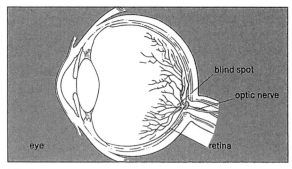

blind spot

blizzard A heavy and long-lasting snowstorm with very strong winds.

blood The red liquid that is pumped by the

heart and circulates in blood vessels such as veins and arteries. Blood carries digested food and oxygen to the cells and carries away wastes such as carbon dioxide. It also kills germs and keeps the body at a constant temperature. The adult human has about ten to twelve pints (about five liters) of blood. About half of the blood consists of a pale fluid called plasma. The other half is made up of red blood cells (called erythrocytes), white blood cells (called leukocytes), and platelets (called thrombocytes). Blood cells are made in the marrow of bones. About 100 million red blood cells are made every minute and live about 120 days.

blood grouping One of several systems for classifying blood. The most important is the ABO system. In this system, blood is classified as A if it contains a substance called antigen A, B if it contains antigen B, AB if it contains both, and O if it contains neither. Another important blood group is the Rhesus or Rh factor. The word comes from the Rhesus monkey in which the blood factor was first discovered. People who have the Rh factor are called Rh-positive; those who do not are called Rh-negative. It is important to know blood groupings before giving a blood transfusion. When blood containing an antigen is given to someone who does not have the antigen, the red cells clump together; this may cause death.

blood vessel A tube in the body through which blood circulates. A blood vessel is an artery, a vein, or a capillary.

bluetooth A wireless technology that enables mobile phones, computers, and other electronic devices to communicate with each other.

Bohr, Niels (1885–1962) A Danish physicist who proposed a model of the atom that is commonly accepted today. The Bohr model of the hydrogen atom consists of a central proton around which a single electron circles. In the Bohr atom, the electron's orbits can only be of certain definite sizes and carry certain definite quantities of energy. In 1922 Bohr received the Nobel Prize in physics. During World War II Bohr escaped to England and then in 1943 went to the United States, where he helped develop the atom bomb. But Bohr was always concerned about the terrible problems that the bomb posed for humanity.

Bohr, Niels

boil 1. PHYSICS. To heat a liquid enough to turn it into a gas. When water is heated and made to boil, it turns into water vapor. The temperature at which boiling takes place is called the boiling point. The boiling point of water is 212°F (100°C). 2. MEDICINE. A pus-filled, painful infection beneath the skin.

bone The hard part of the skeleton of any vertebrate (an animal with a backbone). Bones support the body and protect its soft parts. They also act as anchors for muscles and work with the muscles when the body moves. Long bones, such as those in the arms and legs, have a hollow cavity filled with a soft tissue called marrow. The marrow makes blood cells.

boot The process through which a computer starts or restarts.

boson A class of subatomic particles, such as a photon or alpha particle that has a kind of spin called zero or infinite and obeys what are called the Bose-Einstein statistics.

botany The science that studies plants. Botany is one of the two major divisions of biology. Botany deals with the many different kinds of plants, how and where they grow, and how they adapt to their surroundings. A scientist who studies plants is called a botanist. [*Botany* comes from a Greek word meaning "plant."]

boulder   A large rock detached from underlying bedrock. Boulders are rounded and worn by weather, water and ice. Glaciers can carry large boulders for many miles.

bowel   Also called the intestines. The bowel reaches from the stomach to the anus. Food passes through the bowel and is digested. [*Bowel* comes from a Latin word meaning "little sausage."]

Boyle, Robert   (1627–1691) A British scientist who is often called the father of modern chemistry. He collected and studied gases and formulated Boyle's law, which deals with their properties. He believed that experimentation was necessary in chemistry and was a pioneer in the scientific method.

Brahe, Tycho   (1546–1601) A Danish astronomer who closely observed and tracked the motions of the stars and planets. His observations were remarkably accurate even though he did not use a telescope.

brain   A large mass of nerve tissues that is the center of sensation, thinking, and memory. In human beings and other vertebrate animals, the brain is protected within a skull in the head. Mammals have big brains compared to their size, and humans have the biggest brains of all—about two percent of the body's weight.

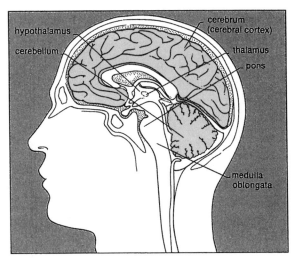

brain

A human brain has many millions of interconnecting nerve cells. The brain mainly consists of the cerebrum or cerebral cortex (the largest part in humans), the thalamus and the hypothalamus, the cerebellum, the pons, and the medulla oblongata. Different parts of the brain do different things. For example, the cerebral cortex is the center of language, senses, thought, and memory.

brass   A hard, yellowish metal that is an alloy of copper and zinc. Brass has been known since Roman times and is widely used today in industry.

breakthrough   A major advance in science, such as Einstein's theory of relativity.

breath   The air that is taken into the lungs and forced out again during breathing

breathing   Taking air into the lungs and giving it out again. A gas called oxygen is in the air and is needed by the body all through life. Oxygen passes through tiny tubes in the lungs into the blood. Another gas, called carbon dioxide, passes out of the blood into the lungs and is breathed out. A resting adult breathes in and out about twenty times a minute. Children usually breathe faster than adults.

breeding   The development o f new breeds of plants or animals with more desirable features. Breeding under controlled conditions has produced plants and animals that are hardy, have greater resistance to disease, and produce high yields.

breeze   A gentle wind.

brittle   Hard and easily snapped or broken. Glass is brittle.

bronchus   One of two tubes (called bronchi) through which air passes from the throat (the trachea) into the lungs. Each bronchus has a lining that makes a sticky substance called mucus, which traps the dust in air. Bronchitis is a disease in which the bronchi are inflamed.

Smoking may cause bronchitis that lasts for a long time and results in damage to the lungs.

bronze A hard, brownish metal that is an alloy of copper and tin. Bronze was used to make many objects by early peoples that lived three thousand years ago. That time has become known as the Bronze Age (about 3000 B.C. to about 800 B.C.)

Brownian motion A constant, irregular motion of tiny particles when suspended in a fluid. The quivering movement of the particles is caused by the random impacts of the surrounding molecules. It was first described by Robert Brown (1773–1858), a Scottish botanist, when he observed through a microscope the movement of pollen grains suspended in water.

browser A software program such as Internet Explorer, Firefox, Chrome, or Safari that accesses and navigates the Internet.

bubble A thin skin of a liquid, such as soapy water, filled with a gas, such as air. Most of a bubble is air. When a soap bubble breaks, only a tiny bit of soapy water is left.

bug 1. ZOOLOGY. An insect that feeds with a sharp, tubelike mouth, which it uses for sucking. 2. COMPUTING. A mistake or a fault in a computer program.

bulb 1. BOTANY. A small, underground plant stem covered by fleshy leaves that store food. Plants such as tulips and daffodils grow from bulbs. 2. ENGINEERING. An electric light bulb. When electricity passes through the filament in a bulb, it becomes so hot that it glows with light.

Bunsen burner A gas burner widely used in schools and laboratories for heating chemicals. The gas is mixed with air by an adjustable valve that makes the flame smokeless and very intense. The burner is named after its inventor.

buoyancy The quality of being able to float on the surface of a liquid. Wood has the buoyancy to float on water. Also, the power of a liquid to keep an object afloat. Seawater has more buoyancy than fresh water.

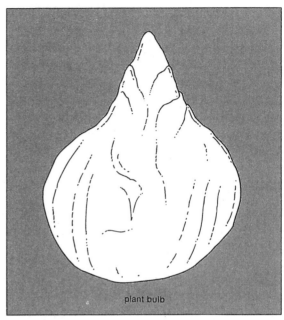

plant bulb

bulb

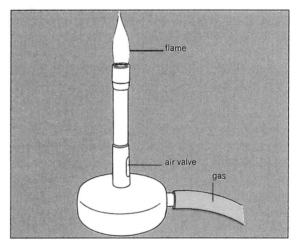

flame

air valve

gas

Bunsen burner

burn To be on fire and give off light and heat. Also, to damage or to injure by heat.

byte A grouping of binary digits that stands for a letter, number, or symbol to a computer. Eight binary digits, or bits, make up one byte.

C

cable, electric A wire or a bundle of wires threaded together that conducts an electric current or an electric signal. The wire is covered and shielded by a tube of insulating material such as plastic. There are many different kinds of cables. Coaxial cable is used for television and radio signals; overhead or underground cables are used to transmit power from generating stations. Multi-stand telephone cables carry many signals at once.

cable television A system of carrying television signals through cables to home receivers.

calcite A common mineral made of calcium carbonate and found all over the world. Limestone, marble, and chalk are varieties of calcite. Cement and some fertilizers are made from calcite.

calcium A soft, silvery-white metallic element found combined in many rocks and minerals, such as calcite, gypsum, and fluorite. Calcium compounds are an important part of bones, teeth, and seashells. Calcium is the fifth most abundant element in the world. It has an atomic number of 20 and an atomic weight of 40.08. Its chemical symbol is Ca.

calculator A machine that does rapid arithmetical calculations. Most mechanical calculators can only add or subtract. The first mechanical calculator was invented by the French scientist Pascal in 1642. A modern electronic calculator can add, subtract, multiply, divide, and do many other mathematical tasks at high speeds. [*Calculator* comes from a Latin word meaning "someone who does arithmetic."]

caldera A large volcanic crater. A caldera, such as Crater Lake in Oregon, is usually caused by a repeated and immense collapse or explosion of a volcano. [*Caldera* was originally a Spanish word meaning "cauldron" or "kettle" and is based on a Latin word meaning "warm."]

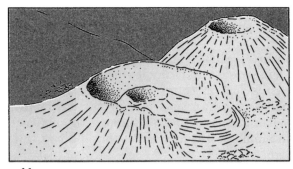

caldera

calendar A way to show the days, weeks, and months in a year. Calendars were first used by the Babylonians and the early Egyptians. The Egyptian calendar had a year of 12 months with 30 days each. Later, five extra days were added at the end of each year to approximate a year of 365 days. The main difficulty in making calendars is that the day (measured by Earth's rotation on its axis), the month (reckoned by the moon's revolution around Earth), and the year (measured by Earth's revolution around the sun) are not dependent on each other. Nowadays we use the Gregorian calendar, named after Pope Gregory, who introduced it in 1582. It divided the year into 365 days and 12 months. Every fourth year is a "leap year" having 366 days. But any century year (1700, 1800, 1900, etc.) is not a leap year unless it is divisible by 400. That means that the years 1600 and 2000, even thought they are century years, are leap years. [*Calendar* comes from a Latin word meaning "the first day of the month."]

calipers An instrument used to measure the thickness of an object. Simple calipers are a pair of metal legs hinged at one end. Vernier calipers look like a sliding wrench and can be read more precisely.

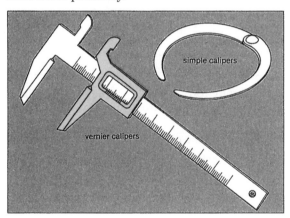

calipers

calorie 1. CHEMISTRY. The amount of heat needed to raise the temperature of one gram of water one degree centigrade. The abbreviation is cal. 2. NUTRITION. A unit that measures the energy supplied by foods. The food calorie is one thousand times as large as the calorie used in chemistry. The abbreviation is Cal. or kcal.

calorimeter An instrument used to measure the heat energy in substances such as food or fuel.

cambium A layer of cells in the stem and

roots of woody plants. As new cells (called xylem and phloem) are formed on both sides of the cambium, the stem and the roots grow thicker.

Cambrian Period The earliest period of the Paleozoic Era, about 544 to 520 million years ago. Cambrian rocks contain fossils of trilobites and other primitive sea animals, showing that some forms of life existed on the earth that long ago. [*Cambrian* comes from the ancient Romans' name for Wales. Adam Sedgwick, a nineteenth-century English geologist, first used this term to name some layers of rock in Wales.]

camera A device for recording a light image digitally on a photoelectric cell or on light-sensitive photographic film. The result is a photograph, a motion picture film, or a digital video.

camouflage A means by which some animals protect themselves by appearing to blend into their surroundings. Some animals have skin colors patterns that make them difficult to see. Other animals, such as the chameleon, change their colors to match the changing background as they move from one place to another.

canal 1. ENGINEERING. A waterway that is built to join rivers or different seas. The Panama Canal is a waterway built by the United States that connects the Atlantic and Pacific Oceans. 2. BIOLOGY, ANATOMY. A tube in the body that carries food, air, or some kind of body fluid. The alimentary canal carries food through the digestive system. The Eustachian tube is an air-filled canal in the ear.

cancer A group of diseases in which body cells multiply wildly and sometimes form lumps called tumors. Cancer often spreads through the body, destroying healthy cells and tissues. Prevention of cancer can be aided by avoiding known causes, including smoking, radioactivity, and cancer-causing chemicals. Cancer is sometimes treated by surgery, drugs (chemotherapy), radiation (radiotherapy), or some combination of these. Drugs and radiation kill or slow down the growth of cancer cells. Some kinds of cancer can be treated and even cured but a great deal of research must still be done. [*Cancer* comes from a Latin word meaning "crab." The ancient physician Galen first used the word for the disease because the swollen veins around a tumor looked like crab legs.]

canine Doglike. Any animal belonging to the family of animals that includes dogs, wolves, foxes, and jackals. In mammals, the pointed teeth used to tear flesh are called canine teeth. Mammals, including humans, usually have four canines, one on each side of the upper and lower jaws.

cantilever A beam of wood, metal, or some other building material that is supported at or near one end only. A diving board is an example of a cantilever. A cantilever bridge is constructed by two cantilevers that are joined together in the middle.

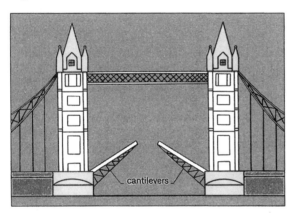

cantilever

canyon A ravine or deep gorge once formed by a river that slowly cut downwards through the land. A canyon is a kind of valley with very steep sides. [*Canyon* comes from a Spanish word meaning "long tube" or "pipe."]

capacitor A device used to store electric charges. A simple capacitor is made with two metal plates separated by an insulator such as air.

capillary One of many tiny blood vessels that carry blood from small arteries to small veins. A capillary is thinner than a hair and can be seen only through a microscope. In the lungs, the blood in capillaries picks up oxygen and releases carbon dioxide. [*Capillary* comes from a Latin word meaning "hair."]

capsule 1. SPACE SCIENCE. A part of a spaceship designed to hold people, animals, or instruments that carry out a mission. 2. BOTANY. A seedcase that develops from a fruit and splits open when ripe. 3. MEDICINE. A small container of a dose of medicine that dissolves when swallowed. [*Capsule* comes from a Latin word meaning "little box."]

carbohydrate Any substance made up of carbon, hydrogen, and oxygen. Sugars and starches in food are carbohydrates. Carbohydrates are made by green plants during photosynthesis. Animals get immediate energy from carbohydrates by eating plants. Carbohydrates make up a third to more than a half of the diet of most people around the world.

carbon A common, nonmetallic chemical element found in all animals and plants. Coal, charcoal, graphite, and diamond are different forms of carbon found in nature. Graphite, used in pencils, is soft; but diamond is the hardest substance known. Carbon has an atomic number of 6 and an atomic weight of 12.011. The chemical symbol for carbon is C. [*Carbon* comes from a Latin word meaning "charcoal" or coal."]

carbon cycle The circulation of carbon atoms in nature. Green plants take in carbon dioxide from the air to make food in a process called photosynthesis. Animals eat the plants. When animals and plants die, they decay and carbon dioxide is released back into the air. Animals and plants also give out carbon dioxide during respiration.

carbon dioxide One of the gases in air. It is produced when carbon combines with oxygen during burning or respiration. Carbon dioxide has no odor and is colorless. It forms bubbles in soda water. The formula for carbon dioxide is CO_2.

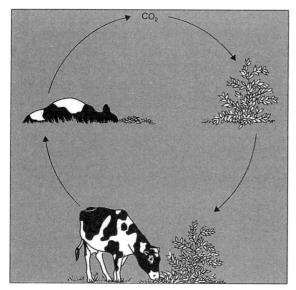

carbon cycle

carbon monoxide   A deadly poisonous gas that has no odor and is colorless. It is produced when a substance containing carbon does not have enough oxygen to burn completely. This may happen in poorly ventilated boilers or in the burning of gasoline by automobile engines. The formula for carbon monoxide is CO.

Carboniferous Period   The warm, rainy period in the earth's history when great swamps grew and then died. The dead plants piled up and later hardened into beds of coal. The Carboniferous Period began about 350 million years ago and lasted for about 65 million years.

cardiac   Relating to the heart. Cardiac muscle is a special kind of muscle that makes up the walls of the heart.

caries   Decayed or softened areas of the teeth caused by bacteria. A large amount of sugar in the diet and a lack of brushing worsens caries and produces cavities in the teeth. Tiny amounts of fluoride in toothpaste help to prevent caries.

carnivore   An animal that eats the flesh of other animals. Carnivores are either of two kinds; trappers, such as pythons and crocodiles, which lie in wait for their prey; and hunters, such as hawks and sharks, which go after their prey.

carrier wave   A constant radio wave that carries sound or picture signals from a transmitting station to a radio or television receiver.

cartilage   The flexible, white gristle that joins one bone to another. Cartilage helps the bones to move smoothly within a joint, such as a knee. The flexible parts of your nose and your ears are made of cartilage. [*Cartilage* comes from a Latin word meaning "gristle."]

cartridge   A small container. A bullet cartridge holds gunpowder; an ink cartridge holds ink for a printer.

cassette   A small case that holds magnetic tape used to record sounds (audio cassettes) or pictures and sounds (video cassettes). Magnetic tape has been mostly replaced by many other kinds of digital recording media including disks.

CAT (CT) Scan   Pictures of structures within the body created by a computer that takes the data from multiple X-ray images and turns them in colored images on a screen. The CAT (computerized axial tomography) scan can reveal some soft-tissue and other structures that cannot even be seen in regular X-rays. Using the same dosage of radiation as that of an ordinary X-ray machine, doctors can see an entire slice of the body with an image that is 100 times sharper than an ordinary X-ray.

catalyst   A substance that changes the speed of a chemical reaction without being changed itself. Enzymes in the body are catalysts that speed up the digestion of food. [*Catalyst* comes from a Greek word meaning "to break down" or "to dissolve."]

caterpillar   The larvae of butterflies and moths are called caterpillars. They are mostly herbivores (plant eaters), and many of them are considered pests in agriculture because of the damage they cause to fruits and other agricultural produce.

cathode The negatively charged electrode of a battery, electric cell, or a cathode ray tube (an old-style television tube, for example). A cathode gives off electrons.

cave A naturally formed open space in rock usually open to the surface through a passageway. Limestone caves that are very large are called caverns.

Cavendish, Henry (1731–1810) An English chemist who discovered hydrogen and showed that water was not a separate element but a compound made of hydrogen and oxygen.

celestial Pertaining to the sky or heavens. The celestial sphere is an imaginary sphere that seems to enclose all the stars and other heavenly objects in the sky. To an observer looking up from Earth, the visible sky forms half of the celestial sphere. The other half of the celestial sphere is seen from the other side of Earth. The celestial poles are the points in the sky right above Earth's North and South poles. The celestial equator is the projection of Earth's equator onto the sphere.

cell 1. BIOLOGY. The smallest unit of living things. It is made up of a substance called pro-

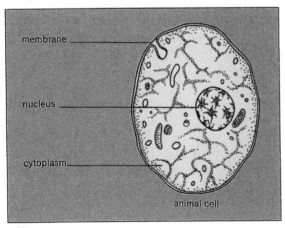

cell

toplasm and surrounded by a thin membrane. Most cells have a central part called a nucleus surrounded by clear fluid called cytoplasm. Some living things, such as bacteria, are single-celled. In many-celled animals and plants, such as humans or trees, different kinds of cells have special purposes. 2. PHYSICS. A part of a battery that stores or makes electricity by chemical means. [*Cell* comes from a Latin word meaning "a small room."]

cell phone A hand-held mobile device used for talking, text messaging, or data communication over a network of base stations known as cell sites.

cellulose The substance that forms the walls of plant cells. In industry it is used to make paper, textiles, cellophane, celluloid, and other plastics.

Celsius scale A way of measuring temperature that sets the freezing point of water at 0° and the boiling point of water at 100°. Also known as centigrade. The scale was named after the Swedish scientist Anders Celsius (1701–1744), who first proposed its use. The abbreviation is C.

cement Cement is a gray powder made from crushed limestone and clay. When mixed with water and sand, it hardens into a rocklike construction material called concrete.

Cenozoic Era The most recent era of geologic time. Mammals, birds, and flowering plants developed during the Cenozoic Era, and the continents moved into their modern-day locations. The Cenozoic began about 65 million years ago and is still going on today. [*Cenozoic* comes from Greek words meaning "recent life."]

center of gravity The point in an object at which the weight seems to be concentrated. A racing car has a low center of gravity and resists tipping over on curves. If an object is supported beneath its center of gravity, it will be balanced.

centigrade scale A way of measuring temperature, at which water freezes at 0° and boils at 100°. Also called Celsius, the abbreviation is C.

central nervous system In animals with backbones, the part of the nervous system made up of the brain and the spinal cord. The central nervous system controls the senses, movement, and all the other activities of an animal.

centrifugal force The force that causes an object turning around a center to move outward from the center. The opposite of centripetal force.

centrifugal force

centripetal force The force acting inward on an object moving in a circle. For example, the opposite of centrifugal force gravity is the centripetal force acting on an Earth satellite.

cerebellum The part of the brain that coordinates the muscles in the body so they can work together, allowing us to move easily. The cerebellum is located behind and below the cerebrum.

cerebrum The largest and main part of the brain. The cerebrum is divided into two halves called hemispheres. The right side of the cerebrum controls the left side of the body, and the left side controls the right side of the body.

Some parts of the cerebrum receive messages from the sense organs and control voluntary movement. Other parts are concerned with language, speech, thinking, and memory.

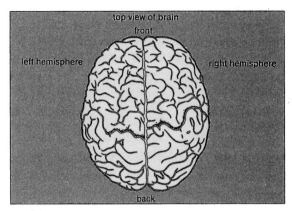

cerebrum

Chadwick, Sir James (1891–1974) An English scientist who received the 1935 Nobel Prize in physics for his discovery of the neutron, one of the three elementary particles found in atoms.

chain reaction A series of chemical or atomic changes in which energy is released. The energy released in an atomic bomb or nuclear reactor is the result of a chain reaction in a radioactive material such as uranium or plutonium.

chalk A soft, white rock made mostly of limestone that contains tiny fossil seashells. Chalk is used in lime and cement, in cosmetics and plastics, and as a fertilizer. School chalk is usually made from calcium carbonate produced in chemical factories.

***Challenger* disaster** The ill-fated launch of the *Challenger* space shuttle on January 28, 1986, the worst disaster in the United States space program The shuttle blew up 73 seconds after lift-off, killing the seven-person crew. Teacher-in-space Sharon Christa McAuliffe was among the fatalities. The cause of the accident was the failure of the O-rings that sealed the joint between two parts of one of the rocket boosters. NASA, the Marshall Space Flight Center, and contractor Morton Thiokol were all faulted for poor management and engineering.

***Challenger* expedition** The first worldwide oceanographic survey. The expedition made many biological, chemical, and physical observations of the oceans. It was headed by Sir Charles Thomson aboard the steamship HMS *Challenger* between 1872 and 1876.

channel The deepest part of a body of water such as a river or stream. Also, a narrow passage of water that connects two larger bodies of water: a strait.

channel

characteristic A distinctive feature or trait of an animal or plant (such as its size, shape, or behavior) that is inborn. For example, a characteristic of hawks is their keen eyesight. [*Characteristic* comes from the Greek word for an instrument used to engrave or stamp a distinctive or identifying mark.]

charge (n.) The amount of electricity held by an object. [*Charge* comes from the Latin word for a wheeled vehicle, commonly used to carry a load.]

charge (v.) To fill with electrical energy or chemical energy. Such energy can be used as a source of electricity, as in an electric cell or battery.

chemical (adj.) Having to do with chemistry. Chemists perform chemical research.

chemical (n.) An element or a compound used in chemistry. A chemical can be represented by a chemical symbol or a formula. For example, the element oxygen is represented by the symbol O, hydrogen by the symbol H, and the compound water is represented by the formula H_2O.

chemical bond The force that holds atoms together to form a molecule of a chemical compound.

chemical change, or reaction A change in the properties of a substance. For example, oxygen is a colorless gas that supports burning, and hydrogen is a colorless gas that burns. When they combine, a chemical change takes place and they form water, which puts out flames.

chemical energy The energy stored in a substance. It is released or absorbed during a chemical reaction.

chemical equation A representation of a reaction that uses chemical formulas and symbols. In a balanced equation, the number of atoms in each element is shown. The equation HC1 + NaOH   NaC1 + H_2O can be read: hydrochloric acid plus sodium hydroxide yields sodium chloride plus water.

chemistry The science of the properties of different substances and the effects they have on each other. A scientist who studies these things is called a chemist. Chemistry deals with elements and their atoms, with compounds and their molecules, and with their reactions.

chemotherapy The use of chemical substance to treat different diseases—in particular, cancer. Chemotherapy sometimes uses drugs that poison and interfere with the growth of germs or cancer cells without doing great harm to normal body cells. Chemotherapy is also used to treat some mental illnesses and other ailments, such as arthritis.

chest The upper front part of the body. The chest is separated from the abdomen by a layer of muscle cells called the diaphragm. [*Chest* comes from a Greek word meaning "basket" or "box."]

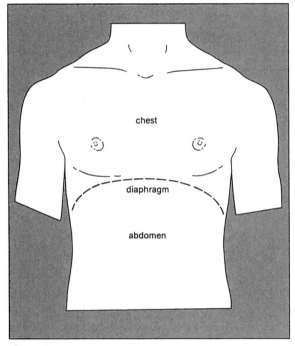

chest

chicken pox A disease found mainly in children that is caused by a virus. Symptoms include a rash of small blisters and a slight fever. The only treatment is rest. Chicken pox is contagious but rarely serious in children.

chip A tiny electric circuit (often smaller than a fingernail) that may contain hundreds or thousands of electronic parts. Chips are the working parts of computers, TVs, quartz watches, robots, and a host of other electronic machines in use today.

chitin The hard, waterproof substance that forms the shell or outer covering of insects, lobsters, and other joint-legged animals. [*Chitin*

comes from the Greek word for a kind of clothing.]

chlorine A greenish-yellow poisonous gas that is bad-smelling and very irritating to the nose and the throat. Chlorine has an atomic number of 17; an atomic weight of 35.453; and its chemical symbol is Cl. Small amounts of chlorine often are used to kill bacteria in water.

chlorophyll The green coloring matter found in many plants. Green plants use chlorophyll and the energy in sunlight to change water and carbon dioxide into sugar and oxygen, a process called photosynthesis. [*Chlorophyll* comes from Greek words meaning "green" and "leaf."]

cholesterol A chemical found in most animal cells. Cholesterol is normally made in the liver and intestines. It is found in all animal tissues, especially the nervous system. It is also found in many foods, such as egg yolk and meat. Many doctors believe that a large amount of cholesterol in the blood leads to diseases of the arteries. They advise eating fewer high-cholesterol and high-fat foods. [*Cholesterol* comes from Greek words meaning "bile" (or gall) and "solid." Gallstones are made of cholesterol.]

chromatography A method of analyzing the different substances in a mixture by separating them. The substances are first dissolved in a solvent. They separate by traveling through an inactive material at different speeds.

chromosome The tiny, threadlike parts of a cell that develop just before the cell divides. Chromosomes carry the genes of heredity that determine the characteristics of an animal or plant, such as eye and hair color, size and shape, and whether the living thing is a cactus or a lion. The gene is on a double strand of the substance DNA. Every living thing has the same number of chromosomes as others of its kind. More complex animals and plants have two identical sets of chromosomes in each cell nucleus. Such animals and plants are called diploid.

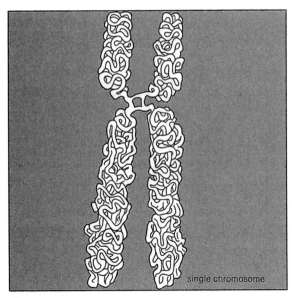
single chromosome

chromosome

chronometer A very accurate mechanical clock or timepiece. Mechanical chronometers were often carried on ships and planes to determine the exact time so that the position of the sun and stars could be used as an aid to navigation. Modern technology is making digital timepieces that are more accurate in determining the exact time.

circuit A path for electricity to travel. A complete path is called a closed circuit. If there is a break in the circuit, it is called an open circuit and the current will not flow. [*Circuit* is based on a Latin word meaning "to go around."]

circuit breaker A device used in place of a fuse to protect electrical power lines or equipment from being damaged by too much current. When the current exceeds a set amount, the breaker opens the circuit automatically and stops the flow of electricity. The advantage of a circuit breaker is that it can be reset: a blown fuse has to be replaced.

circulation In animals that have a circulatory system, the movement of blood around the body.

circulatory system The closed network in the body through which blood and the materials in it travel. In humans, the circulatory system moves blood from the heart through arteries, arterioles, capillaries, venules, veins, and back to the heart.

circumpolar stars To an observer on Earth, the stars that seem to circle the celestial poles and never dip below the horizon.

cirque A steep, bowl-shaped hollow in the earth's surface formed by the advance of a glacier. A lake often forms in the hollow after the glacier has retreated. [*Cirque* is based on a Latin word meaning "round."]

cirrus Describes a cloud, usually high and thin and made of ice crystals. These feathery clouds are sometimes called "mares' tails," because they are thin and wispy like the hairs of a horse's tail.

classification The grouping together of plants, animals, or other objects with similar qualities. In one classification that is widely used, living things are grouped into five kingdoms: monerans (bacteria and blue-green algae), protists (most one-celled organisms), fungi (plants that do not have chlorophyll), plants, and animals. [*Classification* comes from a Latin word referring to a division of people, ships, or military forces.]

clavicle The collarbone. People have two S-shaped collarbones joining the shoulder blade (scapula) to the breastbone (sternum). [*Clavicle* comes from a Latin word meaning "little key." The ancients thought that the collarbone looked like a door bolt or key.]

claw A curved, pointed nail on the toes of some animals such as birds and cats. A claw is used to grab and hold an object.

clay A very tiny particle of soil. Clay particles are smaller than sand or silt particles. Also, a sticky kind of soil that can be shaped when wet and that hardens when dry. Clay soils are used to make bricks and tiles, and they are used in ceramics and pottery.

climate The average weather in an area over a long period of time. Weather conditions include temperature, rainfall or snowfall, sunshine, wind, humidity, and cloudiness. Climates are often classified into five groups: tropical rainy, arid (dry), warm temperate, cold temperate, and polar climates. Much of the southern half of the United States is warm temperate; while the northern half, Canada, and most of Europe are cold temperate. The mid-parts of Africa and South America are tropical rainy. Global warming refers to changes in climate, not the daily weather.

clocks Devices used to tell the time of day. Mechanical clocks first appeared in Europe in the thirteenth century. They used a series of gears and pinions with a weight and a pendulum. In the seventeenth century, the hairspring and the balance wheel were used to make portable clocks and, later, watches. Mechanical clocks have been replaced by other kinds of clocks that use electronic means to tell the time.

clone An animal or plant that has developed from a cell of a single parent. A clone is genetically identical to its parent.

clot A solid mass. A blood clot is formed from the clumping together of blood cells and other material in the blood. A solid clot that forms on the skin stops the bleeding from a damaged blood vessel. A clot within a blood vessel, called an embolism, can interfere with the flow of blood and cause cell damage or even death.

cloud chamber A device used to observe the telltale tracks of atomic particles. Atomic particles leave fog trails in a cloud chamber that look like streaks, rays, or spirals.

clouds Millions and millions of tiny water droplets or ice crystals floating in the air.

When a cloud is at the surface of the ground it is called fog. There are three main types of clouds: Cumulus (puffy) clouds are mountain or mushroom-shaped; Cirrus (wispy, hair-like) clouds are high and feathery; Stratus (layered) clouds are low-lying clouds that make the sky look gray.

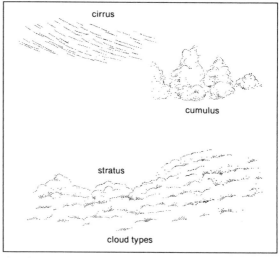

cirrus

cumulus

stratus

cloud types

clouds

coal A hard, black natural material burned as fuel. It is made mostly of the element carbon. Coal was formed many millions of years ago from the remains of tropical and subtropical plants. Different kinds of coal include bituminous (soft coal used in generating electricity and for heating) and anthracite (harder coal, which burns slowly and is preferred in homes).

coal tar A thick, black liquid produced when bituminous coal is processed. Asphalt, disinfectants, fuels, preservatives, and many other different chemicals used in industry and the home are made from coal tar.

cochlea A spiral tube in the inner ear that contains a fluid and nerve endings. In the cochlea, sound vibrations are changed to nerve impulses that are sent to the brain.

cocoon A silky, protective covering spun by the larvae of some insects such as moths and butterflies. Also, the egg cases of spiders and earthworms. We get silk from the cocoon of the silkworm moth.

code A set of symbols or words used to represent letters or numbers. The Morse code, which uses a series of dots and dashes that stands for letters, is one example. Some codes are secret so that they can be used in wartime. In computers, numbers, letters, and other symbols are represented by a series of 1's and 0's. This is called a binary code. Also, the genetic code. The genetic code determines the makeup of the gene.

cold, common A mild illness involving the nose and throat and caused by different viruses. People with colds may have runny noses, coughs, sore throats, and headaches.

cold front The boundary of a cold air mass that pushes toward and under a warm air mass. Clouds often form and rain or snow may fall as the cold front passes by.

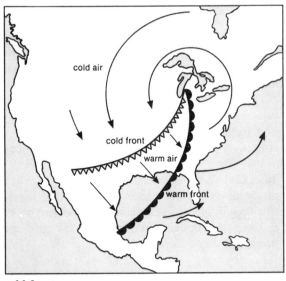

cold front

cold-blooded Refers to the body temperature of reptiles, amphibians, and fish. Cold-blooded animals have body temperatures that change when the temperature of the surrounding water or air changes. Mammals and birds are warm-blooded. Their body temperature remains constant.

colloid A mixture that is halfway between a solution and a suspension of large particles. Also called a colloidal suspension. The particles in a colloid are very tiny, but larger than most molecules. The particles do not actually dissolve, but remain suspended in a gas, liquid, or solid. Fog is an example of a colloidal suspension of tiny water droplets in air. When light rays shine through a colloid, they are scattered and dispersed by the particles. The colloidal particles of dust and other substances in the atmosphere cause the sky to be blue in daytime and sometimes red at sunset and sunrise. [*Colloid* comes from Greek words meaning "gluelike."]

colon The main part of the large intestine in mammals. The final part of food digestion takes place in the colon.

colony A group of the same animals, such as seals or ants, living together in the same area. Also, a grouping of bacteria or other microorganisms growing on a culture plate in a laboratory. [*Colony* comes from the Latin word meaning "an inhabitant" or "settler."]

color The result of the way the brain senses the wavelengths of light entering the eye. The color nerve cells in the eye are called cones and can respond to colors only when they are in bright light. The cones respond to red, green, and blue light. The brain adds together the responses and produces the sensation of the different colors. Only a few mammals, including humans, are able to see colors. [*Color* comes from a Latin word meaning "complexion" or "appearance."]

color blindness or deficiency The inability to tell the difference between certain colors, usually red and green. Color deficiency is due to disorders in the retina of the eye. More males are color deficient to red and green than females. This trait is an inherited characteristic.

coma 1. MEDICINE. A state of unconsciousness caused by a brain injury or an illness.

2. ASTRONOMY. The glowing gases round the nucleus of a comet. [*Coma* comes from a Greek word meaning "deep sleep."]

combustion Burning. The process of catching fire and giving off heat and light when a substance reacts with oxygen in the air.

comet A small space object made of dust and gases. Comets travel around the sun in long, cucumber-shaped paths. Far out in space they are round and dark. When they come near the sun, they begin to glow and some comets grow a "tail." The tails are made of thin gas and dust blown away from the body of the comet by the pressure of sunlight. The most famous comet is Halley's comet, which last visited Earth in 1986. [*Comet* comes from a Greek word meaning "long-haired." To the Greeks a comet seemed to have long hair flowing out behind it.]

comet

command An order to a computer to do something, such as run a program.

community A group of different animals and plants that live together in a particular place, such as a field, a forest, or a coral reef.

compass An instrument used to show direction on Earth's surface. Most compasses are small magnetic needles that line up with Earth's magnetic north and south poles. Compasses are used to help navigate ships and airplanes. Modern compasses often use the satellites in a GPS (Global Positioning System) to show direction.

compound eye A type of many-surfaced eye found in insects, such as bees. Some insects, such as dragonflies, have compound eyes composed of several thousand individual eyes. The result is a combined mosaic image that allows a dragonfly to see a wide area around it.

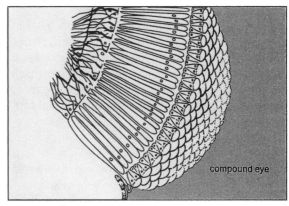
compound eye

computer A computer is a machine that stores large amounts of information and recalls the information quickly when it is needed. It can also do speedy calculations and combine facts in different ways. Every computer has three main ways of working. It can take information, called input, from outside itself. It can work on that information by following a set of instructions called a program. It can show, display, or store results called output. A tiny computer today is more powerful than the room-sized computers that were used by large businesses just a few decades ago. Modern computers are usually linked to other computers around the world through the Internet.

As powerful as modern computers are today, there are many things that a computer still cannot do. It cannot make moral judgments about what's right and what's wrong. A computer does not experience emotions such as love, pity, or happiness. Some things can be done better by computers. Other things can be done better by people. People who use computers can take advantage of the large amount of information a computer makes available to them while using their own judgment about the best way to apply it.

computer languages An artificial language created to express ways of doing things performed by a computer. A computer language is used to write programs that control the way a computer operates. BASIC, JAVA, FORTRAN and C are examples of a computer language.

computer program A set of step-by-step instructions that tell a computer exactly what to do. Computers must be able to understand the special language in which the program is written. The computer has a language program built inside that enables it to understand a program for a particular job.

concave Curved inward. The inside surface of a spoon is concave. The lenses in glasses worn by nearsighted people are concave.

concentration In chemistry, the amount of a substance that is dissolved in a liquid. The smaller the amount of liquid, the more concentrated the solution. For example, the concentration of salt in a glass of seawater increases when some of the water evaporates.

concrete A building material made from cement, sand, pebbles, and water. Concrete can be molded into any shape when it is soft. It hardens into a strong, rocklike substance when it dries. [*Concrete* comes from a Latin word meaning "to grow together" or "to become solid."]

condensation The process by which a gas cools and is changed into a liquid. Clouds are a result of condensation of water vapor in the air. Dew is the result of the condensation of water vapor on cold objects.

condense To change a gas into a liquid by cooling. A liquid takes up less space than the gas from which it condenses.

condenser 1. CHEMISTRY. A piece of apparatus used to change a gas or a vapor, such as steam,

into a liquid by cooling the vapor. A condenser is used to purify, or distill, water and other kinds of liquids. 2. PHYSICS. A device used to store electric charges, usually called a capacitor.

conduct To carry or transmit forms of energy such as heat, electricity, or sound. A copper wire is often used to conduct electricity. Metals are good conductors of heat. The tiny bones in the ear conduct sound waves. [*Conduct* comes from a Latin word meaning "brought together."]

conduction The process by which heat, electricity, sound or some other form of energy can travel through a substance. For example, electricity travels through a wire by conduction.

conifer A tree that produces cones and usually has needle-shaped leaves. Conifers include pines, spruces, and firs, and are usually evergreens.

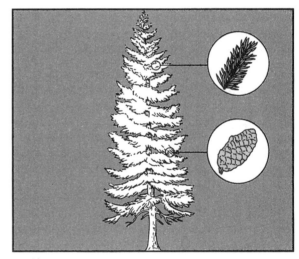

conifer

conservation The protection and care of natural resources such as animals, plants, air, water, minerals, and land. Careful conservation of our environment works to help preserve the natural world for future generations. [*Conservation* comes from a Latin word meaning "to protect" or "to keep safe."]

constellation A group of stars that form a pattern in the night sky. Constellations are usually named after an animal, person or thing in a myth—for example, Ursa Major (the Big Bear), Draco (the Dragon), or Orion (the Hunter). Over the year, the path of the sun takes it through twelve constellations, called the zodiac. Some of the constellations of the zodiac are Gemini (the Twins), Aquarius (the Water Carrier), and Leo (the Lion).

contagious   Spread by contact with a person having a disease such as a cold or the flu. A non-contagious disease, such as hardening of the arteries, is one that is not spread by contact.

continent   One of the six large land areas in the earth's surface. These are North America, South America, Eurasia (Europe and Asia form a single land area), Africa, Australia, and Antarctica. [*Continent* comes from a Latin word meaning "to contain" or "to hold together."]

continental drift   The very slow movement of continents. About 250 million years ago, the continents formed a single land mass called Pangaea. Pangaea broke apart and the continents began to drift away from one another. The surface rock of Pangaea was lighter than the rock deep beneath the earth. When the interior heat of the earth broke the surface rock into huge pieces called plates, the plates moved about, carrying the continents with them. Thus, Pangaea broke apart and the continents began to drift away from one another. The movement is very slow, in most places only an inch every hundred years.

continental shelf   The gradually sloping land under the sea that surrounds each of the continents. The shelf slopes down away from the coast sometimes for hundreds of miles and reaches a depth of about 600 feet. Beyond the shelf is the steep continental slope, which drops down to the deep ocean floor.

contour   A line on a map or globe that traces the surface features of a region. All the points on the same contour line are the same height above sea level. [*Contour* comes from a French word meaning "to go around something" or "to trace its outline."]

control   The part of an experiment that is used to check or compare results. For example, in testing the effect of a fertilizer on plants, some plants will be treated with fertilizer and some will not. The growth of the fertilized plants will be measured and compared to the growth of the unfertilized plants. This is called a control experiment and the unfertilized plants are called a control group.

convection   The transfer of heat from one place to another by the movement of heated gases or liquids. The heated liquid or gas expands and rises. As it rises, the liquid or gas cools and falls. The rising and falling liquids or gases are called convection currents. Some winds are convection currents in the air.

convex   Curved outward. The outside of a ball is convex. Convex is the opposite of concave. A lens with two convex surfaces will focus light to a point. A magnifying lens is convex.

Copernicus, Nicolaus   (1473–1543) A Polish astronomer who proposed that Earth was not the center of the universe as was thought at the time. Instead, Copernicus wrote that Earth, the planets, and the stars orbit round a stationary sun. This is called the heliocentric theory.

Copernicus, Nicolaus

copper   A reddish-brown metal element with a symbol of Cu, an atomic number of 29, and an atomic weight of 63.546. Copper is a good conductor of electricity and heat. It can be made into this wire and is often used in electric wiring.

coral   Small sea animals whose limestone

skeletons form coral rock. Coral forms coral reefs and islands in tropical seas. Coral can be found in many different shapes and colors.

Coriolis effect The change in direction of a moving mass caused by Earth's rotation. The effect is most noticeable with large motions such as winds or ocean currents. In the Northern Hemisphere, winds and ocean currents seem to shift to the right. In the Southern Hemisphere, they seem to shift to the left. The effect was first described in 1835 by Gaspard Coriolis (1792–1843), a French engineer.

cornea The transparent part of the tough coating of the eyeball that protects the iris and the lens. Light passes into the eye through the cornea. [*Cornea* comes from a Latin word meaning "like an animal's horn in texture and appearance."]

corona The outer atmosphere of the sun or some other star. During a total solar eclipse, the sun's corona can be seen as a ring of light.

corpuscle A red or white blood cell or a blood platelet. A red blood corpuscle is also canned an erythrocyte; a white blood corpuscle is also called a leukocyte; and a platelet is also called thrombocyte.

corrosion The slow destruction of metals and alloys by chemical reactions with substances in the surroundings. The corrosion of iron by oxygen in moist air produces iron oxide, commonly called rust. When silver and copper corrode, they are said to be tarnished. [*Corrosion* comes from a Latin word meaning "to chew to pieces" or "to gnaw away."]

cortex The outer part or layer of a body organ such as the brain or kidneys. [*Cortex* comes from a Latin word meaning "the bark of a tree" and later came to mean "rind" or "shell."]

cosmic rays Radiation composed of high-speed, charged particles that come from outer space and bombard Earth's atmosphere. There is still a question about whether cosmic rays are a danger for long flights in space. [*Cosmic* comes from a Greek word meaning "world" or "universe."]

cosmology The study of the universe, including its beginnings, its nature, and the ways in which it changes. Some important cosmologists are Copernicus, Brahe, Kepler, Galileo, Newton, Einstein, and Hubble.

cotton A plant grown in warm climates for the soft, white fibers attached to its seeds. The fibers are woven into threads used to make a cloth also called cotton.

cotyledon A tiny leaf found within a seed. Some seeds have one leaf (monocotyledons) and other seeds have two (dicotyledons). When a seed sprouts, the cotyledons turn green and start to produce food. But they soon fall of as the regular leaves develop.

CPU *C*entral *P*rocessing *U*nit, the "brains" of a computer. A CPU is a special chip that directs the workings of a computer. Different computers may use different CPUs. A home computer has a CPU that is about the size of a fingernail.

crater A steep, bowl-shaped hollow in the ground. On Earth, craters are usually found at the tops of volcanoes. Impact craters are also formed when a large meteorite crashes into a surface. The moon is covered with impact craters.

crescent The thin, curved shape of the moon when seen in its first or last quarter. The crescent moon appears in the west at sunset. Also, Mercury and Venus when less that half of the planet is illuminated.

Cretaceous Period The last geological period of the Mesozoic Era, when large chalk deposits formed, about 135 to 65 million years ago. Dinosaurs died out during the Cretaceous Period, and flowering plants and mammals spread over the earth. [*Cretaceous* is a Latin word meaning "chalklike."]

crevasse A deep crack in the thick ice of a glacier or in the ground after an earthquake. A crevasse in a glacier forms when adjacent paths of a glacier move at different speeds. [*Crevasse* is a French word meaning "a gap" or "a crack."]

Crick, Francis H.C. (1916–2004) An English biochemist who, along with James D. Watson, discovered the shape of the DNA molecule. This led to a better understanding of how different traits are passed down from one generation of living things to the next. Crick shared the 1962 Nobel Prize in physiology and medicine with Watson and also with Maurice Wilkins, who had provided important X-ray data on the DNA molecule.

Crick, Francis H.C.

Cro-Magnon A prehistoric race of people who lived thousands of years ago in Europe during the last Ice Age. Paintings, tools, and bones of Cro-Magnon people have been found in caves in Cro-Magnon, France.

Crookes, Sir William (1832–1919) An English physicist who discovered the element thallium and pioneered the study of cathode rays. The Crookes tube, which he invented in 1876, is the forerunner of the cathode ray tubes found in most television and computer screens.

CRT *C*athode *R*ay *T*ube. The screen of an old style TV.

crust The rocky, outer layer of the earth. The crust is 20 to 30 miles thick and mostly made up of granite and basalt. It is thicker under the continents than it is under the oceans. Another name for the earth's crust is the lithosphere. [*Crust* comes from a Latin word meaning "shell" or "hard surface."]

crustacean A class of joint-legged animals with a hard outer covering. Most crustaceans, including crabs, shrimps, lobsters, and barnacles, live in water. Some, such as wood lice, are land dwellers.

cryogenics The science that deals with very low temperatures and their effect on the behavior of matter. Recent advances in the field of cryogenics have increased our understanding of superconductors—materials that conduct electricity indefinitely at low temperatures.

crystal A solid with its atoms arranged in a definite geometrical shape, such as a cube or a pyramid. Different chemical substances have crystals of different shapes and colors. The science of crystals is called crystallography.

CSI An abbreviation for *Crime Scene Investigation*. CSI is sometimes called forensic science or forensics.

culture A group of microorganisms or living cells growing in a special liquid or jelly. Cultures are usually grown in nutrient agar in a container such as a petri dish.

cumulonimbus Describes a large, billowing cloud having mountainous or anvil-shaped peaks called "thunderheads." The cumulonimbus cloud often brings rain or snow, and sometimes hail or thunderstorms. [*Cumulonimbus* is based on Latin words meaning "a heap or mass" and "cloud."]

cumulus Describes a type of cloud that is thick and fluffy like a cotton ball. Cumulus clouds develop during fair weather when warm, moist air rises upward. [*Cumulus* comes from a Latin word meaning "a heap" or "a pile."]

Curie, Marie (1867–1934) A Polish-born French physicist who, with her French-born husband Pierre (1859–1906), investigated radioactivity and discovered the radioactive elements radium and polonium. The Curies shared the 1903 Nobel Prize in physics. Marie

Curie won another Nobel Prize in chemistry in 1911. The unit for measuring radioactivity is called the curie.

Curie, Marie

current   1. EARTH SCIENCE. A swift stream of air or water. 2. PHYSICS. A flow of electricity. [*Current* comes from a Latin word meaning "to run."]

cuticle   1. ANATOMY, ZOOLOGY. The outer skin of humans and animals with backbones. Also, the strip of skin around the sides and base of a fingernail or toenail. In insects and some other animals without backbones, the hard outer covering of the animal is called the cuticle. 2. BOTANY. A thin, waxy, waterproof layer that covers the outer surface of many plants.

Cuvier, Georges   (1769–1832) A French scientist who founded the science of paleontology, the study of the remains (fossils) of prehistoric life.

Cuvier, Georges

cycle   A chain of events that repeats itself in the same order. 1. BIOLOGY. A repeating series of stages in the life history of plants or animals. For example, the life style of a frog includes the stages of egg, tadpole, and mature frog. Also refers to repeating events in nature, such as the carbon dioxide cycle or the water cycle. 2. PHYSICS. A wave cycle, such as alternating current. Also used to describe a sound wave or a radio-wave frequency. [*Cycle* comes from a Greek word meaning "ring," "wheel," or "circle."]

cyclone   An area of low pressure in which winds blow inward toward the center and in a counterclockwise spiral in the Northern Hemisphere (clockwise in the Southern Hemisphere). Tropical cyclones are severe storms with high winds and heavy rains. In the Atlantic Ocean or Gulf of Mexico, such cyclones are called hurricanes; in the Pacific, they are called typhoons. A tornado is a very small but powerful cyclone. [*Cyclone* comes from a Greek word meaning "whirling."]

cyclotron   A particle accelerator or "atom smasher." It works by using large electric fields to speed up protons or other atomic particles and large magnets to make them move in a spiral path until they crash into a target.

cyst   A small, fluid-filled swelling sometimes found in animal or plant tissue. [*Cyst* comes from the Greek word meaning "bag," "pouch," or "bladder."]

cytology   The science that studies the nature and function of cells. [*Cytology* is based on Greek words meaning "vessel" and "study."]

cytoplasm   The thin, jelly-like substance of which a cell is made. The cell nucleus and other cell bodies are found in the cytoplasm.

D

Daguerre, Louis (1789–1851) A French inventor who in the late 1830s developed the first practical photographic process called the daguerreotype. Daguerre used metal plates coated with silver. The silver was sensitive and turned black when exposed to light. The photo took as long as twenty minutes to take and the subject had to keep absolutely still for the entire time. A weak image developed on the plate and was fixed with a salt solution.

Dalton, John (1766–1844) An English chemist famous for proposing the modern atomic theory. He correctly proposed that atoms of different elements had different weights, and he prepared the first table of atomic weights. In physics, Dalton's law concerns the pressure of gases in a container. Dalton also provided the first scientific description of color blindness.

dam A thick wall or barrier built across a river to control the flow of water. Dams are built of earth and rock, or concrete. The water held in dams can be used as a source of hydroelectric power, irrigation, or drinking water. If a dam bursts, severe flooding can cause great damage to communities down river.

Darwin, Charles (1809–1882) An English naturalist and biologist who first formulated the theory of evolution. As a young man, Darwin sailed around the world between 1831 and 1836 aboard the HMS *Beagle*. On that voyage, his observations convinced him that living things changed or evolved from earlier forms by a process he called natural selection, or survival of the fittest. In 1859 Darwin published *On the Origin of Species*. In the book, he proposed that competition among living things resulted in the survival of those animals or plants that were best fitted to their environment. For the rest of his life, Darwin continued to do research to confirm his theory.

Darwin, Charles

data 1. COMPUTING. The facts or bits of information that you put into or take out of a computer. Data can be in the form of words or numbers or both. The computer can work with the data it has to produce other data. 2. GENERAL SCIENCE. Facts that are collected by observation or experimentation from which theories are sometimes derived. "Data" is plural; the singular is "datum."

database A large amount of information on a particular subject or subjects stored on computer storage devices.

Davy, Sir Humphry (1778–1829) An English scientist who is best known for his invention of a miner's safety lamp known as the Davy lamp. Before the use of the lamp, explosions in coalmines were common because of the hot flames of candles or oil lamps. The Davy lamp used wire gauze around the lamp flame to absorb the heat and prevent the explosive gas found in coalmines from becoming hot enough to explode. Davy also was a pioneer in using electricity to break down compounds into their elements.

Davy, Sir Humphry

dawn Sunrise or daybreak. Dawn is the time when the sky begins to lighten as the sun comes up.

day A unit of time that is equal to one rotation of Earth on its axis, or 24 hours. Also, the time of daylight from sunrise until sunset is commonly called day. The length of time of daylight varies depending on the location and the time of year. For example, in the Arctic, it is always daylight in June and always dark in December.

deafness Difficulty in or failure of hearing. Some people are born deaf; others become deaf during childhood or later life. Deafness may have many causes, including disease, damage to the inner ear due to injury, or the death of nerve cells in old age.

death The end of life of a living organism or a cell in an organism. Death of a human is usually thought of as the time when the heart stops beating, there is no breathing, and the brain stops functioning.

decay 1. BIOLOGY. The rotting and breakdown of dead substances caused by bacteria and other microorganisms. 2. PHYSICS. The change of one radioactive element into another element, such as radium into radon. 3. ASTRONOMY. Describes the changes in orbit when a satellite slows down due to the friction in the atmosphere.

decibel A unit used to measure sound or noise levels (abbreviated dB). A sound that you can just barely hear has 0 dB. Talking quietly has about 20 to 50 dB. A loud shout is about 90 dB. A jet plane taking off has about 110 to 140 dB. Sounds above 140 dB can cause pain and damage hearing. The word comes from "deci"—meaning one tenth—and "bel," a larger unit for measuring sound named for Alexander Graham Bell, the inventor of the telephone.

deciduous Describes trees and other plants that lose their leaves, usually in the autumn before the onset of cold weather. Oaks and maples are two kinds of deciduous trees. [*Deciduous* comes from a Latin word meaning "to fall off."]

decompose 1. BIOLOGY. To decay or rot. Dead animals and plants decompose in the soil or in the water as a result of microbial action. 2. CHEMISTRY. To break down a substance into simpler compounds or elements by chemical means

deep A part of the ocean floor that is more than 6,000 feet (more than 1,800 meters) below the surface waters. The greatest deep is the Marianas trench in the Pacific Ocean, about 36,000 feet (about 10,000 meters) down.

degree 1. PHYSICS. A unit for measuring temperature. One degree Celsius is equal to 1.8 degrees Fahrenheit. 2. MATHEMATICS. A unit for measuring an angle. Used in geography for measuring position on Earth or other planets in latitude and longitude. Also used in astronomy for measuring the position of a celestial body. [*Degree* comes from an Old French word meaning "down a step."]

dehydrate To remove the water from a substance.

delta A fan-shaped land deposit at the mouth of a river. The land collects as the river slows down when it reaches a large lake or the sea. Delta lands, as in the Nile delta, are usually good for farming as a result of the fertile soil deposited by the river. [*Delta,* the fourth letter of the Greek alphabet, is shaped like a triangle. The word is often used to name objects having that shape or occurring fourth in a series.]

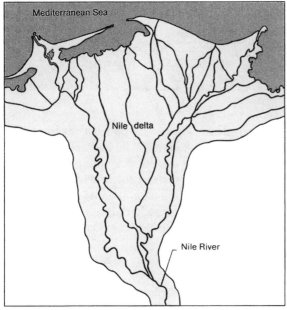

delta

dendrite 1. ANATOMY, ZOOLOGY. Any of the tiny, many-branched endings of a nerve cell. The dendrites carry nerve messages toward the nerve cell body. 2. EARTH SCIENCE. A branching or tree-like pattern in a mineral or rock. [*Dendrite* is based on a Greek word meaning "tree."]

density The mass of a substance compared to its volume. Density is equal to mass divided by volume. For example, a block of lead will weigh much more than an equal volume of wood. That means that lead is denser than wood.

dentine The hard, bony tissue beneath the enamel of a tooth.

deposit An earth material dropped by moving ice (glaciers), water, or wind. Glaciers deposit rocks and other materials on the ground when they melt.

depression 1. EARTH SCIENCE. A low place on the surface of the earth. 2. METEOROLOGY. An area of low atmospheric pressure. 3. MEDICINE. A condition in which a person feels very sad and without hope. This often results in disturbances in sleep and other body functions.

desert A large area of land that has very little rainfall and may be either hot or cold. Plants and animals are limited in number by the scarcity of available water. In cold deserts such as Antarctica, water is trapped in the form of ice. Hot deserts are usually sandy and have no trees. The best known and largest hot desert is the Sahara in northern Africa. Desert plant such as cacti and desert animals such as camels are able to survive by storing water in their body cells and wasting very little water in perspiration and excretion. [*Desert* comes from a Latin word meaning "forsaken."]

detergent A substance that is dissolved in water and used to remove oil and dirt from minerals. Detergents are of two main kinds: soaps and synthetics. Soaps, used since 600 B.C., are made from animal or vegetable fats and oils. Synthetic detergents are usually made from petroleum. They both work the same way by loosening the grease and dirt particles and allowing them to be washed away. [*Detergent* comes from a Latin word meaning "to wipe off" or "to clean."]

Devonian Period The name given to the fourth period of the Paleozoic Era, which lasted from about 400 to 345 million years ago. During the Devonian Period, forests, amphibians, and wingless insects appeared.

dew The small drops of water that form on grass and other surfaces that are cooler that the air. Dew forms usually overnight when air temperatures fall.

dew point The temperature at which the air has all the water vapor it can hold. When air is cooled below the dew point, water vapor forms clouds, fog, dew, or frost.

dextrose A simple form of sugar. Dextrose is also called glucose, corn sugar, or fruit sugar.

diabetes A disease in which the pancreas does not make enough of a hormone called insulin. Insulin controls the amount of sugar in the blood. Too little insulin causes too much sugar to be present in the blood. High blood sugar can lead to ill health and diseases of the blood vessels. Diabetes can be controlled by diet in some cases or by daily injections of insulin in other cases.

diagnosis The identification of a patient's disease or condition after an examination.

diamond One of the crystal forms of the element carbon. Pure diamonds are colorless and used in jewelry. Diamonds are the hardest known substance and on the Mohs hardness scale of 1 to 10 are rated 10. Because of their hardness, industrial (imperfect) diamonds are used for cutting, drilling, and grinding. [*Diamond* comes from a Greek word meaning "hard" or indestructible."]

diaphragm 1. ANATOMY. A thin layer of muscles that separates the chest cavity from the abdominal cavity. The diaphragm moves up and down during breathing. 2. PHYSICS. A device on a camera, microscope, or other optical instrument that controls the size of the opening through which light passes. [*Diaphragm* comes from the Greek word meaning "partition" or "barrier."]

diatom A tiny, single-celled water plant that has a hard shell composed of silica. Diatoms are a kind of algae that may be green or light brown in color. Diatomaceous earth contains large amounts of their skeletons and is used in metal polishes and toothpastes because of its abrasive properties.

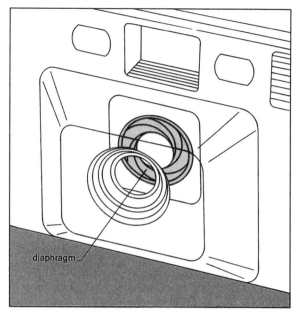

diaphragm

dicotyledon Flowering plants that have two seed leaves (cotyledons). The leaves of a mature plant have a network of veins and parts of flowers in fours or fives, or a multiple of these. Most broadleaf trees, such as apple and maple trees, and many common garden plants such as bean and lettuce plants, are dicotyledons.

diesel engine A kind of internal combustion engine that burns oil. It was patented by Rudolf Diesel in 1892 and is named after him. Diesel engines are mostly used in ships, electrical power plants, large trucks, and heavy machinery. Diesels do not use spark plugs, are heavier than gasoline engines, and make more efficient use of fuel.

diet The food that humans and other animals eat and drink. A balanced diet contains all the nutrients needed for good health, including protein, carbohydrates, minerals, and vitamins. A fairly active adult needs about 2,500 to 3,500 calories each day. A lack of one or another nutrient over a period of time can cause a deficiency disease such as rickets (lack of vitamin D), scurvy (lack of vitamin C), or pellagra (lack of niacin). These diseases strike many poor people in industrial and Third World countries who do not get enough of the right kinds of food. [*Diet* comes from a Greek word meaning "lifestyle."]

diffraction The change in direction of a ray of light around the edge of an object, or through a small opening. White light is split up by diffraction into the colors of the spectrum: red, orange, yellow, green, blue, indigo, and violet. Scientists use a diffraction grating, which is a piece of glass with finely spaced parallel scratches in it, to produce a sharp image of the spectrum in an instrument called a spectroscope. [*Diffraction* comes from a Latin word meaning "broken in pieces" or "shattered."]

diffusion The way in which molecules or atoms of a substance spread through another substance. The process speeds up at high temperatures because the molecules are moving more rapidly. Gases diffuse more rapidly than liquids and liquids diffuse more rapidly than solids.

digest To chemically change foods into simpler substances so that the food can be absorbed into living cells and used for growth and energy. Chemicals in the body, called enzymes, help to digest food.

digestion The process by which living things break down or digest food. Food is usually made up of large molecules that are broken down during digestion into smaller molecules that can diffuse or pass through a cell membrane. [*Digestion* comes from a Latin word meaning "to divide" or "to dissolve."]

digestive system The parts of the body of an animal that take part in the digestion of food. In humans, the digestive system includes the mouth, the esophagus, the stomach, the small and large intestine, and other related organs, such as the liver and pancreas.

digital Information that can be represented as 0s and 1s. Examples of digital devices include computers, CDs and DVDs, new TVs, cameras, cell phones and many more things.

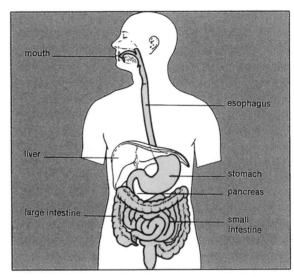

digestive system

digital camera A device for taking still photographs, or video, or both, that stores the image digitally rather than on film by way of an electronic image sensor. The image can be printed and/or downloaded to a computer. A digital camera is also called a digicam. Most cameras used in the twenty-first century are digital. Digital photos are limited by the amount of memory in the camera as well as the optical resolution of the lens and sensor.

dilute To make a substance weaker or thinner by adding water or another liquid.

dimension The shape of an object, such as its length, width, or depth. A book has length, width, and depth, and is called a three-dimensional object.

dinosaur Any one of a large group of extinct reptiles. Dinosaurs included some of the largest and fiercest hunting animals that ever lived, such as Tyrannosaurus. Others were giant, lumbering plant eaters, such as Brachiosaurus and Diplodocus. Still others were small, some no bigger than a chicken or a dog, such as Saltopus. Many had armor plates or scales covering their bodies. Dinosaurs first appeared about 225 million years ago during the Triassic Period. They flourished for 160 million years during the Jurassic and Cretaceous periods. Then, about 65 million years ago, the dinosaurs all died out. There are many theories about their extinction. Some scientists believe great climate changes were responsible; others think an explosion in a nearby star, or a huge comet or asteroid crashing into the earth was the cause. But what really killed the dinosaurs remains one of the great mysteries of science. [*Dinosaur* comes from Greek words meaning "terrible lizard."]

dinosaur

diode   An electron tube or semiconductor with two electrodes. It allows current to pass in one direction only.

direct current   A flow of electricity in only one direction. The abbreviation is DC (or dc). Batteries supply direct current.

dirigible   A large cigar-shaped airship filled with a lighter-than-air gas such as helium or hydrogen. A dirigible differs from a balloon in that it is powered with an engine and can be steered. IT is also called a zeppelin after its pioneer, Ferdinand von Zeppelin (1838–1917). In 1937, the German dirigible, *Hindenburg,* filled with flammable hydrogen, was destroyed by fire. Since that time, dirigibles use nonflammable helium. [*Dirigible* comes from a Latin word meaning "steerable" or "guidable."]

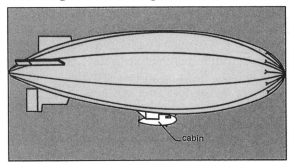

dirigible

discharge   The transfer of electricity from one charged object to another nearby object. The discharge of electricity from a cloud to the ground or to another cloud is called lightning. Also, the using up of the stored electrical energy in a battery.

disease   A sickness or illness in which the normal functions of the animal or plant are disturbed. Diseases can be caused by many things including bacteria and viruses, insect pests (usually in plants), and lack of some important nutrient. Medicine is concerned with the diagnosis and treatment of diseases in people.

disinfectant   A chemical that is used to kill the bacteria and viruses that may cause diseases. Ammonia water, tincture of iodine, and alcohol are common disinfectants used in the home. Disinfectants re not taken internally and some are too strong even for use on the skin.

disk   1. ASTRONOMY. The face of a planet or other object. The disk of Jupiter, for example, can be seen through a telescope. 2. COMPUTING. A magnetic or optical device use to store information. 3. ANATOMY. A round, flat piece of cartilage usually found between the bones (vertebrae) in the spine.

disk drive   A computer device used to record and read digital information from disks. Some drives use small, flexible disks that can be inserted and removed by the user. Other drives use hard disks to store large amounts of information.

dispersion   The separation of light into its

different wavelengths or colors, as when light passes through a prism.

displacement The weight of water or another liquid that is pushed aside by an object in the liquid. The weight of the liquid is equal to the weight in air of the object.

dissect To cut apart an animal or plant or one of its parts in order to study its structure. Dissection is often used in medicine to diagnose and treat disease.

dissolve To cause a solid or a gas to pass into a liquid and form a solution. Sugar dissolves in water to form a sugar solution. The oxygen dissolved in ocean water allows fish to breathe.

distill To heat a liquid until it becomes a gas and then condense the gas back into a pure liquid by cooling it. To distill water is to remove any salts or impurities in it. [*Distill* comes from a Latin word meaning "to trickle down" or "to drip."]

diurnal Happening every day, like the rising of the sun. Diurnal also refers to the daytime activities of plants or animals as contrasted with their nocturnal, or nighttime activities. Diurnal rhythm is a term used to describe the regular changes in the life of an animal or plant that are linked to the 24-hour light and dark cycle.

diverging lens A lens that is thinner in the middle than at the edges. A diverging lens causes light rays to spread out rather than focus together. Glasses for nearsighted people use diverging lenses.

DNA Deoxyribonucleic acid. DNA is an important part of the nucleus of living things. DNA is a long molecule made up of two spiral chains of atoms twisted around each other in a shape called a double helix. The chemical structure of the double helix codes the genetic instructions for the cells of every living thing. Each kind of animal and plant has its own unique DNA. The structure of the

double helix was discovered in England in 1953 by James Watson and Francis Crick at Cambridge University and Maurice Wilkins at the University of London. For their discovery, they received a joint Nobel Prize in 1962.

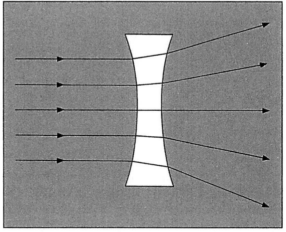

diverging lens

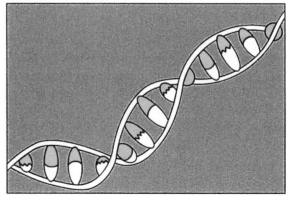

DNA

doldrums Ocean regions near the equator where the winds are light and variable. Often there are dead calms during which sailing ships would lie motionless for days on end. The doldrums are also called the doldrum belt or equatorial belt.

domain A tiny spot in a piece of iron or other substance that acts like a small magnet. Each of the domains has a north and south pole. When the magnetic poles of the domains are lined up with each other, the piece of iron becomes a magnet.

dominant 1. GENETICS. In heredity, a dominant trait is one of a pair of different characteristics that prevails over the other. For example, if a child inherits the trait for brown eyes from one parent and the trait for blue eyes from the other, it will have brown eyes because brown is the dominant trait. 2. ECOLOGY. The plant or group of plants that has the greatest importance in a particular environment. For example, grasses are the dominant plants in a meadow. 3. ZOOLOGY. In some groups of animals, such as a baboon troop, certain individuals that are more important are called the dominant animals.

Doppler effect A change in the frequency of sound or light waves that is caused by the motion of either the source of the waves or observer. It was named after Christian Johann Doppler (1803–1853), an Austrian physicist who first described it in 1842. A train whistle becomes higher in pitch as the train speeds toward you and then lower in pitch as it speeds away. In the case of stars moving away from us, the spectrum of their light is shifted toward the red end. This "red shift" has led to the theory that the universe is constantly expanding.

dormant 1. BIOLOGY. A plant or animal that is resting and not active, such as a seed, or an animal that is hibernating. In winter, many trees become dormant. 2. EARTH SCIENCE. Inactive, such as a dormant volcano.

dorsal The back, or the area near the back, of an animal. The large fin on the upper back

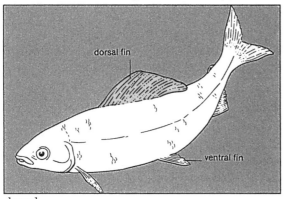

dorsal

of a fish is called its dorsal fin. Dorsal is the opposite of ventral.

DOS *D*isk *O*perating *S*ystem. A program that tells a computer how to send and receive information from a memory storage device called a disk.

dose A correct amount of medicine taken at one time. Also, the time of exposure to harmful radiation such as from a nuclear reactor.

double star Two stars that appear close to each other through a telescope. When double stars revolve around each other, they are called binary stars.

down The soft, fluffy feathers that cover young birds. Also, the soft feathers that lie close to the bodies of adult birds.

drag The resistance acting against an object moving through a gas or liquid. Drag is caused by friction. When you swim, you are slowed by the drag of the water. A parachute is slowed by the drag of the air.

drone 1. ZOOLOGY. A male bee that does no work, is stingless, and produces no honey. 2. AERONAUTICS. A radio-controlled aircraft. [*Drone* may be related to a Sanskrit word meaning "buzz" or "murmur."]

drought A long, dry period of weather where there is not enough rain for crops to grow.

drug Chemicals that affect the way a person feels or acts. Many drugs, such as antibiotics, are taken to treat or prevent a disease. Other drugs, such as aspirin, are used to take away pain or reduce swelling. Still other drugs, such as insulin, replace chemicals that the body needs but is not producing. Certain drugs, such as alcohol or narcotics, are habit-forming. People who become dependant on them may become addicts and drug users.

dry cell An electric battery that consists of an outer zinc case and a paste of chemicals inside. A carbon rod in the middle of the cell forms the positive pole and the zinc case forms the negative pole. Dry cells provide 1.5 volts. A battery can be made with a number of dry cells in series to provide a greater voltage.

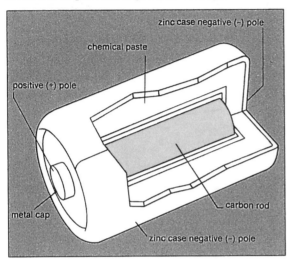

dry cell

dry ice Frozen carbon dioxide (CO_2) having a temperature of $-103°F$ ($-78°C$) or less. Carbon dioxide changes directly from a gas to a solid at its freezing point. Dry ice is often used to keep foods cold while they are being shipped.

duct A tube or pipe in the body for carrying a body fluid, such as a tear duct. [*Duct* comes from a Latin word meaning "led" or "guided."]

ductile The property of a substance that allows it to be drawn out into a wire. Copper and silver are both highly ductile, as are many other metals.

ductless glands Body glands in people and other mammals such as the thyroid that produce chemicals such as hormones. The hormones are released into the bloodstream directly rather than through a duct. Ductless glands are also called endocrine glands.

dune A mound or ridge of loose sand formed by the wind. Dunes are usually found in deserts or along sandy seashores.

duodenum The upper or first part of the small intestine. The duodenum is the shortest and widest part of the small intestine. [*Duodenum* comes from a Latin word meaning "twelve."] The length of the duodenum was first measured by ancient physicians, who found it equal to the breadth of twelve fingers.]

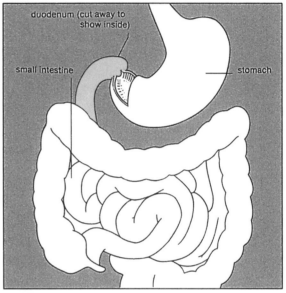

duodenum

dwarf An animal or plant much below the ordinary height or size of its kind. Dwarfism may be a family trait or caused by an illness or a smaller amount of growth hormones than normal.

dwarf star A small star that has a very great mass compared to its size. A single teaspoonful of matter from a dwarf star may weigh more than one ton on Earth.

dye A natural or chemical substance used to give color to something else. Dyes are used to color cloth, paper, plastic, and foods.

dynamite An explosive containing nitroglycerine that is less likely to explode accidentally than pure nitroglycerine. Dynamite is used in construction to clear unwanted buildings or large rocks. It was invented by Alfred Nobel (1833–1896), the Swedish founder of the

Nobel prizes. [*Dynamite* comes from a Greek word meaning "power" or "force."]

dynamo   A machine that changes movement into electric energy. A dynamo usually consists of wire coils moving through a magnetic field. Dynamos are also called generators.

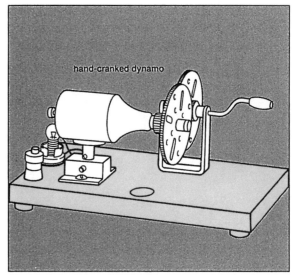

dynamo

ear 1. ANATOMY. The part of the body with which humans and higher animals hear sound. The ear includes the external, or outside, ear that can be seen on either side of the head; the middle ear; and the inner ear. The middle ear is important in maintaining balance as well as in hearing. 2. BOTANY. On a cereal plant such as corn, the ear is the part from which grains develop.

eardrum A thin membrane that separates the outer ear from the middle ear. The eardrum vibrates when sound waves hit it. The eardrum is also called the tympanic membrane or tympanum.

earth Soil or loose land on the surface that is different from rock. Also, the land surfaces on our planet as compared to water, such as oceans.

Earth The planet on which we live and, as far as we know, the only planet in the solar system that supports life. The third planet from the sun, and the largest of the four inner planets (Mercury, Venus, Earth, and Mars), Earth is about 90 million miles (about 150 million kilometers) from the sun. It has a diameter at the equator of about 7,927 miles (about 12,762 kilometers), but is not perfectly round. The diameter from pole to pole is about 26 miles (about 42 kilometers) less that the diameter at the equator. Earth's surface is about 30% land and 70% water. Earth rotates on its axis in 23 hours, 56 minutes, and 4 seconds, and revolves around the sun in 365 days, 6 hours, 9 minutes, and 10 seconds.

Earth satellite Any object in space that orbits Earth. The moon is a natural satellite of Earth. The space shuttle is an artificial Earth satellite.

earth science The study of the earth, the materials of which it is made and the forces acting on it. Earth science involves other sciences, including geology, geography, meteorology, chemistry, physics, oceanography, and sometimes astronomy.

earthquake A shaking or sliding of the ground. Earthquakes are usually caused by the sudden shifting of rock beneath the surface along a fault. The strength of an earthquake is measured on the Richter scale, which numbers from 1 to 10 (the most devastating). In a severe earthquake of more than 7, cracks may open in the ground and buildings may collapse. There have been several earthquakes of 9 or higher including a 9.5 quake in Chile in 1960 and a 9.2 quake in Prince William Sound, Alaska in 1964. Earthquakes and volcanic activity often occur in the same areas of the world. The underground point of an earthquake is called the focus and the point directly above it at the surface is called the epicenter. The study of earthquakes is called seismology. Some seismologists believe that with further study earthquakes one day may be predictable.

earthquake belts The areas around the Pacific Ocean and the Mediterranean Sea containing many active volcanoes and mountains, where earthquakes are most likely to occur. The earthquake belt around the Pacific is sometimes called the Pacific Ring of Fire.

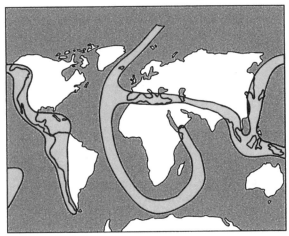

earthquake belts

earthshine The faint light visible on the dark surface of the moon. Earthshine is caused by the sunlight that is reflected on the moon by Earth.

earthworm A kind of worm found in large numbers in forest or grassland soils. An earthworm's body is long and narrow and made of many rings joined together by a softer material. The bottom side of the worm has tiny bristles on each segment. Earthworms eat plant materials in the soil.

ebb tide The outgoing tide away from the shore. Ebb tides expose large sections of the shore that are covered by water when the tides are in. In most parts of the world, there are two ebb tides each day.

echo A sound that bounces back from a hard surface such as a wall or a nearby hill. Also, a radio wave that has been reflected off a surface. Radio wave echoes are the basis of radar. [*Echo* is a Latin word (with the same meaning) that comes from a Greek word meaning "sound."]

echo sounder An instrument used on boats to determine the depth of the water; a type of sonar. A sound pulse is sent down to the ocean floor and its echo is timed. The speed of sound in water is known, so the depth of the water is easily determined. Echo sounders are also used by fishing boats to locate large schools of fish.

echolocation A way of finding the direction and distance of objects by the sounds reflected from them. Bats and some sea mammals such as porpoises give off high-pitched sounds and use echolocation to find food and avoid obstacles. Sonar is a shipboard instrument that uses echolocation to find objects in the ocean.

eclipse When the light from an object in space is hidden by the shadow of another object in space. A solar eclipse happens when the moon comes between the sun and Earth and casts a shadow on part of Earth's surface. A lunar eclipse happens when Earth's shadow falls on the moon. An eclipse is called total if the entire body is hidden, or partial if only part of the body is hidden.

ecliptic The pathway that the sun and the planets appear to travel among the stars during the year.

ecology The study of the relationship between living things and their surroundings.

ecosphere The atmosphere, earth, and water within which living things are found. Also called the biosphere.

ecosystem A small area or community in which each living thing is in balance with its environment. Ponds, seashore, meadows, and forests are all ecosystems.

Edison, Thomas Alva (1847–1931) An American inventor of over one thousand inventions. As a boy, Edison spent only a few months in school, but his teacher thought he was stupid and he left. He educated himself and patented his first successful invention, an improved stock-ticker machine, when he was 22 years old. Among his most famous inventions were the electric light, the phonograph, and an early motion picture system. According to Edison, his success was due to hard work. He said, "Genius is one percent inspiration and ninety-nine percent perspiration."

Edison, Thomas, Alva

effector   A part of the body, such as a leg muscle or an adrenal gland, that does something in response to a nerve message. Also, a nerve that carries a message to a muscle or a gland.

effort   A force needed to do work. In simple machines such as a lever, an inclined plane, or a pulley system, effort is the force that produces motion.

egg   The reproductive cell produced by a female animal. An egg cell must be fertilized by a sperm cell before it will develop. In birds and reptiles, the egg is usually a thin-shelled, oval object that hatches several weeks after it is laid by the female.

Einstein, Albert   (1879–1955) A scientist who was born in Germany, but who fled when Hitler came to power and lived much of the rest of his life in the United States. He also lived and worked for several years in Switzerland where he developed the theory of relativity, which changed the science of physics. His famous quotation, $E = mc^2$, showed that a small amount of matter could be converted

into a huge amount of energy. This led to the invention of atomic energy. He was awarded the 1921 Nobel Prize in physics. Element number 99, einsteinium, is named after him. Many people think that Einstein was the greatest scientist of the twentieth century.

Einstein, Albert

elasticity   The ability of a material to return to its former shape after being bent or stretched. All substances are elastic to some degree, but some metals are very elastic.

electric circuit   A path through which an electric current flows. If a switch in the circuit is open (or "off"), the circuit is not complete and the current will not flow.

electric motor   A machine that produces motion when electricity flows through it. An electric fan, an electric razor, and an electric train all have electric motors.

electricity   A form of energy that can be produced by chemical changes (as with a battery), magnetic induction (as with a generator), friction, or in several other ways. Electricity involves charged particles at rest or in motion. When the particles are in motion the energy is called an electrical current. When the electrical charge is at rest, it is called static electricity. Electrical energy can be converted into light, heat, motion, and other forms of energy. It can also be used to make an electromagnet.

electrode   A terminal that conducts electricity into or out of an electric device, as, for example, the two terminals of a battery, the anode and the cathode.

electrolysis The breaking down of a substance in solution by passing electricity through the solution. For example, water can be broken down into hydrogen and oxygen by electrolysis. In industry, electrolysis is used to plate a thin layer of one metal (such as silver or gold) over another metal.

electromagnetic wave A wave of electrical and magnetic energy that radiates through space. Light waves, radio waves, X-rays, and heat waves are all forms of electromagnetic waves.

electromagnetism Magnetism produced by an electric current. When an electric current flows through a conductor a magnetic field forms. When the current stops, the magnetic field collapses. Also, the science that combines the study of electricity and magnetism.

electron A tiny particle, much smaller than an atom, that is charged with a small amount of negative electricity. All atoms have electrons surrounding the nucleus at different distances. A hydrogen atom has one electron; a uranium atom has 92 electrons. A free electron is one that has escaped from its atomic orbit around the nucleus.

electron microscope An electron microscope uses beams of electrons instead of beams of light to project magnified images on a screen or photographic plate. An electron microscope can magnify an object hundreds of thousands of times, many times more than an ordinary light microscope.

electronics The study of the effect of electronics in motion. Electronics in industry deals with integrated circuits (also known as IC, chip, or microcircuits) that are used in computers, radios, and television. Advanced integrated circuits or "cores" control many different kinds of devices from cellular phones to computers to airplane flight.

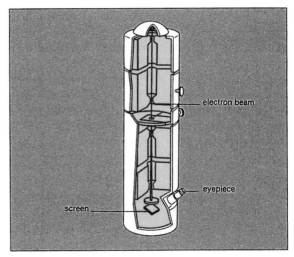

electron microscope

electroscope A device that shows the presence of tiny amounts of electricity.

element A substance that cannot be broken down into simpler substances by ordinary chemical means. Elements are made up of atoms that are alike. There are more than 118 known elements. Oxygen, carbon, copper, silver, and gold are some of the 94 natural elements. The rest are made artificially in particle accelerators. Plutonium and einsteinium are some of the more than 20 artificial elements.

e-mail Electronic mail is a way of exchanging digital messages across the Internet or other computer networks. Originally text only, e-mail now also carries photo, video, and other multimedia content attachments.

embryo 1. ZOOLOGY. An animal in the earliest part of its life before it is born. A human embryo is called a fetus after it is ten weeks old. 2. BOTANY. The partly developed plant inside a seed. [*Embryo* was used by the ancient Greek poet Homer as a word meaning "any young animal." It later came to mean "any fetus." It is believed to come from the Greek word meaning "to grow" or "to swell."]

embryology The division of biology that studies the development of an animal or plant embryo.

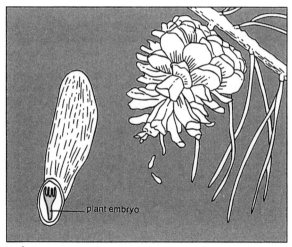
embryo

emf *or* **EMF** *E*lectro*m*otive *f*orce. EMF causes and electric current to flow. It is commonly measured in volts.

emission The discharge or release of heat, light, radio waves, sound, or some other kind of energy from a substance.

emulsion A mixture of two or more liquids that do not dissolve in each other. One of the liquids is suspended in tiny droplets in the other liquid, as when you shake oil and water together. Unless the emulsion is fixed by a special substance, called an emulsifying agent, the two liquids will eventually separate into two layers. Soap and detergents are common emulsifying agents.

endocrine system A system of ductless glands in animals that make chemicals called hormones. Hormones work with the nervous system to control different body functions. Endocrine glands such as the pituitary or the thyroid send hormones directly into the blood or lymph without using a duct.

endoskeleton The skeleton found inside the body of all vertebrates—animals with backbones. The muscles of larger animals are usually attached outside the skeleton. The endoskeleton supports the body and protects the important internal organs such as the brain and the heart. It also gives an animal's body its shape and helps in movement.

energy The ability to do work. Electrical, chemical, mechanical, and nuclear are forms of energy; so are heat and light. All forms of energy are measured by the amount of work done. According to the law of conservation of energy, energy can neither be created nor destroyed, only changed from one form into another. Einstein discovered that matter is a form of energy, and that matter can be changed into heat and light in nuclear reactions. The equation for this, $E = mc^2$, is called the mass-energy equation or the Einstein equation. [*Energy* comes from a Greek word meaning "work."]

engine A machine that changes one kind of energy (usually heat) into another kind of energy (usually movement or mechanical energy). The most common heat engine is the internal combustion engine that uses gasoline to move cars.

engineering The study of how to use new materials, methods, and scientific knowledge to make engines, buildings, bridges, airplanes, and other desired products.

entomology The study of insects.

environment The conditions around a living thing that affect its life, including temperature, water, light, living space, soil, food sources, and the existence of competing species. Humans play an increasingly important part in changing and shaping environments around the world.

enzyme A complex substance found in living things that controls a chemical reaction without being changed itself; a kind of catalyst. Enzymes such as pepsin help break down food so it can be digested. An average cell in the human body contains about three thousand different enzymes.

Eocene Epoch The second epoch or division

of the Tertiary Period in the earth's history, from about 55 million to about 37 million years ago. Ancestors of many modern mammals appeared during the Eocene epoch.

eon Any span of time longer than an era in the earth's history.

epicenter The place on the earth's surface that is directly above the center or focus of an earthquake.

epidemic An illness or infectious disease that attacks many people in an area at the same time. A disease is said to be endemic in an area if it keeps recurring there. A pandemic is an epidemic that strikes in many places across the world.

epidermis The outer layer of the skin of animals and the outer cell layer of plants. The epidermis protects the internal cells from the loss of water, from injury, and from infection.

epiglottis A flap of tissue behind the tongue that covers the entrance to the windpipe during swallowing. This prevents water and food from going into the lungs.

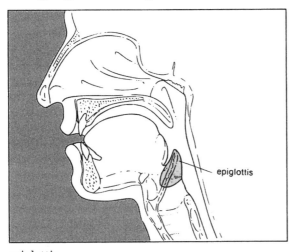

epiglottis

epoch In the earth's history, one of the divisions of time into which a period is divided. We live in the Recent of Holocene, Epoch of the Quaternary Period.

equator An imaginary line that circles the earth midway between the North and South poles. The equator divides the earth into two equal halves, the Northern and the Southern Hemispheres. Every point on the equator is at 0° latitude. The distance around the earth is about 24,901 miles (40,075 kilometers) at the equator.

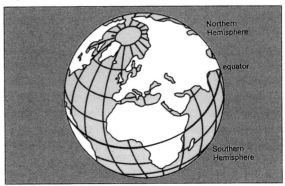

equator

equilibrium 1. PHYSICS. A state of balance. When opposing forces, such as buoyancy and gravity, balance or equal each other, an object is said to be in equilibrium. An unequal force will disturb the balance. 2. CHEMISTRY. A condition in a chemical reaction where no further change occurs.

equinox The two times during the year when the day and night are equal in length everywhere on Earth. It happens at the time when the sun crosses the equator. The spring, or vernal equinox, is about March 21 and the autumnal equinox is about September 23.

era The main divisions of the earth's history (smaller than eons), including the Paleozoic (ancient life) Era, the Mesozoic Era (middle life, sometimes called the age of the dinosaurs) and the Cenozoic (recent life) Era. Each era spans millions of years and is usually divided into periods. [*Era* is a Latin word for the metal objects that the ancient Romans used for counting.]

erg A unit for measuring work or energy. An erg is a very small amount of energy, about the amount given off by a feather dropping on the floor.

erosion   The gradual wearing or weathering of the earth's surface by running water, rain, wind, waves, and other natural forces. In some parts of the world, where forests have been cut down and their living roots do not absorb water, rain falls on the bare ground and running water causes soil erosion. [*Erosion* is based on the Latin word meaning "to chew out" or "to gnaw out."]

erratic   A large rock or boulder that has been carried along by a glacier and then left in another place.

eruption   The discharge of material such as lava or boiling water from inside the earth, as in a volcano or a geyser. An erupting volcano that becomes quiet for a time is said to be dormant.

erythrocyte   A red blood cell. An erythrocyte contains a substance called hemoglobin that carries oxygen to the cells of the body.

escape velocity   The minimum speed that a moving object such as a rocket must reach to escape the gravitational pull of Earth or some other body. The escape velocity of Earth is about 7 miles per second (about 11 kilometers per second); for the moon, about 1.5 miles per second (about 2.4 kilometers per second); and for Jupiter, as much as 36 miles per second (about 60 kilometers per second).

esophagus   The gullet, or tube, through which food passes from the mouth to the stomach.

estivate   To spend the summer in a dormant condition, much like hibernation. Some kinds of snakes and rodents estivate during very hot weather.

estuary   A wide river mouth into which the tide from the sea flows. [*Estuary* comes from a Latin word meaning "tide."]

Eukarya   One of the three major groupings of life (called Domains) on Earth. It is composed of eukaryotes, living things that have a nucleus and other structures called organelles in their cells, such as animals, plants and fungi. The other two Domains are Bacteria and Archaea.

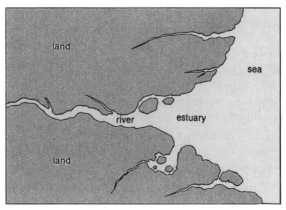

estuary

Eustachian tube   The thin tube that connects the middle ear to the back of the throat. The Eustachian tube equalizes the air pressure on either side of the eardrum because it connects one side with the other. [*Eustachian* refers to the Italian anatomist Bartolomeo Eustachi (1500?–1574), who was the first to study the tube and give a correct and detailed description of it.]

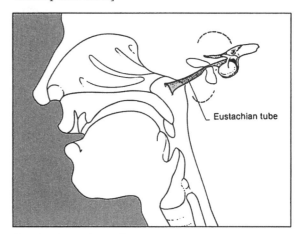

Eustachian tube

evaporate   To change a liquid into a vapor or gas. When water is heated it evaporates quickly. The evaporation of water from oceans, lakes, and other bodies of water is constantly going on.

evening star The planet Venus when it appears soon after sunset in the western sky. The planet Mercury can sometimes also appear as an evening star. These planets are called morning stars when they appear just before sunrise.

evergreen A tree or other plant that keeps its green leaves during the winter. All year round some of the leaves are shed and replaced. Some evergreen trees, such as pines, spruces, and firs, have needlelike leaves that cut down water loss and let snow slide off during winter.

evolution The process of gradual change and development of all kinds of living things through the ages. Charles Darwin developed the theory of evolution more than one hundred years ago, based on the observations he made while sailing around the world aboard HMS *Beagle*. He observed that plants and animals had many more offspring than were necessary to keep the total population the same. Yet the population remained about the same for long periods of time and over several generations. Darwin proposed that while many offspring died, others lived because they were better suited to their surroundings. He called this "survival of the fittest" or "natural selection." Natural selection continues even when the environment changes. Species continue to adapt themselves to their new surroundings over many centuries. Observations that support the theory of evolution have been made by many scientists since Darwin. Simple life probably began to appear on the earth more than three thousand million years ago. Fossils of one-celled life forms have been found in rocks two billion years old. Fossils of more complicated kinds of animals and plants slowly began to appear and change over millions of years. Many of the fossil remains we find today are of animal and plant species that have died out. The animal and plant species that are alive today are those that successfully adapted to their environments. [*Evolution* comes from the English word *evolve*, which is based on a Latin word meaning "to open out" or "to expand."]

excretion The ways in which living things get rid of their wastes from their cells, tissues, and organs. In vertebrate animals (animals with backbones) the kidneys are the main excretory organs. Water and wastes are filtered from the blood and turned into urine. In many one-celled organisms, wastes are excreted directly out of the cell through the cell membrane.

exhale To breathe out, to expel air from the lungs. Exhale is the opposite of inhale, to breathe in.

exobiology The study of possible life on planets other than Earth.

exoplanets Planets that circle distant stars beyond our own solar system are called exoplanets or extrasolar planets. We have discovered a bit fewer than 500 exoplanets but astronomers are constantly discovering more of them.

exoskeleton The hard, outer covering of some animals such as insects, lobsters, crabs, and other joint-legged animals. An exoskeleton gives the body of an animal its shape and protects the organs inside. The shell of a turtle is an exoskeleton.

exosphere The outermost zone of Earth's atmosphere, just past the ionosphere. Its altitude is greater than 300 miles (500 kilometers).

expand To get larger. Gases and metals expand when heated.

expanding universe The theory that the galaxies are moving away from each other.

experiment A planned way of testing a hypothesis or discovering something in science. An experiment is usually done to solve a problem or to find out new information. Also, to carry out or perform an experiment. [*Experiment* comes from a Latin word meaning "to put something to a test in order to discover something about it" or "to prove something that is already known."]

expiration Exhalation. Breathing air out of the lungs.

explosion A violent bursting due to pressure produced suddenly, as when a bomb explodes. Materials that are able to explode, such as gunpowder or nitroglycerine, are called explosives. [*Explosion* comes from a Latin word meaning "thunderous clapping."]

extinct 1. BIOLOGY. Any kind of animal or plant that no longer exists. The dinosaurs are extinct. 2. EARTH SCIENCE. No longer active or expected to become active, as in an extinct volcano. [*Extinct* comes from a Latin word meaning "something that has been blotted out of existence or silenced forever."]

eye The organ of sight in humans and other animals. Although many different forms of eyes are found in animals, they usually have a lens system linked to a light receptor system (nerves) that is connected to the brain. A human eye consists of a ball-shaped eyeball in a bony socket in the skull. It is kept moistened by tear ducts and is moved by special eye muscles.

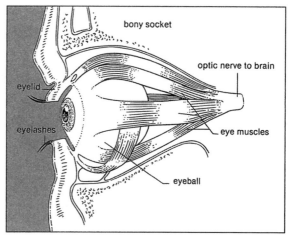

eye

eyelashes The short hairs along the outer edges of the eyelid in mammals. Eyelashes protect the eye from dust and other particles.

eyelids The flaps of skin (upper and lower) that cover the eye when it is closed. Eyelids can close to protect and keep the eye moist. In humans, the tear duct lies under the upper lid. Tears enter the eye and wash away dust and particles that could damage the eye.

eyepiece The lens or lenses in a telescope, microscope, or other optical instrument that is nearest the eye of the user.

facet 1. ZOOLOGY. One of the small flat surfaces that make up the compound eye of an insect. Some insects have compound eyes with a thousand or more facets. 2. EARTH SCIENCE. A polished surface of a gemstone such as a diamond or a sapphire. 3. ANATOMY. A small, flat surface on a bone.

Fahrenheit The temperature scale on which the freezing point of water at sea level is 32° and the boiling point 212°. The abbreviation is F. The Fahrenheit thermometer was developed by Gabriel D. Fahrenheit (1686–1736), a German scientist. To convert degrees Celsius to degrees Fahrenheit multiply by ⅝ and add 32 (F = ⅝ C + 32).

Fallopian tube In female mammals, either of a pair of thin tubes through which egg cells pass from the ovaries to the uterus.

fallout Radioactive particles in the atmosphere that settle to the ground after a nuclear explosion. Radioactive fallout results in radiation burns and has other harmful long-term effects such as causing an increase in cancer rates.

family 1. BIOLOGY. A group of living things with similar characteristics used by scientists in the classification of animals and plants. The name of each animal family ends with the suffix –idea, while each plant family ends with the suffix –acae. For example, house cats, lions, and tigers belong to the cat family (called Felidae). A family is further divided into genera (singular, genus). Also, a group of animals made up of a male and female and their offspring. 2. CHEMISTRY. A group of chemical elements that have similar properties. Neon, argon, xenon, and krypton belong to a family of elements that are chemically inactive. [*Family* comes from a Latin word meaning "household."]

famine A disastrous shortage of food that causes starvation and death among many people. Famines are often caused by a lack of sufficient rainfall over a long period of time, which causes crops to fail.

fang A long, pointed tooth used by meat-eating animals to hold or tear their prey. Also, the curved, hollow tooth of a poisonous snake that ejects venom.

Faraday, Michael (1791–1867) An English scientist best known for his experiments with electricity and magnetism. Faraday showed that electricity could be generated by passing a wire coil through a magnetic field. This is called electromagnetic induction. Most electricity is made in big generators by this method today.

farsightedness The condition of being able to see distant objects more clearly than objects at close range. Also called hyperopia, it can be corrected by using a converging lens.

fat A greasy substance found in the tissues of certain animals and plants. Fats are found in foods such as butter, oil, and margarine. Fats are usually solid at room temperature; those that are liquid are called oils. Fats are a high-energy nutrient in food. Animal tissue made up mainly of fat is sometimes called blubber.

fathom A unit of length used for measuring the depth of waters. There are 6 feet in a fathom.

fatigue 1. PHYSIOLOGY, ZOOLOGY. A temporary feeling of tiredness after overexertion. Fatigue disappears after a period of rest. 2. PHYSICS. The tendency of solids, particularly metals, to crack under repeated stress. You can create metal fatigue in a wire by bending it back and forth in the same spot until the wire breaks.

fatty acid A group of organic acids that contain carbon, hydrogen, and oxygen. Fatty acids are found in animal and plant fats and oils. In the body, fatty acids are produced when fat is digested.

fault A crack or break in the earth's crust. A fault is caused by movement of the rock formations that make up the crust. The San Andreas fault in California stretches for one thousand miles from Mendocino to the Gulf of California. Earthquakes often occur along faults. [*Fault* comes from a Latin word meaning "to fail."]

fauna All of the animals found in a particular place or at a particular period in the earth's history; for example, the fauna of a coral reef or the fauna of the Mesozoic Era.

feather One of the light, thin growths that cover the skin of birds. No other animal has feathers. Feathers usually have a partly hollow, central shaft and many barbs. Feathers help to insulate and waterproof a bird's body. They are moved by muscles and used in flight. Pennae feathers are the outer, stiff feathers that give an adult bird its shape and markings and make flight possible. Plumulae, or down feathers, are soft and curly and lie close to the skin.

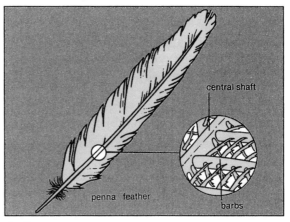
feather

feces The solid wastes remaining after food is digested. Feces are held in the large intestine and expelled from time to time through the anus.

feedback The process by which a system controls itself by using its own output. For example, the brain uses feedback from the muscles of the body to correct the messages it sends out to control the muscles. Many electronic instruments and electromechanical devices use feedback to correct and control their output.

feeler A long, jointed growth found on the heads of insects and some other animals. Also called an antenna. Feelers are sense organs for touch and smell.

feldspar Any of a large group of common rock-forming minerals. Feldspars contain silica, aluminum, oxygen, and varying amounts of other minerals. They are light in color and weather to form fine clay particles. Feldspars are found in granite and basalt rocks.

female 1. ZOOLOGY. The sex that lays eggs or bears offspring. 2. BOTANY. A plant, or the organs of a plant, that need to be fertilized in order to have offspring.

femur   In humans, the bone of the leg between the hip and the knee. Commonly called the thigh bone, it is the largest bone in the body. In other vertebrate animals, the femur is a similar bone in the hind leg.

fermentation   The chemical change by the action of yeast that converts sugar into alcohol. Fermentation takes place in the making of wine, beer, and other alcoholic drinks.

Fermi, Enrico   (1901–1954) An Italian scientist who won the Nobel Prize in physics in 1938, the year he came to the United States. Fermi built the first atomic reactor for the United States in 1942 during world War 11. Later in the war, he helped develop the atom bomb.

Fermi, Enrico

fern   A green plant with roots, stems, and feathery leaves called fronds. Ferns do not produce flowers or seeds. They reproduce from tiny spores on the underside of the leaves. About ten thousand different kinds of ferns grow all over the world today, usually in damp places. Many millions of years ago, giant ferns grew to the size of tall trees in the hot, humid conditions of the Carboniferous Period. [*Fern* comes from a Sanskrit word meaning "wing" or "feather."]

fertile   1. BIOLOGY. Able to produce young, seeds, or fruit. For example, a fertile animal can have young. A fertile plant can produce seeds. Also, able to develop into a new individual. Baby birds hatch from fertile eggs. 2. ECOLOGY. Soil that is rich in nutrients and able to produce crops easily.

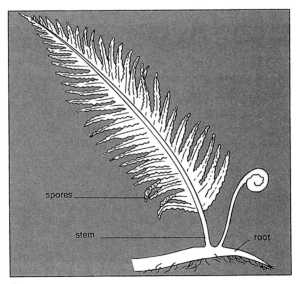

fern

fertilization   The act of combining the egg cell of a female animal or a plant with a sperm cell of a male animal or the pollen cell of a plant. From these two cells, called gametes, fertilization produces a cell called a zygote, which is able to develop into a new organism.

fertilize   To make the soil rich by adding nutrients called fertilizers. Also to combine a female gamete (an egg cell) with a male gamete (a sperm cell) to produce a zygote (a cell able to develop into a new organism).

fertilizer   Any material added to the soil to provide food for plants. The elements supplied in large quantities in fertilizers include nitrogen, phosphorus, and potassium. Too much fertilizer added to the soil can harm the environment when it enters lakes and ponds. The nutrient-rich water leads to excessive growth of algae. This process, called eutrophication, depletes the water of oxygen and may kill pond animals and other pond plants.

fetus   A mammal embryo in the later stages of development in the uterus, when it begins to look like an adult mammal. A human embryo is usually called a fetus from three months' growth to the time of birth.

fever A rise in the body temperature above normal (98.6°F or 37°C in humans). Fever is usually caused by an infection or disease. Drugs such as aspirin help to reduce fever. [*Fever* probably comes from a Latin word meaning "warm."]

fiber 1. PHYSICS. A thin thread of natural (cotton, wool, carbon) or artificial (nylon, polyester, glass) material. 2. PHYSIOLOGY. Plant materials that are not easily digested by humans. 3. ANATOMY. A threadlike part of a nerve or muscle cell.

fiber optics The science that deals with the passing of light through strong, very thin, bendable glass or plastic fibers. Each fiber is thinner than a human hair. A bundle of such fibers can be bent into curves to "see" into difficult-to-reach places. As light travels through the fibers, a bright, clear image is reflected back through another bundle of the fibers. An endoscope is a fiber optic instrument that doctors use to see inside the human body. Engineers also use fiber optics to peer inside engines without having to take them apart. Fiber optic cables are important in transmitting telephone signals and computer information.

fibrin A white, tough, elastic protein formed when blood clots. Fibrin becomes a mesh of small fibers, which helps to prevent further bleeding from a cut. Fibrin is formed from fibrinogen, a protein in blood plasma.

fibula The outer and smaller of the two long bones in the lower leg, between the knee and the ankle. Also, a similar bone in the hind leg of animals.

field 1. PHYSICS. A space through which a force such as magnetism or gravity operates. A magnet has a magnetic field around it. A planet has a gravitational field around it. 2. OPTICS. The area in which things can be seen through a microscope, telescope, or other optical instruments. Also called a field of view.

filament 1. PHYSICS. A very fine thread. The thin tungsten wire in an incandescent electric light bulb, which glows white-hot when the light is on, is called a filament. 2. BOTANY. In flowers, the fine stalk of the stamen that supports the anther. [*Filament* comes from a Latin word meaning "thread."]

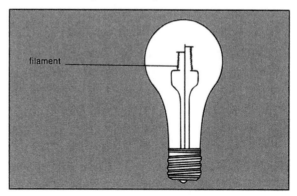

filament

file 1. INDUSTRY. A steel tool with a rough surface used for grinding or smoothing a hard material. 2. COMPUTING. A collection of data or information stored under a special heading.

film 1. PHOTOGRAPHY. A thin strip of plastic with a light-sensitive coating used in cameras to take photographs. 2. CHEMISTRY. A very thin layer or coating of one material on another material. Oil released in the ocean will spread and form a thin film on top of the water. 3. PHYSICS. A material used to make integrated circuits and other electronic devices. [*Film* is descended from a Greek word meaning "skin."]

filter 1. CHEMISTRY. A material with tiny holes in it that is used to separate solids from a liquid. The filter holds back the solids, and the liquid passes through. Paper, charcoal, and sand are common filters. 2. PHYSICS. A device that allows certain electronic frequencies to pass through and holds back others. 3. OPTICS. An optical filter is sometimes used to change the color of the light that passes through the lens of a camera or other optical instrument.

filtration The removal of solid particles from a liquid or the air by passing it through a filter. The filtration of drinking water removes particles of soil and other impurities.

fin 1. ZOOLOGY. A moveable, flat, winglike part of the body of a fish or other water animal. A fin sticks out from the body and is used for steering, swimming, and balancing in water. 2. AERONAUTICS. A fixed, flat surface that helps to keep an aircraft steady. The tail fin on an airplane helps to keep the plane from spinning around. [*Fin* comes from a Latin word meaning "feather" or "wing."]

fingerprints Impressions of the loops and whorls that make up the ridges of a person's fingertips. Since no two people have exactly the same fingerprints, a set of fingerprints left on an object can be used to identify the person who held it.

fiord A long, narrow, deep bay with very steep sides. Fiords are found along the coastlines of Norway, Scotland, Alaska, New Zealand, and Chile.

fiord

fire The light and heat given off when an object burns.

fireball 1. ASTRONOMY. A very bright meteor. 2. PHYSICS. The large, glowing cloud of dust and gases produced by an atomic bomb or other explosion.

fish A cold-blooded animal with a backbone that lives in water and breathes through gills. Fish are usually covered with scales and have fins for swimming. Most fish lay eggs in the water; others produce eggs inside their bodies and give birth to living young. Fish live in the oceans or freshwater rivers, lakes, and ponds. There are about thirty thousand different kinds of fish, more than all the other vertebrate animals put together. The ancestors of modern fish first appeared in the seas more than 500 million years ago.

fission 1. PHYSICS. The splitting of the nucleus of a heavy atom of an element such as uranium or plutonium. Nuclear fission results in the release of a huge amount of energy. Fission powers the atom bomb and atomic energy plants. 2. BIOLOGY. When a cell divides into two or more parts of about the same size. In simple one-celled organisms, fission is a form of asexual (one parent) reproduction in which the body of the parent divides into two parts. Each part becomes a new individual.

flagellum A long, whiplike tail or part of some cells and simple organisms such as certain bacteria and protozoa. The flagellum lashes back and forth or rotates and drives or pulls the organism through the water. [*Flagellum* is the Latin word for "a whip" or "a lash."]

flame test A simple method for testing for some chemicals. Certain substances burn with a characteristic color, such as yellow for sodium and green for copper. The color indicates the substance is present.

flammable Able to burn easily. Gasoline and alcohol are flammable liquids. Flammable and inflammable mean the same thing.

flap An aircraft control area at the trailing edge of the wings. Flaps are lowered when landing to increase lift. They are kept raised during normal flight.

flare A violent explosion on the surface of the sun. A solar flare is associated with a sunspot or group of sunspots. Flares last for only a few minutes but send out huge waves of radiation into space. When the radiation hits Earth it can cause disturbances in radio and television reception.

flash A light source used in photography. A flash is used when there is not enough light from the surroundings. A flash sends out a short but bright flash of light. Modern cameras usually use electronic flash units, which can be used repeatedly.

flask A glass container with a narrow neck used in laboratories.

Fleming, Sir Alexander (1881–1955) A British bacteriologist and doctor who, in 1928, accidentally discovered the antibiotic drug penicillin. Later, penicillin was isolated by two other scientists, Australian-born Howard Florey and German-born Ernst Chain. Fleming, Florey, and Chain received the Nobel Prize in medicine in 1945.

Fleming, Sir Alexander

flex To bend a joint by using the flexor muscles. A person stretches these muscles to flex an arm, leg, or the body.

flexible To be able to bend without breaking. Rubber is a flexible material, as are strips of metal.

flight To travel for long periods in the air.

Most birds, some insects, and bats can fly by flapping their wings. A few fish and some mammals can glide through the air for a short distance. Leonardo da Vinci was the first person to try a scientific design for a flying machine. But it wasn't until the late eighteenth century that people flew in the Montgolfier brothers' hot-air balloons. The first true heavier-than-air flight was made by Orville and Wilbur Wright in 1903.

flight path The track that an aircraft or spaceship takes through the air or space. The flight path of the *Voyager* spaceship goes past Jupiter, Saturn, Uranus, and Neptune and then goes out of the solar system.

flint A fine-grained, hard mineral. Flint, a form of quartz, makes a spark when it is struck against steel.

flipper A broad, flat limb used by some water animals for swimming. Seals, whales, turtles, and penguins have flippers.

float To stay up or at the surface of water, another liquid, or air. An object will float if it weighs less than an equal volume of the water or other fluid it is in.

floe A sheet of floating ice in the ocean formed by the freezing of seawater. Many floes are found in the North Atlantic and around Antarctica.

flood plain A stretch of flat land bordering a river and made of the sediment deposited during floods. A flood plain is similar to a delta.

flora All of the plants found in a particular place or at a particular period of the earth's history. The flora of a meadow includes grasses. The flora of the Carboniferous Period includes giant ferns.

flow The continual movement in a current or stream of fluids such as air or water. Also, the movement of a current of electricity through a conductor. [*Flow* comes from a Greek word meaning "to swim" or "to sail."]

flower The part of a plant that contains its reproductive parts. Inside a flower are male parts called stamens and female parts called pistils. Tiny grains of pollen from a stamen fertilize a pistil. Fruits and seeds come from fertilized pistils.

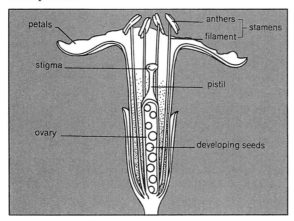

flower

fluid A substance that flows. Any gas or liquid such as air, water, oil, or syrup is a fluid. A fluid takes the shape of its container.

fluorescence The ability that some substances have to give off light when they are exposed to ultraviolet or X-rays. Fluorescence is often green or blue but can be different colors depending on the substance. The fluorescent light disappears when the exposure to ultraviolet rays stops.

fluoridation The adding of small amounts of fluoride to water or to a substance such as toothpaste in order to reduce tooth decay.

fluoride A chemical compound of fluorine and another element, usually a metallic element. Fluorite is a natural mineral made of fluoride.

flywheel A large, heavy wheel used in machines for storing mechanical energy. A flywheel in an automobile smoothes the power output of the engine.

focus 1. PHYSICS. The point at which rays of light or other radiation meet. Also called the focal point. The distance from the focus to the center of the lens is called the focal length. The sun's rays can burn a piece of paper that is placed at the focus of a convex lens. 2. EARTH SCIENCE. The origin of earthquake waves. [*Focus* is the Latin word for a hearth, the center of the ancient Roman household.]

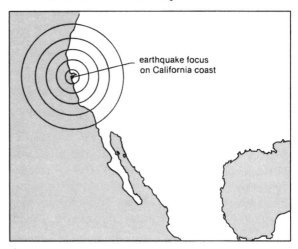

focus

foehn A warm, dry wind that blows down the northern slopes of mountains such as the Alps. On the eastern slopes of the Rocky Mountains, the same kind of wind is called a Chinook.

fog A thick mist or cloud of tiny water drops near the ground.

foliage All the leaves of a plant or of many plants.

follicle 1. BOTANY. A kind of dry fruit such as milkweed, that splits down one side only to release the seeds. 2. ZOOLOGY. A small sac, gland, or pit in the body. A hair follicle is a small pit in the skin from which a hair grows. [*Follicle* comes from a Latin word meaning "a little bag."]

food Any animal or plant substance taken in by a living thing that is used for energy, growth, or other life process. Food may supply nutrients such as proteins, carbohydrates, vitamins, minerals, and fats.

food chain A series of living things in which each one feeds upon the one below it and in turn is eaten by the one above it. A food chain starts with a green plant that is eaten by an animal. That animal, in turn, is eaten by another animal that comes after it in the chain and so on. Larger animals such as sharks, lions, and humans are the final links in many food chains.

food web A group of interrelated food chains in a particular area or community. Animals may feed on more than one other plant or animal. In turn, they may be eaten by many other animals. Food webs are very complex even in small communities.

foot 1. ANATOMY. The end part of a leg on which an animal walks. 2. ZOOLOGY. The muscular part of the body of mollusks such as snails, clams, and oysters. A mollusk uses its foot for moving about.

force A push or a pull that makes an object move, or change its speed or direction if it is already moving. Common forces that make objects move are wind, flowing water, or a gasoline engine.

forebrain The front part of the brain. The forebrain includes the cerebrum, the thalamus, and the hypothalamus.

forensic science The use of many different kinds of science to look for clues or answer other questions of interest in legal matters such as criminal trials, often involving the analysis of evidence found at crime scenes. Forensic science is often shortened to forensics. CSI uses forensics to help solve mysteries in crimes.

forest A large group of trees growing close together along with various kinds of other plants. A conifer forest is made up mostly of one kind of tree such as pine, spruce, or fir. A mixed forest is made up of many kinds of trees. Other kinds include rain forests—found in very hot, rainy regions—and deciduous forests, with trees such as oak, maple, beech, birch, and elm.

formation The act of shaping or developing. Growth comes from the formation of new cells in the body. Clouds are formations of tiny drops of water. A rock formation is a layer of related or identical rocks.

formula A way of showing a chemical compound or the molecule of an element. For example, the formula H_2O tells us that there are two hydrogen (H) atoms for every one oxygen (O) atom in a molecule of water. [*Formula* comes from a Latin word meaning "a form" or "a model."]

fossil The hardened traces or remains of an animal or plant naturally preserved in the ground. A fossil may be a leaf, a bone, a skeleton, or even an entire animal or plant. A fossil can also be a footprint or some other trace of an animal. We learn about the living things of the past, such as the dinosaurs, by studying their fossils. [*Fossil* comes from a Latin word meaning "something that is dug up."]

fossil fuel A fuel found in the ground, such as coal, oil, or natural gas. Coal is the compressed remains of tropical and subtropical plants that lived millions of years ago during the Carboniferous and Permian Periods. Oil and natural gas also formed millions of years ago from the compressed remains of animal and plant plankton.

Foucault pendulum A pendulum made up of an iron ball at the end of a long steel wire. When it is set swinging it keeps swinging in the same path while Earth rotates underneath it. The pendulum was first demonstrated in 1851 by J.B.L. Foucault, a French scientist. It was the first direct evidence that Earth rotates. Many science museums display Foucault pendulums.

fovea A tiny area in the center of the retina where daylight vision is sharpest. It contains many cones but no rods. The cones are nerve cells in the eye responsible for seeing color and for clear vision. The fovea is sometimes called the "yellow spot." [*Fovea* is a Latin word meaning "a little hole."]

fracture 1. MEDICINE. A break, crack, or split in a bone. Fractures are caused by sudden bending or twisting and sometimes by underlying disease. 2. EARTH SCIENCE. A break or crack in rock layers due to folding or faulting. Also, an irregular break or crack in a rock or mineral.

Franklin, Benjamin (1706–1790) An American scientist and statesman. Franklin flew a kite in a storm in 1752 to demonstrate the electrical nature of lightning. His inventions include the lightning rod, the Franklin stove, and bifocal glasses.

Franklin, Benjamin

freeze To change from a liquid to a solid by being cooled below the freezing point. When water freezes it turns into ice.

freezing point The temperature at which a liquid becomes a solid. The freezing point of water is 32°F or 0°C.

frequency In physics, the number of complete cycles per second of any periodic wave motion. Frequencies are measured in hertz (Hz), or cycles per second. Sounds that humans can hear range from 20 to about 20,000 Hz. Different radio and television stations broadcast at different frequencies so that they do not interfere with one another. Alternating current in the United States is 60 Hz; in Europe it is 50Hz. [*Frequency* comes from a Latin word meaning "something that occurs constantly or repeatedly."]

freshwater Water that is not salty, found naturally in lakes and rivers. The bullfrog is a freshwater animal.

Freud, Sigmund (1856–1939) An Austrian neurologist and psychiatrist, Freud is known as the founder of psychoanalysis. In 1938, Freud fled from Nazi anti-Semitism to England, where he continued to write, teach, and practice as a psychoanalyst. Freud's ideas about people's behavior are based on a part of the mind called the unconscious. Freud tried to explore the unconscious mind by analyzing dreams and allowing his patients to freely associate meanings with their dreams. Nowadays, psychoanalysis is one method that psychiatrists use to explore and treat mental problems that people may have.

Freud, Sigmund

friction The resistance caused by moving the surface of one object over the surface of another. Friction slows down movement and produces heat. Since there is less friction with smooth surfaces than with rough surfaces, oil or grease is used to reduce friction between the moving parts of a machine.

front The boundary between two different air masses. Fronts are regions of clouds and precipitation. A warm front is where a warm air mass advances pushing a cold air mass. A cold front is where a cold air mass pushes a warm air mass. An occluded front is where a mass of warm air is surrounded and pushed aloft by cold air. [*Front* comes from a Latin word meaning "forehead."]

frost Feathery ice crystals that form when water vapor condenses on a surface colder than the freezing point of water. Frost forms beautiful patterns on windowpanes in cold climates.

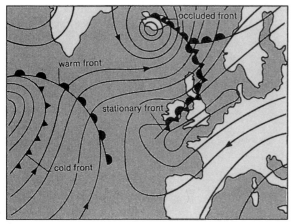

front

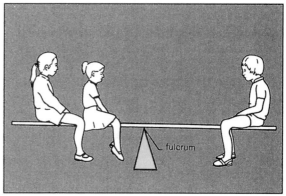

fulcrum

frostbite Damage to the skin and tissues caused by freezing. Frostbite can cause injury to exposed parts of the body, face, ears, nose, and fingers. Sometimes the area goes numb. In severe cases, the tissues may die and then drop off.

fruit A fruit is a ripened ovary of a flowering plant after it is fertilized. Apples, peaches, pears, oranges, tomatoes, and berries are all fruits.

fry A young fish or group of fish, such as guppy fry. [*Fry* comes from a Gothic word meaning "descendants" or "offspring."]

fuel A substance that can be burned to produce heat or power to run machines. Wood, coal, and oil are fuels. Recently, fuel has also come to mean nuclear fuels, such as uranium, that produce heat in atomic power plants. [*Fuel* comes from a Latin word meaning "fire."]

fulcrum The support on which a lever turns or rests. The fulcrum of a seesaw is in the center.

fungus A simple plant with no leaves, flowers, or the green coloring matter chlorophyll. Fungi (the plural of fungus) include all kinds of mushrooms, yeasts, molds, mildews, toadstools, and rusts. Because fungi have no chlorophyll to make their own food, they usually feed upon dead or decaying plants and animals. Some kinds of fungi have only one cell, while others are a mass of threads called hyphae. Fungi usually reproduce by sending out tiny spores that grow into new plants.

funnel A piece of laboratory apparatus with a wide mouth and a thin tube. A funnel is used to pour liquids into narrow-necked jars or test tubes.

fur The soft, thick hair covering the skin of many mammals such as wolves and rabbits. Fur is a good insulator and keeps the animal warm. Some animals such as seals and leopards are caught and killed for their fur. This has threatened some kinds of fur-bearing animals with extinction. [*Fur* probably comes from an Old French word for the fur lining or trimming with which clothes were adorned.]

fuse A safety device placed in an electric circuit to prevent the wires from overheating. A fuse is a piece of thin wire that heats up and melts if too much current passes through it. The open fuse breaks the circuit until it is replaced. In many places, circuit breakers that can be reset are now used instead of fuses. [*Fuse* comes from a Latin word meaning "spindle."]

fuselage The body of an aircraft without the wings or the fins.

fusion 1. PHYSICS. Nuclear fusion is the process by which the nuclei of atoms are joined together to make a heavier nucleus. This results in the release of a huge amount of nuclear energy. The hydrogen bomb relies on a nuclear fusion reaction. 2. BIOLOGY. The joining together of two or more cells, as in fertilization. 3. CHEMISTRY. The melting together of two or more solids to form a new substance. Bronze is made by the fusion of copper and tin.

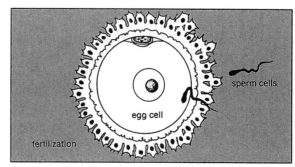

fusion

G

g-force A way of measuring the force that a body feels from gravity and the body's acceleration. At rest on Earth's surface, the force of gravity is 1 g., the body's weight. During liftoff, astronauts feel a force several times greater than 1 g. In orbit, the astronauts feel a force of 0 g. because they and their ship are freely falling together, even though Earth's gravity still pulls both with a force nearly equal to 1 g.

galaxy One of millions of star systems, each containing many billions of stars, planets, clouds of dusts and gas, and other space objects. Our sun is only a medium–sized star among 100 billion other stars in the Milky Way galaxy. [*Galaxy* comes from a Greek word meaning "milk."]

gale A strong wind that blows at speeds of more than 32 miles per hour and less than 63 miles per hour (51 to 101 kilometers per hour). On the Beaufort wind scale, gales are assigned forces from 7 to 10 depending on their speed.

Galen of Pergamun (130–200 A.D.) A Greek doctor of ancient times. Galen made many original studies and observations about anatomy and physiology. He was the first scientist to experiment on the functions of muscles and nerves.

galena A metallic gray mineral containing lead and sulfur. Galena is the most common lead ore.

Galileo Galilei (1564–1642) An Italian scientist who laid the foundations of modern science. Galileo relied on careful observation and experimentation instead of taking the word of earlier authorities.

Sitting in the cathedral of Pisa, the young Galileo timed the swinging of a lamp on a long chain against his pulse. He found that all swings, both large and small, took the same time. This observation led to the use of pendulums as timers in clocks.

Galileo Galilei

Later, Galileo dropped balls of different weights from the top of the Leaning Tower of Pisa. He found that all the balls, no matter what they weighed, took the same time to fall. Through these experiments and others, Galileo discovered the laws of falling bodies and of projectiles.

Galileo was one of the first to build a telescope and to use it to study the heavens. He was the first to see the craters on the moon, the moons of Jupiter, the rings of Saturn, sunspots, and the phases of Venus. Galileo's observations supported the ideas of Copernicus, who said that the sun, not Earth, was the center of the solar system. Galileo's work led to a confrontation with the Church, and Galileo was forced to renounce his Copernican ideas. But to the end of his life, Galileo still believed his ideas were correct.

gall A swollen growth that appears on plants. Galls are caused by insects, mites, fungi, or bacteria.

gall bladder A small sac attached to the liver in which bile is stored. When food reaches the stomach, the gall bladder contracts, sending bile through the bile duct to the duodenum (a part of the small intestine). There the bile helps to digest fat by breaking it down into smaller particles.

gallon A unit of liquid measure. In the United States, a gallon is equal to four quarts or 3.78 liters. In the United Kingdom, a gallon is equal to 4.5 liters and is called an imperial gallon.

Galvani, Luigi (1737–1798) An Italian doctor and anatomist who discovered that a frog's leg, severed from its body, twitched when touched with an electric current. Galvani was incorrect in some of his ideas about "animal electricity," but his name is still used as part of many terms in electricity, such as galvanize and galvanometer.

galvanize To deposit a layer of zinc over an iron or steel surface to prevent rusting. A galvanized object usually has been dipped into hot, molten zinc.

galvanometer An instrument used to detect or measure a small electric current. A galvanometer can also be used to tell the direction of the current.

gamete A male or female sexual reproductive cell. A male gamete (sperm cell) unites with a female gamete (egg cell) to form a new individual (zygote). A male gamete is usually small and able to swim in water. A female gamete is usually larger and does not move. [*Gamete* comes from a Greek word meaning "marriage."]

gamma ray An electromagnetic ray with a very short wavelength and high frequency, given off by the nucleus of decaying radioactive atoms. Gamma rays have great energy and can pass through thick iron or concrete. The rays are harmful to people but they are also used in limited doses to kill cancer cells.

ganglion A group of nerve cells that form a nerve center outside of the brain or spinal cord in humans and other animals. Some simple animals such as worms have a ganglion in each segment of their bodies. Each ganglion acts much like a little brain for that segment.

gas One of the three ordinary states of matter; the others are solid and liquid. The molecules of a gas move about rapidly and freely. A gas will expand to fill up and take the shape of its container. Oxygen and nitrogen are gases at room temperature. Air is a mixture of gases. When the temperature of a gas is lowered enough, it becomes a liquid. If the temperature is lowered even further, it usually becomes a solid. In the high temperatures of stars or in nuclear explosions, atoms are torn apart and the hot gases become a fourth state of matter, called plasma.

gasoline A highly inflammable liquid used as a fuel in automobiles and other motor vehicles. Gasoline is made from petroleum. In some countries, gasoline is called petrol.

gastric Having to do with the stomach. Gastric glands in the lining of the stomach produce gastric juice, which contains body chemicals necessary for digestion. Gastritis is an inflammation of the lining of the stomach. The gastrointestinal tract, also called the gut or the alimentary canal, is the body tube through which food passes.

gear A wheel with teeth along its edge. A gear's teeth fit into the teeth of another gear. As one gear turns, the other gear turns in another direction. If the gears are different sizes, they will turn at different speeds. A set of gears can be used to change speed, power, or direction. A metal rod called an axle is connected to the center of each gear. The axle can be used to drive the wheels of a car or other vehicle. [*Gear* probably comes from an Old English word meaning "to make something ready for use."]

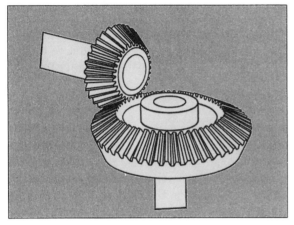

gear

Geiger counter An instrument that detects radioactive particles. It is used to find uranium under the surface of the earth and to check for radiation. The counter was named after Hans Geiger (1882–1947), the German physicist who invented it.

gelatin A jellylike protein found in animal bones and other parts of the body. It is extracted by boiling the bones in water. After the gelatin in the water cools, it forms a clear solid. Gelatin is used in photography and in making jellies and other foods. It is also used to make glue and to grow bacteria in laboratories.

gem A precious or semiprecious stone used in jewelry or decoration. Gems are usually hard, transparent minerals that can be cut and polished. Diamonds, sapphires, rubies, and emeralds are some of the many kinds of gems.

gene A tiny part of a chromosome in the nucleus of a cell that carries genetic information. Genes are passed on by parents to their offspring. A gene controls a particular characteristic of a living thing such as the height of an animal or plant, its color, or the shape of its parts. There are thousands of genes in every cell.

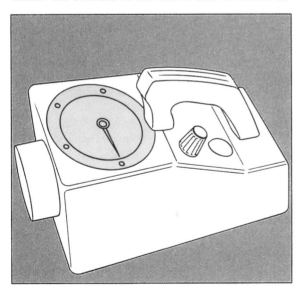

Geiger counter

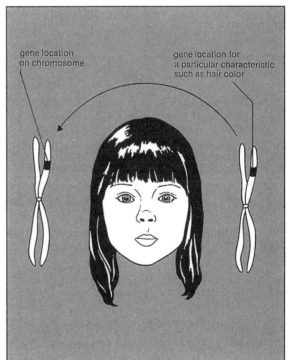

gene location on chromosome

gene location for a particular characteristic such as hair color

gene

generation   A group of living things that have the same parents; also, a single stage in a family's history. Sisters, brothers, and their cousins belong to the same generation. Their parents belong to the generation before them. And their children belong to the generation after them.

generator   A machine that changes motion or mechanical energy into electrical energy.

genetic code   The various combinations of chemicals in the DNA of a chromosome. The genetic code controls the makeup of genes.

genetic engineering   The controlled change of genetic material to create organisms with new or desired characteristics. Also called gene-splicing or recombinant DNA technology. Geneticists try to produce desirable new traits or eliminate undesirable traits in living things by combining pieces of different DNA molecules to form a new DNA molecule. The technique was developed at Stanford University and the University of California in the 1970s.

genetics   The science that studies the way living things inherit the characteristics of their parents. Genetics has to do with genes and their influence. The controlled breeding of farm animals and the development of new strains of plants are some of the ways in which genetics is used.

genome   The complete set of genes in an individual. The human genome has between 20,000 and 25,000 genes, far fewer than was expected before it was completely mapped in the Human Genome Project finished in 2003. Even though the HGP is finished, scientists are still studying the data.

genus   A group of plants or animals that are related to each other. A genus is classified into different species. The scientific name of an animal or plant is its genus (written with a capital letter) and then its species (written with a small letter). *Canis familaris* is the scientific name of the domestic dog. *Canis lupus* is the gray wolf. [*Genus* is a Latin word, derived from a Greek word meaning "a class of things."]

geography   The study of the physical features of the world such as mountains, rivers, lakes, and oceans. Also, the study of climates, mineral resources, plant and animal life, and of people and their activities.

geology   The science that deals with the study of rocks and minerals, the history of the earth, and the ways in which the earth has changed over millions of years. A scientist who studies these things is called a geologist. Geologists dig into the earth's crust to examine the layers of soil, rocks, and minerals. The fossils they find offer clues to life that existed in the past.

geomagnetism   The magnetic field of Earth. Also, the science that studies Earth's magnetism. Geomagnetism causes a compass needle to point towards Earth's magnetic poles.

geostationary   Describes a satellite that orbits Earth at a speed that exactly matches the speed of Earth's rotation and is in an equatorial orbit. This keeps the satellite always above the same point on Earth's surface. To an observer on the ground, the satellite appears to be stationary in the sky.

geothermal   Describes the heat that comes from deep inside the earth. Hot springs and geysers are caused by geothermal energy. Some communities use geothermal energy for heating and to generate electricity.

geriatrics   The branch of medicine dealing with the elderly. Geriatrics is one of the branches of a science called gerontology that studies aging and old age.

germ   A tiny living thing, too small to be seen without a microscope, which can cause disease. Germs include bacteria and viruses. Scientists sometimes use the term microorganism rather than the word germ. [*Germ* comes from a Latin word meaning "a sprout" or "a bud."]

germinate To start to grow, develop, or sprout. In order to germinate, a seed needs water, warmth, and air. After germination, it becomes a new plant called a seedling.

gestation The period of time between conception and birth of a mammal embryo in the uterus. The birth of a human baby occurs after a gestation period of about nine months. Other mammals have different gestation periods, ranging from two or three years for elephants to several weeks for small rodents.

geyser A natural, hot water, underground spring that frequently erupts with a stream of hot water and steam. Most geysers erupt irregularly. Other geysers, such as Old Faithful in Yellowstone National Park, erupt at fairly regular intervals. [*Geyser* was named for a hot spring in Iceland and means "gusher" in Icelandic.]

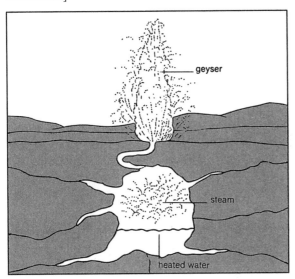

geyser

gill The breathing organ of many water animals such as fish, crabs, and tadpoles. Gills are rich in tiny blood vessels. When the animal breathes, oxygen passes in and carbon dioxide passes out through the thin walls of the gills.

gizzard A small, second stomach or sac found in the digestive system of birds and some invertebrate animals such as earthworms. The gizzard usually holds bits of sand or gravel, which help grind up food for digestion.

glacial Having to do with ice or glaciers. A glacial epoch is the same as an ice age.

glacier A huge river or sheet of ice that usually moves very slowly down a mountain or over the land. Glaciers form when the snowfall over a period of years is greater than the amount that melts during the summer. The largest glacier in the world is the ice cap that covers Antarctica. The study of glaciers is called glaciology.

gland An organ in a human or an animal that produces special body chemicals that help the body function. Some glands, called exocrine glands, have tubes or ducts that carry the chemicals. Tear glands, sweat glands, the liver, and the kidneys are exocrine glands. Other glands, called ductless or endocrine glands, pass chemicals straight into the blood. The pituitary and the adrenal are endocrine glands. [*Gland* comes from a Latin word meaning "acorn."]

glass A hard, transparent, brittle substance. Commercial glass is made from sand, sodium, and lime heated at high temperature until the substances melt and become liquid. The liquid can be shaped into bottles, sheets, or many other forms. As it cools, glass hardens and becomes a solid.

glider An aircraft with wings that uses air currents to keep it aloft. Gliders do not have engines. They are launched by being towed from the ground like a kite or from the air by an airplane.

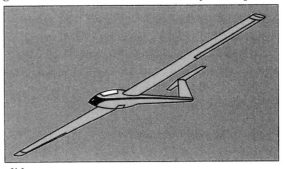

glider

global warming   The term used to describe the rapid changes in Earth's climate in recent decades. Global warming does not refer to weather, which happens every day. It refers to climate, which is the average weather in a particular place over a period of years. It's possible that the weather on any day in any place might be cool or cold, but the average weather, the climate, is getting warmer.

glucose   A simple sugar found in fruit, green plants, and the blood of animals. Green plants make glucose from carbon dioxide and water, using the energy of sunlight. This process is called photosynthesis. Glucose provides animal cells with energy. Plants make both starch and cellulose from glucose. Glucose is also called dextrose or grape sugar. [*Glucose* comes from a Greek word meaning "sweet."]

glue   A liquid used to make things stick together. Glue is an adhesive made from animal or plant materials such as bones, hides, flour and water, or soybeans.

glycogen   A form of starch stored in the liver and the muscles of vertebrate animals. When needed, the body changes glycogen into glucose and uses it for energy.

gneiss   A common kind of metamorphic (changed) rock. Gneiss contains bands of quartz, feldspar, and other minerals.

gold   A shiny, bright, yellow, heavy metal. Gold is a precious metal used to make coins and jewelry. It can be drawn into fine wire or beaten into a thin sheet called gold leaf. Gold is resistant to corrosion and is used in dental work and electronic circuits. Gold has an atomic number of 79 and an atomic weight of 196.967. Its chemical symbol is Au.

gonad   The organ in animals that produces reproductive cells called gametes. The female gonad is the ovary, which produces eggs. The male gonad is the testis, which produces sperm cells. There are two gonads in every animal.

gorge   A deep, narrow passage between hills, usually with a river or stream flowing through it. A gorge is steep and often rocky. Also called a canyon, ravine, or gulch.

GPS   GPS stands for *G*lobal *P*ositioning *S*ystem. It is a system of 27 earth-orbiting satellites that are arranged so that at any time, anywhere on Earth, there are at least four satellites "visible" in the sky. This allows receivers in planes, cars, boats, cell phones, cameras, and many other electronic instruments to pinpoint their precise location in the world. More and more devices include a GPS receiver to track their location.

gradient   1. PHYSICS. The way in which temperature, air pressure, or other quantity changes as you move from place to place. On a weather map, the air pressure gradient is shown by the spacing between the lines called isobars. 2. GEOLOGY. A slope of the surface of land or a river. [*Gradient* comes from a Latin word meaning "step."]

graft   1. BOTANY. To insert a part of one plant into the stem of another similar plant so that it will grow there in place. Grafts are used to produce superior fruit trees or plants with desirable flowers or strong roots. 2. MEDICINE. To take a piece of skin or bone from one place in the body and transfer it to another place or another body, where it will grow. Burn victims often receive skin grafts to replace skin that has burned off.

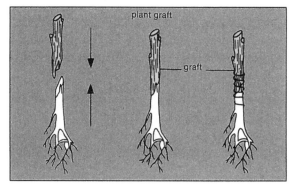

graft

grain   A single seed or fruit of a cereal group such as corn, wheat, rice, or oats. Grains are important foods throughout the world and, because they provide essential nutrients, are part of a balanced diet. Grains are eaten by both people and livestock.

gram A small unit of mass in the metric system (abbreviated g). One gram is equal to the mass of a cubic centimeter of water at a temperature of 4°C. The weight of about 28 grams is one ounce. [*Gram* comes from a Greek word meaning "a little weight."]

granite A common kind of igneous (fireformed) rock. Granite is very hard and contains quartz, feldspar, and a small amount of other minerals. Granites range in color from gray to pink or even red. [*Granite* comes from an Italian word meaning "grainy."]

granule 1. BIOLOGY. Small grains or particles found inside animal and plant cells. A granule may be a food particle in the cell. 2. GEOLOGY. A rounded piece of rock larger than a grain but smaller than a pebble. 3. PHYSICS. Any small, hard piece of material.

graph A diagram that shows the relationship between two different things, such as temperature and the time of day. Graphs can use lines, bars, or circles to represent amounts.

graphite A soft, black, shiny mineral. Graphite is a form of carbon, and it—not lead— is used in pencils. Graphite is also used to lubricate parts of machines to reduce friction.

grass A green plant with long, narrow leaves and jointed stems. Plants such as wheat, corn, oats, bamboo, and rye are all different kinds of grasses.

gravel Pebbles and broken bits of rock that are larger than sand. Gravel is used in construction work and in the making of concrete.

gravitation One of the fundamental forces of nature. Every object in the universe has a gravitational attraction for every other object in the universe. Newton's law of universal gravitation states that the attraction between two objects is proportional to the product of their masses and inversely proportional to the square of the distance between them. That means that more massive objects attract a given mass more than less massive objects do, and that closer objects have a greater attraction for each other than distant objects.

gravity The force that attracts things to move towards the center of the Earth, the moon, or a planet as the result of gravitation. Gravitation is the attraction of every bit of matter; gravity is the gravitational attraction of larger bodies in space, such as planets and moons. Gravity is what causes people and objects to have weight on Earth. Gravity makes objects fall towards Earth at an increasing speed of 32 feet (9.81 meters) per second for every second it is falling. This acceleration (increase in speed) is usually labeled g. [*Gravity* comes from a Latin word meaning "heavy."]

greenhouse effect The increase of temperature on Earth's surface due to the absorption of the sun's radiation in the atmosphere. The greenhouse effect occurs when the carbon dioxide and water vapor in the atmosphere trap the heat and prevent it from being lost in space. Global warming is happening because of the greenhouse effect.

Greenwich mean time Local time at the Greenwich meridian (the time in Great Britain). Greenwich time had been used as a time standard throughout the world for many years. Since 1972, GMT has been replaced by Universal time, which is based on atomic clocks.

Gregorian calendar The calendar in use today. In the Gregorian calendar, an ordinary year has 365 days and a leap year 366 days. It replaces the Julian calendar used before 1582, which had an error of 11 minutes a year. The Gregorian calendar has an error of only 26 seconds per year.

ground 1. EARTH SCIENCE. The surface of the earth. Ground is also any loose material such as soil found on the surface. 2. PHYSICS. An electrical conductor connected to the earth. Also, an electrical ground is the common path of an electrical circuit.

group 1. CHEMISTRY. A number of elements with similar properties. A group of elements forms a vertical column on the periodic table of elements. Group O consists of the six inert gases: helium, neon, argon, krypton, xenon, and radon. 2. BIOLOGY. A number of animals or plants sometimes classed together because of similar characteristics or a special relationship. Frogs and freshwater fish can be said to be a group of pond animals.

growth The increase in size and weight of a plant or animal in the course of its life. Growth takes place because of an increase in the number, size, and/or type of cells. Growth rings in a tree trunk can be used to tell the tree's age. Also, a cancer or tumor in an animal or plant is sometimes called a growth.

grub The larva, or wormlike form, of an insect. A grub hatches from an egg and later develops into a pupa or chrysalis, and then into an adult.

guard cell In plants, either of two cells that control the size of the stomata, tiny openings on the underside of a leaf. The shape of the guard cell changes according to the amount of water in the plant. If the plant becomes drier, the guard cells close the stomata, allowing less water vapor to leave the plant.

gulf A large area of the ocean that is surrounded on three sides by land. A gulf is usually larger than a bay.

gullet The tube leading from the mouth to the stomach, also called the esophagus. Muscles around the gullet contract in waves to push food down to the stomach. The gullet is part of the gut or alimentary canal.

gum 1. ANATOMY. The flesh around the roots of the teeth. Gum is often called the gums.

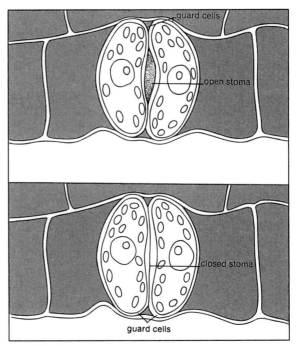

guard cell

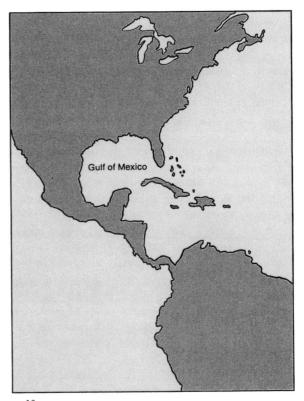

gulf

2. BOTANY. A sticky material given off by certain trees and other plants. Gum is sometimes used as an adhesive, to stick things together. Chewing gum is a sweetened, flavored gum.

gut The alimentary canal in animals. Food passes through the gut and is broken down by digestive juices. The digested food is absorbed into the body and carried to the cells by the blood. Undigested food passes out of the gut through the anus.

gut

Gutenberg, Johann (1400–1468) A German printer who invented printing from moveable

Gutenberg, Johann

type. The bibles that Gutenberg printed by this method that still exist are among the most valuable books in the world.

gymnosperm A class of plants whose seeds are not enclosed in a fruit or a seed case. Pines, firs, spruces, and other conifers are gymnosperms.

gynecology A branch of medicine dealing with diseases of women. Gynecology and obstetrics (the care of a woman during pregnancy) are often practiced by the same physicians. A doctor who specializes in gynecology is called a gynecologist.

gyrocompass An instrument used for navigation that uses a motor-driven gyroscope instead of a magnetic needle. A gyrocompass points to true north instead of magnetic north.

gyroscope A device that consists of a heavy wheel or disk mounted on an axle that can turn freely. When a gyroscope wheel is made to spin rapidly, the gyroscope resists a change in the direction of its axis. Gyroscopes are used in ships, planes, and rockets to keep then on a steady course.

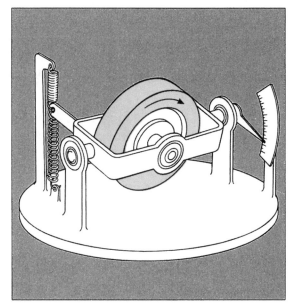

gyroscope

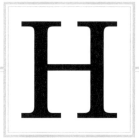

habit A usual or instinctive way that animal or plants have of behaving or growing. A habit of some birds is to build nests. A habit of ivy is to grow around a tree trunk. Habit is also used to describe learned behavior. People can learn a habit by becoming conditioned to doing something at a particular time or in a particular way. Some people have a habit of scratching their heads when they are thinking or a habit of singing in the bathtub.

habitat The natural surroundings of a particular area or community of lining things. A rocky seashore is a habitat for many kinds of sea plants and animals. [*Habitat* comes from a Latin word meaning "to frequent a place or dwell in it."]

hail Frozen raindrops that look like pellets of ice. Hail forms in thunderclouds, where raindrops are frozen; they grow in size as they are tossed about by strong winds. Hailstones are larger pellets or balls of hail that fall during a hailstorm. Hailstones may grow as large as oranges or grapefruit. [*Hail* comes from a Greek word meaning "pebble."]

hair 1. ZOOLOGY. A fine, threadlike filament that grows from the skin of mammals. The color of hair depends upon a pigment it contains called melanin. Hair provides warmth and protection for mammals. Whiskers are facial hair. Fur is thick, soft, fine hair found on certain mammals. Humans have fine hair all over their skin except for the palms of their hands and the soles of their feet. 2. BOTANY. A fine, threadlike growth from the outer layer of roots. Water and dissolved minerals pass through the root hairs into the plant.

half-life The length of time it takes to decrease an amount of radioactivity by half. After two half-lives, the number of radioactive particles will be one quarter of the original amount, and so on. Depending upon the substance, half-lives can range from a tiny fraction of a second to many millions or even billions of years. The half-life of uranium-235 is 713 million years.

Halley's comet A well-known comet named in honor of the English astronomer Edmund Halley (1656–1742), who plotted its path and predicted its return. Halley's comet returns every 75 or 76 years. It was last seen from Earth without a telescope in 1986.

halo A ring of light sometimes visible around the sun or the moon. The halo occurs when the light rays of the sun or moon are bent or refracted by ice crystals that make up cirrus clouds high in the atmosphere. [*Halo* comes from a Greek word meaning "a disc or shield."]

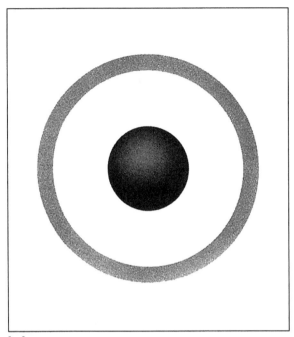

halo

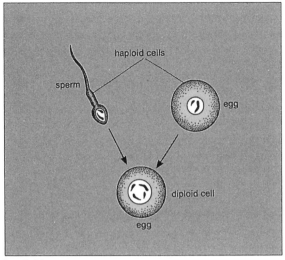

haploid

halogen Any element in a group of non-metallic elements that includes fluorine, chlorine, bromine, iodine, and astatine. Halogens combine with metals to form salts.

hammer In anatomy, the malleus bone: one of three tiny bones in the middle ear of mammals, shaped something like a hammer. The bones (the hammer, the anvil, and the stirrup) pass along sound vibrations from the eardrum to the inner ear.

hand The part of the arm beyond the wrist. It has many small bones, which divide into five fingers with the thumb at right angles to the other four. The hand is used for grasping. The skin of the hand is especially sensitive to touch.

haploid Describes a cell that has a set of unpaired chromosomes. The number of chromosomes in that plant or animal cell is called the haploid number. Haploid cells are produced by a process called meiosis and are also called gamete or germ cells. In sexual reproduction, the nuclei of two haploid cells unite to form a diploid cell with two sets of chromosomes in one nucleus.

hard The quality of being firm or solid, such as rocks and most metals.

hard disk drive A device used to store large amounts of digital data in a long-lasting form. It consists of one or more rapidly rotating disks on a spindle within a case.

hard water Water that contains mineral salts such as calcium carbonate and does not easily lather with soap. Hard water makes washing difficult; soft water makes washing easier.

hardness The degree to which a mineral or other substance resists being scratched. The degree of hardness of a mineral is measured on the Mohs scale, named after Friedrich Mohs (1773–1839). Mohs used ten minerals as reference points, from talc (1), the softest, to diamond (10), the hardest.

hardware The physical parts that you can actually see and touch in a computer such as the keyboard, the screen and a mouse or other pointing device. Not every computer or computing device has the same kind of hardware. The term is used to contrast with software, the word for computer programs.

hardwood The heavy dense wood that comes from trees with broad, flat leaves such as oak, maple, and cherry. Needle-leaf trees such as pine and fir usually produce lighter softwood.

Harvey, William (1578–1657) An English physician who discovered the circulation of blood. He showed that the heart acts as a pump that circulates the blood endlessly around the body. He also showed that valves in the heart and in the veins permit blood to flow only in one direction. Harvey also made important studies in reproduction and the development of the embryo.

Harvey, William

hatch To crack out of an egg, as when a baby bird or reptile bites or pecks through the shell and breaks free to be born. Also, to warm eggs and produce young. Many birds sit on eggs to hatch them. Many reptiles, such as turtles, bury their eggs in the warm ground to hatch them. The young reptiles break through the soft, leathery shell.

hay fever A common allergic disease, usually caused by an allergy to grasses, but may also be triggered by the pollen of trees, weeds, flowers, and other plants. Hay fever is often seasonal.

head 1. ANATOMY. The top part of the body of an animal. It contains the brain, eyes, ears, nose, and mouth. 2. ASTRONOMY. The coma and nucleus of a comet. 3. BOTANY. A closely packed cluster of flowers that grows together from the main stem, as in a daisy or dandelion. 4. EARTH SCIENCE. The source of a river or other flowing water. 5. TECHNOLOGY. The part of a tape

recorder or computer disk drive that reads or writes the signal.

headache A common ache or pain that affects the head or neck. Among the many possible causes of headache are fever, tension, or illness.

health Freedom from illness or disease in an animal or plant. A state of health is the condition in which all the important factors for life are present, and the animal or plant is functioning normally. [*Health* comes from an Old English word meaning "whole" or "unhurt."]

hear To receive sounds through the ear and transmit the resulting nerve impulses to the brain.

hearing The ability to hear. During the process of hearing, sound waves pass into the outer ear and are funneled through the eardrum, causing the bones of the middle ear to vibrate. The vibrations are picked up by nerve cells, and messages are sent to the brain through the auditory nerves. The brain interprets the messages. Animals such as dogs and bats hear sounds that humans cannot.

hearing aid A device used to make sounds louder for hard-of-hearing people. New kinds of hearing aids are tiny devices placed entirely in the ear.

heart A vital, muscular organ in higher animals that pumps blood around the body. In vertebrates, (animals with backbones) the heart has chambers. Fish have a two-chambered heart, reptiles a three-chambered heart. Humans, other mammals, and birds have a four-chambered heart. In humans, the heart has two chambers, called auricles or atria, which receive blood and two chambers, called ventricles, which pump blood.

heart attack An obstruction in a coronary artery. Since the coronary arteries supply the heart with oxygen and nutrients, an obstruction may cause serious illness or sudden death. A heart attack is often called a coronary.

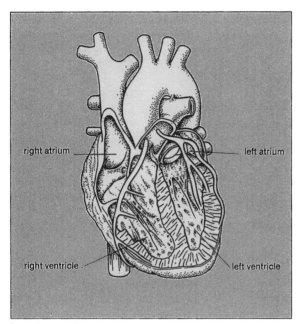

heart

heat A form of energy consisting of the movements of the molecules in a substance. Heat passes from a warmer object to a colder object by conduction (by contact through substances), radiation (electromagnetic waves that travel through transparent objects and even through empty space), or convection (the flow of hot fluids). Heat can change a solid into a liquid and a liquid into a gas. Heat can be transformed into other kinds of energy such as mechanical, the energy of motion.

heat shield On space ships or space shuttles, a device used to prevent them from burning up when they reenter Earth's atmosphere. Heat shields protect the vehicles either by flaking away when they are heated at reentry or by being made of special materials that absorb or radiate heat away from the ship and that do not melt or break easily at high temperatures.

heating The supplying of heat, especially to an enclosed space to produce a comfortable temperature for people or animals. In earlier times, open fires in fireplaces in homes were the most common kinds of heating. Later, coal and gas flames were used to heat rooms. Central heating systems are now the most common in industrialized countries. From a single boiler heated by the combustion of gas, oil, or coal—or by electricity—hot air, hot water, or steam is pumped around a system of pipes and radiators through the entire structure.

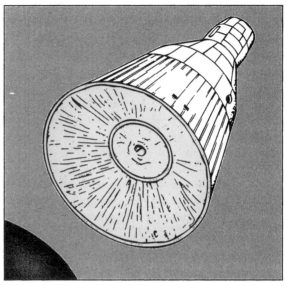

heat shield

heavy 1. PHYSICS. Having a high mass or density. Uranium and gold are heavy elements A proton in an atom is 1,836 times as heavy as an electron. 2. CHEMISTRY. Having a greater atomic or molecular mass than the more common same substance. Heavy water is much like ordinary water but about 1.1 times as heavy.

Heisenberg, Werner Carl (1901–1976) A German mathematical physicist who is said to be the father of quantum mechanics, the science that deals with the interaction of matter and

Heisenberg, Werner Carl

radiation, the structure of the atom, and the motion of atomic particles. He is most famous for the uncertainty principle (1927), which states that there is a limit to accuracy when measuring simultaneously the position and momentum of an atomic particle.

helicopter An aircraft that is able to take off straight up, hover in midair, and fly in any direction without turning in that direction. Different than a fixed-wing airplane, helicopters can be used in congested places in cities or on small landing places where airplanes would not have enough room to take off or land. Helicopters have large, rotating blades that rotate horizontally. Most helicopters also have a tail-mounted vertical rotor that prevents the aircraft from spinning around. The first successful helicopter flight was made in 1939 by Igor Sikorsky (1889–1972), a Russian-born American aircraft designer.

heliocentric Having the sun as the center. The heliocentric theory of Copernicus placed the sun at the center of the solar system.

helium A colorless, odorless, chemically inactive gaseous element. Helium is lighter than all other elements except hydrogen. It is the second most abundant element, present in large amounts in the sun and other stars. Because it is lighter than air and does not burn, helium is used in airships and balloons that float in the air. Helium has an atomic number of 2, at atomic weight of 4.003, and its chemical symbol is He.

helix 1. PHYSICS. A spiral or coil shape like that of a screw thread or a snail shell. The DNA molecule has the shape of a double helix, each spiral wrapped around the other. 2. ANATOMY. The rim of the outer ear.

Helmholtz, Hermann Ludwig von (1821–1894) A German physicist and physiologist who was one of the first to formulate the law of conservation of energy. This law states that energy can be neither created nor destroyed, although it can be changed from one form into another. Helmholtz also invented the opthalmoscope,

an instrument for examining the inner parts of the eye.

Helmholtz, Hermann Ludwig von

hematite A reddish-brown mineral composed of iron oxide. Hematite is the most common iron ore.

hemisphere 1. EARTH SCIENCE. Half of Earth's surface. The Americas are in the Western Hemisphere. Antarctica is in the Southern Hemisphere. 2. ANATOMY. One of the two halves (left or right) of the cerebrum of the brain.

hemoglobin The substance in the blood of humans and many other animals that carries oxygen from the lungs to body cells. When hemoglobin is carrying oxygen, it is bright red. When it gives up the oxygen, it turns a darker, bluish red. A lack of sufficient hemoglobin produces an illness called anemia.

hemophilia An inherited disorder of blood clotting found only in males, but carried by females who do not suffer from the disease. Because a person suffering from hemophilia does not form enough of a particular blood-clotting factor (called factor VIII), even a small cut will continue to bleed for a long time. There are similar diseases, caused by the lack of other clotting factors, from which either sex may suffer equally.

hemorrhage A large loss of blood. A hemorrhage can be blood loss either within or outside the body. [*Hemorrhage* comes from a Greek word meaning "burst blood."]

hemp A plant that grows in Asia, the fibers of

which are used to make strong rope and a kind of coarse cloth. Narcotic drugs such as marijuana are made from the dried leaves and flowers of the plant.

hen A female bird, especially the chicken or other domestic fowl.

Henry, Joseph (1797–1878) An American physicist best known for his studies of electromagnetism. Henry discovered magnetic induction and invented a powerful electromagnet and one of the first electric motors. The unit of inductance is named the henry in his honor.

herb A flowering plant that does not have a woody stem. The leaves, stems, roots, or flowers of various herbs are used for flavoring food and for medicinal purposes.

herbivore Any animal that feeds mostly on plants. Cows, sheep, and horses are called herbivorous animals.

herd A group of large animals that feed and live together, such as cattle or elephants.

hereditary Describes a trait in animals or plants that is transmitted by means of genes from parents to offspring. Hair color and eye color are hereditary. The size of an animal or plant is primarily hereditary.

hermaphrodite An animal or plant that has both male and female reproductive organs. An earthworm is a hermaphrodite. [*Hermaphrodite* comes from the Greek myth of Hermaphroditus, whose name combines the names of his parents, Hermes and Aphrodite. Hermaphroditus was united with a female nymph, thereby combining both male and female characteristics in one body.]

heroin A powerful, habit-forming drug. Morphine, a form of heroin, is used in medicine to lessen severe pain for short periods of time. People who abuse the drug become addicted to its use. Early death is common among heroin addicts.

herpetology The scientific study of reptiles, such as snakes and lizards, and amphibians, such as frogs and toads. A scientist who studies reptiles and amphibians is called a herpetologist.

hertz A unit of frequency of radio waves. One hertz (Hz) is equal to one cycle per second. The unit is named after Heinrich R. Hertz (1857–1894), a German physicist who was the first to broadcast and receive radio waves.

hibernate To go into a deep sleep and remain inactive during the winter. Animals that hibernate, such as bears or woodchucks, can live on the food stored in their bodies until spring comes. Hibernation is the state of being in this condition during the winter. [*Hibernate* comes from a Latin word meaning "winter."]

hide The thick skin of animals such as cattle, elephants, and alligators.

Higgs boson The Higgs boson is a hypothetical, massive subatomic particle with zero electric charge. The proof of the existence of a Higgs boson would explain the masses of elementary particles.

high tide The level or time of the tide during which the ocean reaches to its highest level at the shore. Tides vary with the phases of the moon and the position of the sun. Most shores have two high and two low tides each day.

high-pressure area A mass of air that has a high barometric pressure. Air flows from high-pressure areas to low-pressure areas. High-pressure areas usually produce clear weather.

hinge joint A joint such as the elbow or a door hinge, which allows a back-and-forth motion.

hip The part of the human body that covers the joint where the thigh is attached to the body. In other mammals, the hip is where the hind leg is attached to the body.

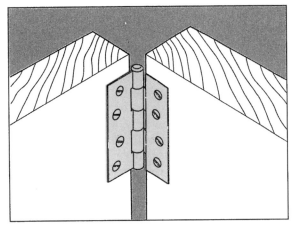

hinge joint

Hipparchus (about 130 B.C.) A Greek thinker who is considered to be the father of astronomy. Hipparchus drew up the first catalog of stars, made a good estimate of the distance and size of the moon, and invented several astronomical instruments.

Hippocrates (about 460–377 B.C.) A Greek physician who is considered to be the father of medicine. He is the author of a number of books on medicine. The Hippocratic oath, a statement of medical ethics and practice still used today, is named after him.

Hippocrates

hive A colony of bees or the place in which bees live.

Holocene Epoch The most recent epoch of the Cenozoic Era. It has lasted about ten thousand years from the end of the last ice age up to and including the present. Also known as the Recent Epoch.

hologram A three-dimensional image that can be seen from different angles by changing the viewpoint. Holography is the method that uses a laser beam and a photographic plate to make a hologram.

homeostasis A stable, normal internal condition that is maintained in a living thing even though changes take place in the environment. For example, mammals are said to maintain homeostasis because they keep their internal temperatures fairly constant even though it may be cold or hot around them.

hominid The family of animals of which modern-day humans are the only surviving species.

Homo sapiens The scientific name for modern humans. The surviving species of the primate family Hominidae.

Hooke, Robert (1635–1703) An English experimental scientist who was one of the first to use a microscope and who invented many other useful devices. His careful drawings and descriptions of the microscopic pattern of cork introduced the word "cells" to biology. He is remembered for Hooke's law, which states that the change in the length of an elastic object is proportional to the stress on it. He is also known for proposing a law of gravitation that helped Newton formulate his theories.

Hooke, Robert

horizon The apparent line where the sky seems to meet the land or the sea. It is impossible to see beyond the horizon because the earth is curved. The higher you are from the surface, the more distant is the horizon. [*Horizon* comes from a Greek word meaning "boundary" or "limit."]

horizontal Flat or level and parallel to the horizon.

hormone One of many different chemical substances such as insulin, adrenalin, and steroids that affect growth, behavior, and various other body functions. Hormones are made by glands such as the adrenal, the pituitary, and the thyroid. Many hormones, including cortisone, can be made synthetically. Hormones and the glands that make them are called the endocrine system. Plant hormones such as auxins and gibberellins are substances that control growth in a plant.

horn 1. A hard growth on the forehead of many kinds of grazing animals such as cows, moose, and antelopes. Horns are often curved and pointed and found in pairs. 2. The hard substance that makes up an animal's horns, a person's fingernails, a horse's hoofs, and a bird's beak.

horsepower The most commonly used unit for measuring the power of an automobile engine or an electric motor. The term was introduced by James Watt. One horsepower is equal to 550 foot-pounds per second, or about 746 watts. One foot-pound is equal to the work done by one pound of force moving an object one foot.

horticulture A branch of agriculture concerned with growing flowers, fruits, and vegetables.

host An animal or a plant that provides food for a parasite.

hot spring Hot water and steam that bubble out of the ground. The underground water is heated by hot, molten rock, called magma, within the earth. Hot springs are also called thermal springs. Hot springs are most often found in regions where volcanoes and earthquakes occur.

hour A unit of time equal to 60 minutes or 3,600 seconds. One day is divided into 24 hours.

Hovercraft A vehicle that rides over land or water on a cushion of air. The air is pushed downward from the bottom of the Hovercraft by fans. A tough skirt attached to the vehicle holds the air beneath it. Hovercrafts are used as ferries and for military purposes.

HTML HTML stands for *H*yper *T*ext *M*arkup Language. It is the main type of computer language used for pages on the Internet. It is used for structuring text and allows images and other objects such as interactive forms to be embedded in the text.

Hubble, Edwin Powell (1889–1953) An American astronomer who developed the modern idea of the expanding universe. Hubble's constant is a ratio between the distance of a galaxy and the rate at which it is moving away from an observer. The Hubble Space Telescope, launched in April 1990, is named after him.

Hubble, Edwin Powell

Hubble Space Telescope (HST) A NASA space telescope that was launched in 1990. Hubble is the largest and best known of NASA's space telescopes, which include the Spitzer Space Telescope, the Chandra X-ray Observatory and the Compton Gamma Ray Observatory. Hubble has presented to the public some of the most extraordinary images of outer space ever seen.

hull 1. BOTANY. The outer covering of a seed or fruit. 2. ENGINEERING. The frame or body of a ship or an aircraft. Also, the outer part of a rocket or spaceship.

human being A man, woman, or child. A member of the species *Homo sapiens*.

human-computer interaction HCI is the study of the contact between people and computers. It includes both software (computer programs) and hardware (screens, keyboards, mice, joysticks and the like).

Humboldt, Alexander von (1769–1859) A German naturalist who traveled for five years through South America collecting plants, animals, and rocks, and making scientific observations. In his most important book, *Kosmos*, Humboldt tried to show how all of nature was interrelated.

humidity The water vapor or moisture in the air. The relative humidity is the ratio of water vapor in the air compared to the amount of water vapor the air could hold at a particular temperature. When the air has all the water vapor it can hold, the relative humidity is 100%. Humidity is measured by an instrument called a hygrometer.

humus A dark-brown or black part of soil formed by decaying leaves and other parts of plants. Humus is rich in nutrients needed by growing plants.

husk The dry outer covering of a number of different kinds of seeds or fruits, such as the covering of an ear of corn or the shell of a walnut.

Huygens, Christian (1629–1695) A Dutch scientist who proposed a theory that light travels in waves rather than particles. Huygens was also the first to use a pendulum to regulate clocks. He worked on improving telescopes, discovered the surface markings on Mars, and was the first to observe that the "halo" that Galileo had seen around Saturn was really a system of rings.

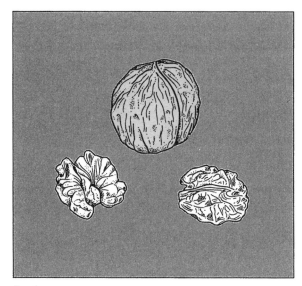

husk

Huygens, Christian

hybrid An offspring produced when two different varieties or species of plant or animal are bred together. Hybrids have one or more characteristics that are different from those of either of their parents. A mule, which is the hybrid offspring of a female horse and a male donkey, is a rare example of two species interbreeding. [*Hybrid* was a term used by Romans for the offspring of a tame sow and a wild boar.]

hydrate A compound containing a definite proportion of water. Many salts, such as copper sulfate and sodium carbonate, combine with water to produce hydrates.

hydraulic Having to do with water or other liquids. Also describes a machine, such as a hydraulic press, that operates because of the pressure of liquids. Hydraulics is the name of the science that deals with the use of liquids.

hydrocarbon A chemical compound that contains only hydrogen and carbon. Most hydrocarbons form the group comprising petroleum, natural gas, and coal gas. Gasoline is a mixture of hydrocarbons.

hydroelectricity Electricity produced by using water power. Hydroelectric power uses the flow of water over a waterfall or a dam to turn a large turbine. The turbine drives a generator that produces electricity. At present, hydroelectric power is the source of about one third of the world's electricity.

hydrofoil A winglike structure usually mounted beneath a boat. When the boat goes quickly, the hydrofoil lifts the boat almost entirely out of the water just as a wing lifts an airplane. Because this reduces the drag (resistance) of the water, a hydrofoil boat can travel at much higher speeds than a conventional boat.

hydrofoil

hydrogen The simplest and lightest element. Hydrogen is a gas that has no color, taste, or odor. It burns easily and combines with oxygen to produce water. Hydrogen atoms make up about 90% of the universe. In our sun and other stars, energy is produced by the nuclear fusion of hydrogen atoms. Hydrogen has an atomic number of 1 and an atomic weight of 1.008. Its chemical symbol is H.

hydrogen bomb A very powerful bomb whose energy is produced by the nuclear fusion of hydrogen atoms. (An atomic bomb produces energy by nuclear fission.) Hydrogen bombs were first developed in the United States in the late 1940s and early 1950s and have since been tested also by the Soviet Union, Great Britain, France, and China.

hydrology A science that deals with the waters of the earth. Hydrography is that branch of hydrology that deals with seas, lakes, rivers, and other large bodies of water.

hydrometer An instrument used to measure the density or specific gravity of a liquid. Hydrometers are often floated in saltwater aquariums to check the density of the salt water.

hydroponics The science of growing plants without soil in water that contains all the necessary plant nutrients.

hydrosphere The water part of Earth's surface and atmosphere. The hydrosphere contains all of Earth's waters including the oceans, lakes, rivers, icebergs, glaciers, and ground water, and the water in the atmosphere.

hygrometer An instrument used to measure the amount of water or humidity in the air.

hyperon One of a class of subatomic particles that are highly unstable and have masses greater than neutrons.

hyperopia A condition of the eye known as farsightedness. Hyperopia can be corrected by using spectacles that have converging lenses.

hypothalamus   The central part of the base of the brain under the thalamus. The hypothalamus contains the part of the central nervous system that controls body temperature, hunger, and thirst. It also produces hormones that influence the pituitary gland.

hypothesis   A proposed explanation or reason for something that has been observed. A hypothesis is like an educated guess. It is used in the scientific method of solving problems.

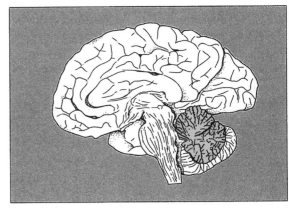

hypothalamus

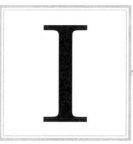

I

ice Frozen water. Ice forms at the freezing point of water, 32°F or 0°C at normal atmospheric pressure. Ice is a colorless solid that is less dense that water and floats on it.

ice ages The times in the past when ice sheets or glaciers covered large parts of the earth's surface. Ice ages last for a few million years and seem to come in cycles. An ice age is often interrupted by shorter, more temperate "interglacial" periods. During the most recent ice age, which ended about twelve thousand years ago, much of Northern Europe and North America looked the way Antarctica does today—a frozen and bleak landscape. No one knows whether we are now warming up and moving out of the ice age or whether we are just in a shorter interglacial period.

ice cap A covering of ice over a large area of land such as Antarctica. Ice caps are large glaciers that flow outward in all directions from their centers. Also called an ice sheet.

ice storm A storm in which rain freezes and forms a coating of ice on surfaces it strikes. An ice storm is one of the most dangerous kinds of winter weather. It can cause transportation accidents, injure or destroy trees and bushes, and kill unprotected animals.

iceberg A large mass of ice floating in the ocean. Icebergs break off, or "calve," from glaciers that reach the sea. In the Southern Hemisphere, huge flat pieces of ice break off the Antarctic ice sheet and form icebergs that may be 100 miles (160 kilometers) or more across. In the Northern Hemisphere, icebergs are smaller and more chunky. About nine tenths of an iceberg lies below the surface of the water and poses a danger to ships that come too close. In 1912, The *Titanic* collided with an iceberg in the North Atlantic Ocean and sank in a few hours. More than 1,500 people lost their lives.

ichthyology The scientific study of fish. A branch of zoology. A scientist who studies fish is called an ichthyologist.

ichthyosaur Any of a group of extinct fish-like reptiles that lived during the Triassic to the Cretaceous periods, about 225 to 65 million years ago. An ichthyosaur had a streamlined body, finlike limbs, and a tail like a fish.

icicle A pointed piece of ice that hangs down from trees, houses, or other objects. An icicle comes from water that drips and then freezes.

igneous rock One of the three main kinds of rock, formed from the cooling and hardening of magma or lava that comes from within the earth. Granite and basalt are common examples of igneous rock.

ignition The process of setting fire to something. An ignition system in an automobile usually uses spark plugs to set fire to a mixture of fuel and air.

illusion A mistaken or incorrect interpretation of information received by the senses, such as an optical illusion. Using one kind of illusion called perspective, an artist can make a viewer believe that one object in a drawing is more distant than another in the same picture.

image A picture of an object formed by a mirror or the lens of an optical instrument such as a camera or telescope.

IMAX A motion picture film and projection format that is much larger and of greater clarity than most conventional film systems. A standard IMAX screen is 72 x 52.8 feet (22 x 16.1 meters) but there are some that are much larger. There are currently hundreds of IMAX theaters in countries across the world.

immature Not fully grown. A young animal or plant is immature.

immunity The resistance of the body to disease bacteria, viruses, poisons, and other harmful substances. Immunity occurs when the body produces substances called antibodies, which fight specific foreign molecules that invade the body. An attack of some diseases, such as measles, usually gives a person a resistance against further attacks of that disease. Immunity can also be given by vaccination against a specific disease. Sometimes immunity can cause problems, as when the body tries to reject the foreign tissue of kidney or heart transplants. High doses of chemicals are used to suppress the body's immunological defenses. In autoimmune diseases such as lupus, the body produces antibodies that attack its own cells and tissues. The AIDS virus attacks and destroys cells in the body's immune system. [*Immunity* comes from a Latin word meaning "exempt."]

immunology The branch of medicine that deals with the immune system.

impact crater A crater that is produced by the powerful collision of a meteorite and the ground. Meteor Crater in Arizona and the craters on the moon are impact craters.

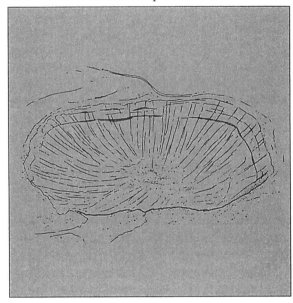

impact crater

impedance The resistance to the passage of electricity in an alternating-current circuit. [*Impedance* comes from a Latin word meaning "something that gets in the way of your feet and blocks your path."]

impermeable Describes a material that does not allow gases or liquids to pass through it. Shale is a kind of rock that is impermeable to water.

implant To graft or set an organ, a piece of tissue, or any living or artificial material into the body (pronounced im-PLANT). Also the organ, tissue, or material that is grafted (pronounced IM-plant). Body implants that have been successful include living kidneys and both mechanical and living hearts.

impulse 1. PHYSIOLOGY. An electrical and chemical signal passed along a nerve cell to another nerve call or to a muscle, or from a sensory organ to the brain. 2. PHYSICS. A surge of force or power that lasts for a short time. For example, a short burst of electrical power that may blow a fuse in a circuit is called an impulse. Also, the product of a force multiplied by the length of time the force acts.

inactive Describes a substance that does not easily react with other elements or compounds. Any of a group of elements called the noble gases are inactive. These include helium, neon, argon, and krypton.

inbreeding Breeding from closely related plants or animals. Inbreeding is sometimes used to develop a special desirable feature such as milk production in a cow or color in a flower. But inbreeding can often cause undesirable characteristics such as lowered resistance to disease.

incandescence The light given off by a substance when it is heated to a high temperature. An incandescent lamp bulb gives off light because the high temperature of its metal filament makes it glow.

incidence The falling of a ray of light or some other form of radiation upon a surface. The angle formed by the ray and a line perpendicular to the surface is called the angle of incidence.

incisor A tooth in mammals that has a sharp, chisel-shaped edge. Human beings normally have eight incisors, four each in the front of the upper and lower jaw.

inclined plane A kind of simple machine sometimes made from a plank or other flat surface set at an angle to the ground. It is often used to roll a wheelbarrow or move a car to a higher or lower level. An inclined plane allows you to overcome a large force by applying a smaller force over a long distance.

incubate 1. ZOOLOGY. To sit on eggs in order to hatch them by keeping them warm. Female birds usually do the incubating, but often male birds take their turn. 2. BIOLOGY, MEDICINE. To keep eggs, delicate living things, or cultures of microorganisms such as bacteria at a warm

inclined plane

temperature and under the proper living conditions. The special heated container that does this is called an incubator. A special kind of incubator is used to care for weak or premature infants.

indicator A substance that changes its color or some other property when certain chemicals such as acids or bases are present. One common indicator is a substance called litmus, which turns blue in the presence of a base and red in the presence of an acid.

indigenous Describes an animal or plant that lives or grows naturally in a certain region, climate zone, kind of soil, or body of water. Animals or plants that are introduced into a region by people are called aliens. Corn is indigenous to the Americas. Kangaroos are indigenous to Australia.

induction The production of electricity or magnetism in an object, caused by an electric current or a magnetic field in a nearby object, but not by direct contact.

induction coil A device used to generate high voltage and make sparks. It is often used along with spark plugs in gasoline automobile engines.

inert Describes a substance that does not react chemically with other substances. [*Inert* comes from a Latin word meaning "powerless" or "ineffective."]

inertia The tendency of an object not moving to remain still, and of a moving object to continue to move, unless acted upon by some outside force. "Mass" is the term used to measure an object's inertia. A heavy object, one with more mass, has more inertia than a lighter one. The same force applied to two objects of different weight produces a greater change in the motion of the lighter object.

infect To cause a disease by passing on bacteria, viruses, worms, or some other agent. Persons with colds or ringworm can infect other people with their illness.

infectious Describes a disease spread by the passing of germs, fungi, viruses, or some other agent from the sick person to the healthy one. Influenza, chicken pox, and measles are infectious diseases.

infertile 1. BIOLOGY. Unable to produce offspring. 2. EARTH SCIENCE. Describes something so poor in nutrients (for example, soil) that plants cannot grow in it.

infinity An amount so great it is without definable limits.

inflammable Able to burn easily. Gasoline is highly inflammable. Inflammable and flammable mean the same thing.

infrared radiation Rays that are invisible to the human eye but that can be felt as heat if absorbed. Infrared rays have wavelengths just a bit longer that the rays of red light we can see. Most of the heat that we feel from sunlight or an incandescent lamp bulb is from infrared rays. Infrared rays can pass through clouds and fog without being scattered as much as visible light rays.

ingest To take food into the body so it can be digested. The act of taking food into the body is called ingestion.

inhabit To live in a particular place. Penguins inhabit Antarctica. Sharks inhabit the seas.

inherit To receive the characteristics of parents or ancestors. Inherited characteristics are received from the gametes (sexual cells) of parents. The receipt of these characteristics is called inheritance. The science that studies inheritance is called genetics.

injection A substance given through the skin by using a syringes and needle. Injections are usually of drugs or vaccines into a muscle or a blood vessel. Diabetic persons usually take insulin by injection.

ink A liquid or paste containing dyes used for writing or printing. Writing inks were first used more that three thousand years ago in China and Egypt.

inner ear The part of the ear innermost in the head, containing the organs of hearing and balance. The inner ear contains the cochlea, which is involved with hearing, and three semicircular canals, which are involved with balance. They are filled with fluid and lined with nerve cells. Vibrations or changes in the fluid stimulate the nerve cells, which send nerve impulses to the brain, which interprets them as sounds or body movements.

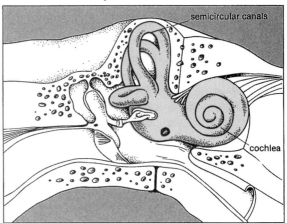

inner ear

inoculation The act of injecting or placing microorganisms into living things or into a culture medium. In medicine, inoculation is used to establish immunity against an infectious disease such as polio or measles.

inorganic Describes any substance that does not come from living things. For example, metals and minerals are inorganic substances, but wood is organic because it comes from trees. Inorganic chemistry is the science that studies the chemical properties of all the elements and compounds that do not come from living things. Many scientists consider any chemical that does not contain both carbon and hydrogen to be inorganic (substances that do contain these two elements are called hydrocarbons).

input 1. PHYSICS. The work applied to a machine. In a machine, the input is equal to the effort multiplied by the distance that the effort moves. 2. ELECTRICITY. The electrical power fed into an electronic device. 3. COMPUTING. A program or some other information fed into a computer or other data-processing machine. The term is often used with output in a computer, as with an input/output (I/O) device such as a disk drive. Also, to enter information into a computer.

insect Any of a group of small animals with three pairs of jointed legs and three body parts: the head, thorax, and abdomen. Insects usually have one or two pairs of wings at some time during their life. Flies, grasshoppers, butterflies, beetles, ants, and bees are insects, but spiders, centipedes, and millipedes are not. There are over a million different kinds of insects, more than all other kinds of animals put together.

insecticide A substance for killing insects. Some insecticides such as DDT have been found to last a long time in nature and are harmful to other animals.

insectivore An animal such as a shrew or a mole that feeds mainly on insects.

insolation The radiant energy received from the sun. Insolation warms Earth.

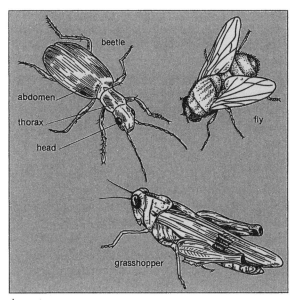

insect

insoluble Describes something that does not dissolve in liquid, usually water. Oil is insoluble in water.

inspiration Inhalation or breathing in.

instinct An aspect of human or animal behavior that is not learned. For example, ants have a nest-building instinct and spiders have a web-building instinct.

instrument A device used to measure, record, control, or do something. A thermometer is an instrument used to measure temperature. A barograph is an instrument used to record changes in atmospheric pressure. A thermostat is used to control temperature.

insulate Top surround or enclose with a material that prevents the passage of heat, electricity, or sound through it. Rubber or plastic is used to insulate an electric cable. The material used to insulate is called an insulator or insulation. [*Insulate* comes from a Latin word meaning "island."]

insulin A hormone, made in the pancreas, that regulates the use of sugar and other carbohydrates by the body. Also, a drug containing that hormone, made from the pancreas of animals. Diabetic persons are treated with the drug insulin.

integrated circuit A complicated electrical circuit put onto a single chip of silicon or other semiconducting material. Computers and other advanced electronic machines use many such chips.

intelligence The ability to solve problems, learn new information, and reason. Human beings are the most intelligent animals on Earth, but there are many other intelligent animals, including apes and dolphins. So-called "intelligence tests" actually measure a number of factors such as numerical ability, verbal ability, memory, and the ability to reason. These tests are of some use in limited ways but are of little value in comparisons between ethnic groups or social classes. [*Intelligence* comes from a Latin word meaning "the ability to discriminate among many things and understand them."]

intensity The amount or strength of heat, light, electricity, or sound per unit of area or volume in a given time. The brightness of a light or the loudness of a sound is called its intensity.

interference The interaction of light and other electromagnetic waves, sound, and water waves with each other. Interference causes larger waves when two crests meet, but the waves cancel each other if a crest meets a trough. Lasers use the principles of interference and coherence (having waves of a similar phase that remain compact) to produce very powerful lights. [*Interference* comes from a Latin word meaning "collision."]

interferon A protein substance produced by human or animal tissues following a virus infection. Interferon prevents the virus from reproducing. It is currently being used to help treat many diseases involving the immune system.

intergalactic Describes the space between and around the galaxies.

interglacial The time between two periods when the glaciers are advancing.

internal combustion engine The most common engine now in use, in which the fuel is burned inside the engine. Jets, rockets, gasoline engines, and diesel engines are internal combustion engines. By contrast, a steam engine, in which the fuel is burned outside the engine, is called an external combustion engine.

international date line An imaginary line agreed upon as the place where the day changes. The line runs north and south through the Pacific Ocean, mostly along the 180th meridian. East of the international date line is one day earlier than west of it.

International Space Station (ISS) An internationally developed and maintained space research station that is in orbit around Earth. The station is expected to remain in use until 2020. It can be seen from Earth as a bright light moving across the sky.

Internet A worldwide system of interconnected computer networks. It uses the standard Internet Protocol Suite (TCP/IP) to link billions of users across the planet. The Internet is a network of networks that connect public, government, private, school, business and other networks. The Internet carries a huge amount of information and services including the World Wide Web (WWW) and supports e-mail (electronic mail).

internode The part of a stem or branch between one leaf and the next.

interplanetary Between the planets. Interplanetary space is within the solar system and outside the atmosphere of any planet or the sun.

interstellar Between or in the region of the

stars. Interstellar space begins where interplanetary space ends.

intertidal Living or located between the high-water mark and the low-water mark of the tides.

intestine A tube that extends from the stomach to the anus, made up of the small intestine and the large intestine. The place where food is digested and absorbed, the intestine is part of the alimentary canal.

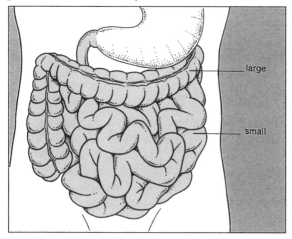

intestine

invention An original process or a device for doing something new or improving the way it was done before. Some of the earliest inventions were primitive tools such as knives and processes such as writing. Some modern inventions include radar, lasers, spaceships, and pocket computers. A person who invents something is called an inventor.

invertebrate An animal that does not have a backbone. Insects, worms, and shellfish are invertebrates; mammals, reptiles, and birds are vertebrates.

invisible light Light waves such as infrared or ultraviolet that cannot be seen by the human eye. Special kinds of instruments can be used to produce images of objects using infrared or ultraviolet light.

iodine A nonmetallic element that takes the form of shiny, blue-black crystals. Iodine belongs to a group of elements called halogens. When warmed, iodine crystals give off a violet gas with a sharp odor. Iodine is used in medicine, in making dyes, and in photography. Iodine solution, which is sometimes used as an antiseptic, is made from iodine dissolved in alcohol. Iodine has an atomic number of 53 and an atomic weight of 126.905. Its chemical symbol is I.

ion An electrically charged atom or group of atoms. Because electrons have a negative charge, negative ions form when atoms gain electrons; positive ions form when atoms lose electrons. Acids, bases, and salts separate into positive and negative ions when they dissolve in water. For example, table salt (sodium chloride), when dissolved in water, forms positive sodium ions and negative chlorine ions.

ion propulsion A theoretical way of propelling spacecraft on long, interplanetary or interstellar trips. Also called ion drive.

ionic bond In a compound, an attraction between two ions with opposite charges. The sodium and chlorine atoms in table salt are held together by ionic bonds.

ionosphere A part of Earth's upper atmosphere that contains large numbers of ions. The ionosphere extends from about 50 to 650 miles (roughly 80 to 1,080 kilometers) above the surface. The ionosphere consists of several layers that reflect radio waves back to Earth. This is important in long-distance radio communication.

iridium A hard, white metallic element that is about twice as heavy as lead. It is used along with platinum to make jewelry and alloys that resist corrosion. Platinum-iridium bars have been used to make international standards of length. Iridium has an atomic number of 77 and an atomic weight of 192.22. Its chemical symbol is Ir.

ionosphere

iris The colorful part of the eye around the pupil. The iris expands and contracts, controlling the amount of light entering the eye through the pupil.

iron A hard, silver-gray, metallic element. Iron is strongly magnetic and the most common metal on Earth. When mixed with carbon and other elements, it becomes steel. Iron corrodes in moist air to become rust, iron oxide. Iron can be galvanized (coated with zinc) or protected in other ways to slow down rusting. In the human body, iron is found in the hemoglobin of red blood cells. Iron has an atomic number of 26, an atomic weight of 55.847, and its chemical symbol is Fe.

irradiate To expose something to some kind of radiation such as ultraviolet rays or X-rays. Food products are sometimes sterilized by irradiating them with gamma rays. The act of irradiating is called irradiation.

irrigate 1. AGRICULTURE. To water soil and crops by using pipes or channels rather than by relying on rainfall. The water can be pumped from wells or piped from faraway rivers or lakes. Irrigation makes it possible to grow crops in places that have little or no rain. Several hundred million acres of farmland throughout the world are irrigated. 2. MEDICINE. To wash parts of the body, tissues, or organs with water or solutions.

island A body of land, smaller than a continent, that is completely surrounded by water. Curving chains of islands are called island arcs.

isobar A line drawn of a weather map connecting points that have the same air pressure (as shown on a barometer) at a given time. Isobars are used to help predict the weather.

isolate To set a sick person apart, usually to prevent a disease from spreading. Also, to separate a chemical substance, an organism, or a cell from others in a mixture of substances, organisms, or cells.

isomers Chemical compounds that have identical composition and formulas but different arrangements of atoms in their molecules. For example, sugars such as sucrose and lactose, which have the same formula but different chemical properties, are called isomers.

isometrics Exercises in which muscles are tensed against a resistance but not moved at the joints. The muscles remain at the same length when they are kept under tension this way.

isostasy The tendency of the earth's crust to be in a state of balance, or equilibrium, caused by equal pressure from above and below. For example, high mountains pushing downward have deep roots of the same material holding up the great weight above.

isotherm A line drawn on a weather map that connects points that have the same air temperature at a given time.

isotope Two or more forms of an element that have the same atomic number and the same chemical properties but different numbers of neutrons and different atomic masses. Hydrogen and heavy hydrogen are isotopes.

isthmus A narrow strip of land with water on both sides that connects two large land areas. The best known are the Isthmus of Panama and the Isthmus of Suez.

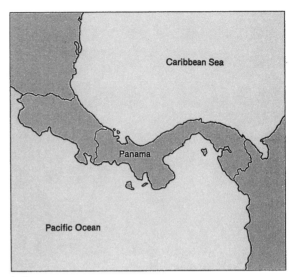

isthmus

J

jade A hard, glistening mineral, usually green but also white, brown, or yellow. Jade is either of two kinds: jadeite or nephrite. It is used as a gemstone in jewelry and artistic carvings.

Japan current A large warm ocean current that starts near the Philippines and flows past Japan and then across the Pacific Ocean. In Japan, it is called the Kuroshio current.

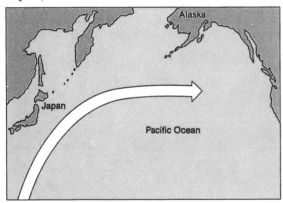

Japan current

jaundice A yellow color in the skin and white of the eye that is a symptom of a disease of the liver. The yellow coloring is caused by the presence of a bile chemical called bilirubin in the blood.

jaw The upper or lower bones of the mouth that hold the teeth in place in people and cer-

tain animals. The upper jaw is called the maxilla. The lower jaw, called the mandible, is hinged and moveable.

Jenner, Edward (1749–1823) An English scientist and physician who pioneered the use of vaccination in preventing certain diseases. After studying many cases of a mild disease called cowpox, he inoculated a young boy with cowpox, which made the child immune to the more deadly diseases of smallpox. This method of inoculating a mild form of a disease to prevent a more harmful disease is still in use today.

Jenner, Edward

jet A high-speed stream of a fluid, such as gas or water, discharged from a small opening or nozzle. Jet propulsion is the thrust produced by a jet. You can demonstrate jet propulsion by blowing up a balloon and then releasing it and watching it move. A jet engine uses jets of burning gases to provide thrust to an aircraft, watercraft, and some land vehicles.

jet stream A high-speed air current that usually travels from west to east at altitudes of seven to fifteen miles. Jet streams move in wavelike motions at speeds ranging from 100 to 300 miles (160 to 480 kilometers) per hour. They influence the movement of weather systems around the world. Aircraft traveling eastward sometimes fly along with a jet stream to increase their speed.

joint 1. ANATOMY. A place in the body where two or more bones are joined or connected so that they can move freely. Hinge joints, such as in the fingers or elbow, allow a back-and-forth motion. Ball-and-socket joints, such as in the hip or shoulder, allow a rotary motion. 2. BOTANY. In plants, the part of a stem where a branch or leaf grows.

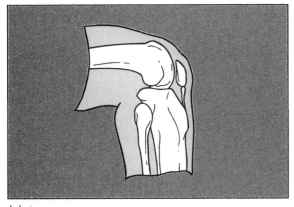

joint

joule In physics, a unit of work or energy. It was named after James P. Joule (1818–1889), a British physicist who showed that heat energy and mechanical energy are equivalent forms of energy.

Jovian Having to do with the planet Jupiter.

jugular Of the neck or throat. The jugular veins are two major veins, one on each side of the neck.

Julian calendar A calendar put into effect by Julius Caesar in Rome in 46 B.C. and used in some European countries for fifteen hundred years. In the Julian calendar, the year is divided into 365 days, with a "leap year" of 366 days every fourth year. After small changes by Pope Gregory XIII in 1582, it became the Gregorian calendar, the basis of the calendar used in most countries today.

jungle A tropical forest with dense growth of plants. Jungles are usually found in tropical rainforest areas and along riverbanks or in swamps.

Jupiter The largest planet in the solar system. More than 1,300 planets the size of Earth could fit inside Jupiter. Jupiter is the fifth planet from the sun, about 483 million miles (778 million kilometers) away. It takes Jupiter nearly 12 years to go once around the sun. Jupiter has a family of at least 63 moons and influences the orbits of more than 50 comets. The four largest of Jupiter's moons, Io, Europa, Ganymede, and Callisto are called the Galilean moons because they are the ones that Galileo first saw through a small telescope 400 years ago.

Jurassic Period The middle period of the Mesozoic Era, lasting from about 190 to 135 million years ago. During the Jurassic , dinosaurs roamed the earth and birds first appeared. The name comes from the many fossils from this period found in the rocks of the Jura mountains of Switzerland and France.

juvenile hormone A chemical substance found in some insects, such as butterflies and moths, which controls the change from caterpillar to adult. A butterfly will remain a caterpillar for the rest of its life unless the juvenile hormone stops being produced in its body.

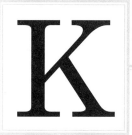

kelvin A unit of temperature in which a degree is the same size as a degree Celsius. The only difference is that temperatures in kelvins equal temperatures in degrees Celsius less 273.15. Zero degrees kelvin is absolute zero (the coldest possible temperature, about −459.67°F or −273.15°C), while zero degrees Celsius is defined as the freezing point of water. The unit was named after William Thomson Kelvin (1824–1907), a British physicist who proposed the absolute temperature scale. Its abbreviation is K.

Kepler, Johannes (1571–1630) A German astronomer and mathematician who proposed three laws describing the motions of the planets in the solar system. He showed that the planets went around the sun in elliptical paths (something like stretched circles).

Kepler, Johannes

kernel The softer part of a plant seed that can grow into a plant. A kernel is protected by an outer covering, or husk.

kerosene *or* **kerosine** A colorless kind of oil made from petroleum. Kerosene is used as a fuel in jet engines.

kidney In vertebrate animals, one of a pair of organs that act as filters to remove waste products from the blood. The wastes are then sent to the bladder and excreted in the urine. In humans, the kidneys are two bean-shaped organs located on either side of the backbone at waist level.

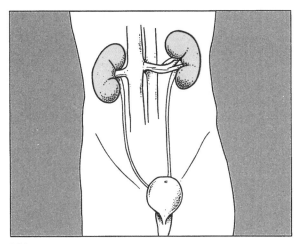

kidney

kilo In the metric system, a prefix meaning one thousand of whatever unit follows. Examples are kilogram (1,000 grams, or about 2.2 pounds), kilometer (1,000 meters or about .6 mile), and kilowatt (a unit of electrical power equal to 1,000 watts).

kinetic energy The energy contained in moving objects such as molecules, waves, wind, boats, and trains.

kingdom The largest unit in the classification of living things or in the more recent three-domain system, the rank below domain. In the five kingdom system, there are animals, plants, fungi, protists, and monerans. The five kingdoms are sometimes combined with two empires: Prokaryota (living things that don't have a cell nucleus) and Eukaryota (living things that have a cell nucleus).

knee The joint in the leg between the thigh and the lower leg. The knee is formed by the joining of the thighbone and the shinbone, and it is protected by the patella, or kneecap.

knot 1. PHYSICS. A unit of speed defined as one nautical mile per hour (1.1 land miles per hour). 2. BOTANY. The joint of a plant stem or part of a tree from which a branch has grown. Also, in a cross-section of wood, the place where a branch has grown.

Koch, Robert (1843–1910) A German physician and scientist regarded as the father of medical bacteriology. He isolated a particular strain of bacteria and proved that it alone causes the disease anthrax. He also discovered the kinds of bacteria responsible for tuberculosis and cholera. Koch received the 1905 Nobel Prize in physiology and medicine.

Koch, Robert

krypton A colorless, gaseous element that does not easily form compounds with other elements. Krypton belongs to a group of elements called noble or inert gases. It is used in lasers and to fill certain kinds of electric light bulbs. Krypton has an atomic number of 36 and an atomic weight of 83.80. Its chemical symbol is Kr.

Kuiper Belt A disk-shaped region in the outer solar system lying beyond the orbit of Neptune containing thousands of small icy bodies, some of which are considered "dwarf planets" because they orbit the sun, and others which periodically visit the inner solar system as comets. Named after Dutch-born American astronomer Gerard Kuiper (1905–1973) who first speculated that there was such a region in our solar system.

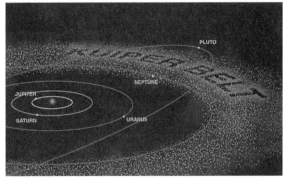

Kuiper Belt   *Image courtesy of NASA.gov*

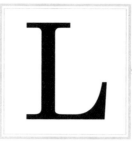

laboratory A special place used for scientific work and experiments.

laccolith A large body of igneous rock, usually granite, that has formed from the pressure of underlying molten rock (magma). A laccolith is forced upwards between layers of sedimentary rock, forming a dome-shaped mass.

lactose A sugar found in milk. When bacteria turn the lactose into lactic acid, milk turns sour and curdles.

lagoon A shallow, saltwater lake either found within an atoll or separated from the sea by low-lying sandbanks. Also, a small freshwater lake or pond connected to a larger lake or river.

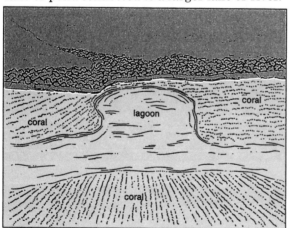

lagoon

lake A large body of water entirely or nearly surrounded by land.

Lamarck, Jean Baptiste (1744–1829) A French biologist who attempted to classify living things, especially insects, worms, and microscopic animals. The work led him to formulate an early theory of evolution more that

Lamarck, Jean Baptiste

fifty years before Darwin. Lamarck thought that living things developed new attributes—such as a longer neck in giraffes—in response to the need for them (giraffes stretched their necks to eat the leaves atop tall trees). He also thought that these acquired characteristics were inherited. Most scientists today do not accept Lamarck's theory of the inheritance of acquired characteristics. But many still feel that he deserves a place in the history of biology because of his important work in classifying animals.

large intestine The lower part of the digestive system between the small intestine and the anus. The large intestine is a wide tube about five feet long that consists of the cecum, the colon, and the rectum. In the large intestine, undigested food is eliminated, and water and salts are absorbed back into the body.

larva The early stage in the development of those insects that change greatly in shape when they become adults. A caterpillar is the larva of a butterfly or moth. Also, the early form of certain other animals that change greatly in shape during their lives. A tadpole is the larva of a frog or toad.

larynx The upper end of the windpipe in humans that forms the Adam's apple in the neck. The larynx contains the vocal cords. The movement and vibration of the vocal cords produce the sound of a voice. Also, a similar structure in other animals, particularly mammals.

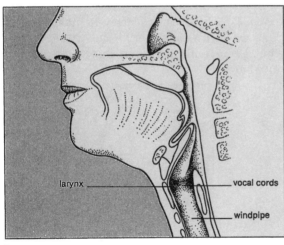

larynx

laser *L*ight *A*mplification by *S*timulated *E*mission of *R*adiation. A device that produces a narrow and intense beam of light. Light rays usually spread out in all directions, but in lasers the light rays are in step with each other and move in the same direction. Laser light is used in holography, in cutting or melting hard materials, in surgery, in compact disc players, and in transmitting communication signals, among many other functions.

latent heat The amount of heat absorbed or released by a substance when it changes state, as from a solid to a liquid, or a liquid to a gas. Latent heat does not change the temperature of a substance. For example, ice remains at 32°F (0°C) until it absorbs enough latent heat to change to water.

lateral Of, at, or on the side of an object. Also, from the middle and branching toward the side, as with the lateral roots of a tree. A lateral moraine is a mass of loose earth and rocks deposited along the sides of a glacier.

lathe A machine tool used to shape wood or metal in different diameters along the length.

latitude The distance north or south of the equator measured in degrees. The equator is at 0°. The North and South poles are at 90° north and 90° south. [*Latitude* comes from a Latin word meaning "breadth" or "width."]

lattice The three-dimensional, regularly repeating arrangements of atoms, molecules, or ions that makes up the structure of a crystal of a substance such as salt. [*Lattice* comes from an Old French word meaning "framework."]

launch vehicle The rocket used to send a satellite into orbit, or a space probe into outer space. The launch vehicle for the *Apollo* moon probes was the *Saturn* rocket. [*Launch* comes from a Latin word meaning "things that were hurled or flung."]

lava The molten rock that flows through volcanoes and cracks in the earth's surface. Also, the rock formed by the molten material after it hardens. Rough lava rock is called *aa* (AH-ah—Hawaiian for "rough"). Shiny, ropy lava rock is called *pahoehoe* (pah-Ho-ee-ho-ee—Hawaiian for "satiny"). [*Lava* comes from a Neapolitan word meaning "a torrent of floodwater."]

Lavoisier, Antoine Laurent (1743–1794) A French scientist who was one of the founders of modern chemistry. Lavoisier showed that burning substances combine with a gas in the air, which he named oxygen. He also discovered that water is composed of hydrogen, the flammable gas, and oxygen, the burning-supporting gas.

law, scientific A statement of what always happens under certain conditions. For example, Newton's third law of motion states that for every action there is an equal and opposite reaction.

layer 1. EARTH SCIENCE. A bed, or stratum, of rock. Also, a region of the atmosphere. 2. ANATOMY. A tissue of a certain thickness spread over a definite body area, such as the epithelial layer of the skin.

LCD *L*iquid *C*rystal *D*isplay. A type of display in pictures, words, or numbers on a small screen, such as a calculator or a digital watch face. The pictures become visible when a small electric current passes through liquid crystals in the display.

leach (out) To dissolve out minerals from soil, ashes, or rocks by slowly running water. Heavy rains can leach nutrients out of soils so that they cannot support much plant growth. [*Leach* comes from an Old English word meaning "to water sometimes."]

lead A soft, heavy, bluish-gray metal. Lead is found in the mineral galena and is used in alloys such as pewter. It is also used for soldering and in paints. Lead is an element whose symbol is Pb; its atomic number is 82; its atomic weight is 207.19. It melts at 327.5°C. Pb is from the Latin *plumbum* from which the word plumbing is derived.

lead poisoning A disease caused by too much lead in body tissues and in the blood. Lead poisoning can cause convulsions, anemia, and upset stomachs. Young children sometimes become seriously ill from lead poisoning when the eat chips of old lead-containing paint.

leaf A green, thin outgrowth of a tree or other plant that grows on a stem or comes up from the roots. The shape of a leaf may vary from plant to plant, but its basic functions are similar: Leaves take in carbon dioxide from the air or water and use the light of the sun to carry on photosynthesis. Leaves may also perform other functions. In the Venus's-flytrap, the leaves catch insects.

LED A *l*ight-*e*mitting *d*iode (LED) is a light source used in many electronic devices such as television and computer screens as well as being used in lighting.

Leeuwenhoek, Antonie van (1632–1723) A Dutch scientist who was the first to observe parts of plants and animals, tiny insects, blood cells, and bits of dust through a microscope. He wrote, "In the year 1675, I discovered living creatures in rainwater, which had stood for a few days in a new pot." He saw "many little animals, very prettily moving." Some "shot through water like a pike." Others "spun round like a top." Still other seemed to make "not the least motion." Today we call the "little animals" that Leeuwenhoek saw in rainwater protozoa and bacteria.

Leeuwenhoek, Antonie van

leg One of the limbs that some animals use to support themselves and move. In humans, the leg is the lower limb that is attached to the trunk of the body by the hip joint. The major bones of the leg are the femur (from the hip to the knee), and the tibia and the fibula (from the knee to the ankle joint). The powerful muscles of the legs are used in walking, running, and jumping.

legume Any plant in the pea family that bears pods containing a number of seeds. Legumes include peas, beans, alfalfa, lentils, and soybeans. Clumps of nitrogen-fixing bacteria present on the roots of legumes take nitrogen from the air and convert it into nitrates.

lens 1. OPTICS. A curved piece of glass or other transparent material that is used to focus light rays (a converging lens) or spread them (a diverging lens). Lenses are used in eyeglasses, cameras, microscopes, telescopes, and other optical instruments. 2. ANATOMY. A transparent part of the eye directly behind the iris that focuses light rays on the retina. 3. PHYSICS. A device that focuses radiation other than light, such as an electron lens. Also, a system or group of such lenses.

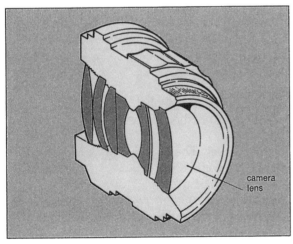

camera lens

lens

Leonardo da Vinci (1452–1519) An Italian Renaissance engineer, naturalist, sculptor, painter, and architect. Da Vinci was an acute observer of the natural world and was particularly interested in anatomy. He made detailed sketches of devices like the flying machine and the diving suit hundreds of years before they were invented. He also designed many simple machines such as pulley systems to make work easier.

Leonardo da Vinci

leucocyte A white blood cell.

leukemia A form of cancer in which the white blood cells multiply uncontrollably and anemia, bruising, and infection result. Recent advances in treatment have greatly improved the chances of children's survival of the disease.

lever A simple machine that multiplies effort or force to move a load or decrease resistance. A lever is a bar that turns on a fixed support called a fulcrum. A first-class lever is like a seesaw. The fulcrum is in the middle. You can raise a load at one end by pushing down at the other end. A second-class lever is like a wheelbarrow. You apply the effort at one end, the fulcrum is at the other end, and the load is in

lever

the middle. A third-class lever is like a baseball bat. The fulcrum is at one end (where you hold the bat at the bottom), you apply the effort in the middle, and the resistance (the ball) is at the other end. [*Lever* comes from a Latin word meaning "lightweight."]

lichen   Lichens are really two kinds of plants growing together: algae and fungi. Algae are green plants that provide the food, and fungi provide the water and prevent algae from drying out. Lichens look somewhat like mosses and grow in patches on rotting wood, on the barks of trees, and even on bare rocks.

life   The quality that organisms such as plants and animals have that makes them different from rocks or metals and dead organisms. Some of life's properties are reproduction, growth, metabolism, and response to stimuli. Even though we know much about life, there are still arguments about its exact definition.

life cycle   A series of changes through which living things pass as they are born, grow older, reproduce, and die.

life history   The record of the stages of development of an organism as it goes through its life cycle.

lift   In aerodynamics, an upward force such as that which acts on the wings of an airplane due to the flow of air over it. [*Lift* comes from an Old English word meaning "air" or "sky."]

lift-off   The first moment in which a rocket or other aircraft leaves the ground.

ligament   In humans and other vertebrates, a band of strong, flexible, white tissue that connects bones and muscles at body joints such as the knee and elbow. Ligaments also hold organs of the body in place. [*Ligament* comes from a Latin word meaning "binding" or "connecting."]

light   A form of electromagnetic radiation. Light travels through space at a speed of about 186,000 miles (just under 300,000 kilometers) per second. According to Einstein's theory of relativity, that is the fastest anything can travel. Humans and other animals can see because of special light-sensitive cells in their eyes. White light is a mixture of different colors called the visible spectrum. The visible spectrum ranges from what we see as deep violet to what we see as deep red.

light-year   A unit of distance measurement used in space. It is the distance that light travels in one year, about 5.9 trillion miles (about 9.5 trillion kilometers). The closest star to us other than our sun is about 4.3 light-years distant.

lightning   A powerful discharge of electricity in the atmosphere that results in a flash of light in the sky. Most lightning occurs between two parts of a cloud; some occur between a cloud and the ground; and a few occur between two clouds. Thunder is the sound produced by the rapid expansion of air due to the heat from a lightning flash.

lignite   A soft, brownish form of coal, sometimes called brown coal.

limb   1. ANATOMY. A leg, arm, or wing; a part of an animal's body that is not the head or the trunk. 2. BOTANY. A large branch of a tree. 3. ASTRONOMY. The edge of the disk of the sun, moon, or other celestial body.

lime   1. ANATOMY. A white, solid compound made up of calcium and oxygen. Lime is usually a white powder formed by heating limestone or shells. It is used to make mortar in construction and on farms and lawns to make the soil less acidic. 2. BOTANY. A small green fruit similar to a lemon.

limestone   A sedimentary rock made up mostly of the mineral calcite (calcium carbonate). Caves and caverns often form in deposits of limestone. Limestone is used in building and in the steel and chemical industries.

limnology   A branch of biology that deals

with the study of freshwater bodies such as lakes and ponds and the plants and animals that live in them.

linen A yarn and fabric made from the fibers of the flax plant.

linkage The association of two or more genes on the same chromosome. Linked genes are carried from generation to generation so that several traits may be inherited together in a group. For example, the genes for red-green color deficiency or hemophilia are linked to the male sex chromosome.

Linnaeus, Carolus (1707–1778) A Swedish botanist and physician who proposed a scientific system for the classification and naming of living things. Many of his ideas and scientific plant names are still in use today.

Linnaeus, Carolus

lipid Any of a group of compounds that includes fats, oils, or waxes. Lipids are found in all plants and animals. Lipids have an oily feel and are not soluble in water.

liquid One of the three states of matter, along with solid and gas. Unlike a gas, a liquid has a definite volume at a given temperature. Unlike a solid, a liquid does not have a definite shape. A liquid will take the shape of the container in which it is put. At usual room temperatures, water is a liquid.

Lister, Joseph (1827–1912) A British physician who pioneered antiseptic surgery. Before his time, operations almost always resulted in severe infections that threatened the life of the patient. Lister was the first to use carbolic acid to sterilize the operating instruments and the wound. This technique of operating in a sterile environment is one of greatest milestones in modern-day medicine.

lithium A soft, silvery-white element. Lithium is the lightest metal and is used in lubrication of machinery; in making ceramics and other materials; and in medicine to treat certain mental illnesses. Lithium has an atomic number of 3 and an atomic weight of 6.941. Its chemical symbol is Li.

lithosphere The solid part of Earth, as contrasted with the atmosphere (the air) and the hydrosphere (the water). The lithosphere is composed mainly of rocks. Also, the earth's crust and upper mantle to a depth of about 60 miles (100 kilometers).

litmus A colored material, which comes from plants called lichens that is commonly used as an acid/base indicator. Litmus turns blue in the presence of a base and red in the presence of an acid. [*Litmus* comes from an Old Norse word meaning "to dye" or "to color."]

littoral Concerning the region along a shore or coast, particularly the area between the high and low tides. Littoral animals and plants live in the intertidal zone.

liver A large, reddish-brown organ in the body of vertebrates. The liver has many functions. It makes bile, which helps in fat digestion. It assists in absorbing and storing sugar (which it changes into glycogen), minerals, and vitamins. It cleans the blood of poisons and waste products, destroys old red blood cells, and makes blood proteins such as clotting factors and enzymes.

lizard A reptile that usually has a long body, a slender tail, and four limbs. Most lizards live in tropical or semitropical climates. Chameleons and iguanas are two kinds of lizards.

load   1. PHYSICS. The force or weight moved by a pulley, lever, or other simple machine. Also, the weight carried by beams or other structural parts of a building. 2. COMPUTING. To enter a program into a computer's working memory.

loam   Fertile soil that is ideal for growing plants. The richness of the loam will depend on the proportion of sand, clay, and humus it contains.

locomotion   The ways in which living things move from place to place. These may include walking, running, flying, swimming, wriggling, and burrowing. Locomotion helps animals survive by enabling them to find food, seek shelter, flee harm, and find a mate.

locus   The place on a chromosome where a particular gene is always located.

lodestone   A piece of a naturally magnetic rock, also called magnetite. Magnetite has a north and south pole and turns to align itself with Earth's magnetic poles. About the twelfth century, early mariners started using primitive compasses made from lodestones.

longitude   A measurement in degrees east or west on Earth's surface. Lines of longitude are usually measured from 0° to 180° east and west from the line of longitude, called the prime

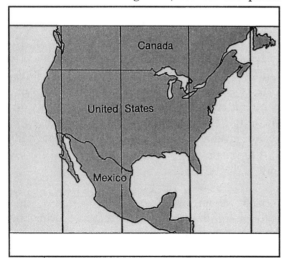

longitude

meridian, that passes through the Observatory in Greenwich, England.

loop   1. ELECTRICITY. A complete electric circuit. 2. COMPUTING. In a computer program, a means by which the same operation may be repeated a number of times before the computer goes on to the next step.

Lorentz, Hendrik Antoon   (1853–1928) A Dutch physicist who explored the relationship among light, electricity, and magnetism. His work on motion, called the Lorentz equations, laid the foundations for Einstein's special theory of relativity. Lorentz received the Nobel Prize for physics in 1902.

loudspeaker   An instrument that changes electrical signals into sound waves. Used in radios, television sets, telephones, and many other products, loudspeakers are often just called speakers.

low tide   The lowest level of ocean water on a beach or shore. Also, the time when the tide is lowest.

low-pressure region   An area of the atmosphere that has a low air pressure as measured by a barometer. Low pressure is often associated with precipitation such as rain or snow.

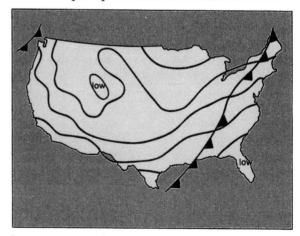

low-pressure region

low-temperature physics   A branch of science that deals with the behavior of materials at temperatures below about 90 kelvins, the boiling point of oxygen. At such low temperatures, electrical conductivity, magnetic properties, and other characteristics of materials change in unusual ways. Scientists are carrying on a great deal of research into superconductivity of different substances at low temperatures.

lubrication   The use of a slippery substance called a lubricant between two moving surfaces. The lubricant allows them to move more freely against each other and reduces friction and wear. Engines, gears, wheels, and other moving parts of machines are often lubricated. Common lubricants are oil, grease, silicones, and powdered graphite. [*Lubrication* comes from a Latin word meaning "slippery."]

lumen   1. PHYSICS. A standard unit of the measurement of light intensity. 2. BIOLOGY. The space inside a hollow organ, such as the inside of a blood vessel or inside the wall of a plant cell.

Lumiere, Louis   (1864–1948) A French pioneer of motion picture photography. Along with his brother Auguste, he invented an early motion picture system and made the first movie in 1895.

luminescence   Light without much heat; so-called cold light. Luminescence includes the light from television screens and chemicals that glow in the dark, as well as the light of glowworms and fireflies.

luminous   To give off light. The sun and an electric light bulb are luminous.

lunar   Having to do with the moon, such as lunar mountains or lunar craters. A lunar month is the time it takes the moon to make one revolution around Earth, about 28 days.

lungs   A pair of breathing organs in the chest of humans and many other vertebrates. The lungs are spongy and full of tiny air sacs called alveoli. Air is drawn into the lungs through the windpipe, or trachea. Oxygen from the air passes into the blood, and carbon dioxide passes out of the blood and into the air as the lungs deflate. The lungs are not muscular and do not move by themselves. They inflate or deflate along with the movements of the ribs and the diaphragm.

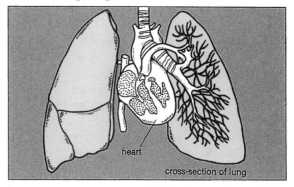

heart

cross-section of lung

lungs

luster   The reflection of light from the surface of a mineral. There are different types of luster, including metallic, silky, dull, and vitreous (like glass).

Lyell, Sir Charles   (1797–1875) An English geologist. In his book *The Principles of Geology,* Lyell contended that natural forces such as erosion and the movement of glaciers were still at work changing the earth's surface. This was an argument against the theory that the earth changed only as a result of great catastrophes in the past.

lymph   A clear fluid that flows inside the bodies of humans and other vertebrates and contains white blood cells, which destroy bacteria. Lymph bathes the tissues of the body and then collects in the lymphatic vessels, which empty into the blood system. Lymph nodes, or lymph glands, are located along the lymph vessels in various parts of the body. The nodes filter the lymph of harmful substances. [*Lymph* comes from a Latin word meaning "clear" or "transparent."]

M

Mach number A number that compares the speed of an aircraft to the speed of sound in air. Near Earth's surface, a Mach number of 1 is equal to a speed of about 750 miles per hour. Speeds greater than Mach 1 are called supersonic speeds. Mach number was named after Ernst Mach (1838–1916), an Austrian physicist who experimented on airflow.

machine A device that does work by transmitting or changing energy or motion. Simple machines include the inclined plane, the axle, the lever, and the pulley. More complex machines may consist of many various moving parts working together. Also, any mechanical or electrical apparatus for doing useful work.

machine language A set of instructions in the binary system that a computer can use immediately. Other kinds of computer languages, such as BASIC, first have to be translated by the computer into machine language before they can be used.

macroclimate The climate of a large region such as the northeastern United States or Western Europe. Weather forecasts usually are given for macroclimates.

macromolecule A large, complex molecule made up of many smaller molecules linked together. DNA is a macromolecule. Polymers such as nylon and polyethylene are also macromolecules.

macroscopic Large enough to be visible to the naked eye. An organ such as the heart is macroscopic. The tissues and cells of the heart are microscopic.

Magellanic Clouds Two irregular galaxies that are the nearest to our own Milky Way galaxy. They were named after the sixteenth-century explorer Ferdinand Magellan. The Clouds are visible as small patches of cloudy light in the sky of the Southern Hemisphere. In 1987, a supernova blazed into view in the Large Magellanic Cloud. It will be studied for many years as it fades and changes.

maggot The legless, wormlike larva of a fly. Maggots often live in rotting food or other decaying materials.

magma The hot, molten rock beneath the earth's crust. Magma forced out of the earth in volcanic eruptions is called lava. When magma cools, it forms igneous rocks such as basalt or rhyolite.

magnesium A silvery-white metallic element that is very lightweight and very active chemically. Magnesium can be drawn into thin wires or flattened into thin sheets. It burns in air with an intense white light. It is the eighth most abundant element and is found in nature combined with many different minerals. Magnesium has an atomic number of 12 and an atomic weight of 24.312. Its symbol is Mg.

magnet An object that produces a strong magnetic field and attracts iron, steel, nickel, and cobalt. If objects made from those materials are themselves magnets, the force can attract or repel them. Invisible lines of force extend between the two poles of a magnet. Lodestone is a rock that is a natural magnet. "Permanent magnets" can retain their magnetic properties for many years.

magnetic field The space around a magnet in which its magnetic lines of force act. Magnetic fields can be produced by permanent magnets or by sending a wire coil (electromagnetism). Earth, other planets, and stars have magnetic fields that extend millions of miles into space, becoming weaker and weaker as distance increases. The behavior of magnetic fields around planets and stars remains an unsolved mystery.

magnetic pole 1. PHYSICS. Either of two poles of a magnet: a north pole (or north-seeking pole) and a south pole (or south-seeking pole). Magnetic force is concentrated near the poles. The like poles of a magnet repel each other; unlike poles attract. 2. GEOPHYSICS. The two poles on Earth to which a compass needle points. Earth's magnetic poles are not in the same places as its geographic poles. The north magnetic pole is located in the Arctic about 75° north latitude and 100° west longitude. The south magnetic pole is in Antarctica about 66° south latitude and 140° east longitude. The magnetic poles "wander" or shift. They have reversed many times over the billions of years that Earth has existed.

magnetic tape A thin, plastic film coated on one side with a magnetic material. It is used to store electromagnetic signals that can be changed into sounds, pictures, or other information by tape recorders, video cassette recorders, computers, and other machines.

magnetism A force of nature that involves certain materials such as iron or steel, and also comes from the movement of an electric current. Magnetism is associated with forces of both attraction and repulsion. A magnet behaves as if there are two poles at which its force is concentrated, unlike gravity, which spreads from a single center of force.

magnetite A brownish iron ore that is attracted to a magnet. When magnetite itself is a magnet, it is called a lodestone.

magnifying glass A convex (outwardly curved) lens or a system of lenses used to make an object appear larger. A magnifying glass is a simple microscope. A magnifying lens can also be used to focus or direct light and heat to a point.

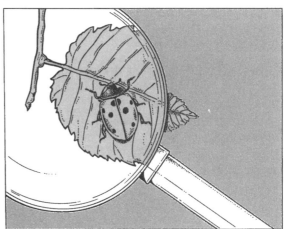

magnifying glass

magnitude 1. ASTRONOMY. The brightness of a star. First magnitude stars are the brightest. The dimmest stars we can see without a telescope are called fifth or sixth magnitude. Large telescopes can be used to help photograph stars as dim as twentieth magnitude. Each unit of magnitude is about two and one half times brighter than the next. 2. GEOLOGY. The force of an earthquake. The most common method of measuring earthquakes is the Richter magnitude scale. Quakes that are felt by most people commonly measure between 4 and 8 on that scale.

maize   The corn plant, a kind of grass. Also the grain produced by the corn plant.

malaria   A tropical disease caused by a protozoan parasite. The parasite is picked up by the *Anopheles* mosquito from the blood of infected people or animals it has bitten. It then passes the parasite on to other people. Malaria victims have repeated attacks of high fever, sweating, and chills. It is treated by drugs such as quinine or atropine. [*Malaria* comes from an Italian word meaning "bad air," which was once thought to cause the disease.]

male   1. ZOOLOGY. An animal that is of the sex that produces sperm, by which the female's eggs are fertilized. 2. BOTANY. A flowering plant that has a structure called a stamen, which produces pollen grains (male sex cells of plants).

malleable   Describes the property of metals and alloys that allows them to be bent into various shapes or rolled into thin sheets without breaking. Gold, silver, and copper are very malleable.

malnutrition   A condition in which humans or other animals do not get enough of the right kinds of foods. Poor people all over the world suffer from some kind of malnutrition.

Malpighi, Marcello   (1628–1694) An Italian physician and biologist who discovered capillaries, the smallest kinds of blood vessels. Malpighi was one of the first scientists to use a microscope to explore the anatomy of the human body.

mammal   Any of a kind of vertebrate warm-blooded animal that usually has hair or fur. A female mammal gives birth to living young and feeds them with milk from her mammary glands. Humans, elephants, horses, dogs, cats, bats, and whales are all mammals. [*Mammal* comes from a Latin word meaning "breast."]

Malpighi, Marcello

mammary glands   The glands in the breasts of female mammals that produce milk for their young.

mammoth   A very large, extinct mammal that looked like a hairy elephant. During the ice ages, about 100,000 years ago, wooly mammoths lived on the plains of Europe and North America. During the past century several frozen bodies of mammoths have been dug up in the ice ground of Siberia. The last of the mammoths died out about 30,000 years ago.

man   1. An adult male human. 2. *Homo Sapiens*. The human species, both male and female. The most numerous and widespread of all the primates, man alone among animals makes tools and communicates by means of language. Man is supposedly the most intelligent of all animals.

mandible   The lower jaw of a vertebrate animal. Also, a special kind of mouth part in insects and certain other invertebrates. Mandibles are used to bite and crush foods. [*Mandible* comes from a Latin word meaning "to chew or bite."]

manometer   An instrument used to measure the pressure in fluids.

mantle   1. ZOOLOGY. The fold or flap of soft material in the body wall of a mollusk. The mantle contains glands that make the material which forms the shell. Also, the back feathers and folded wings of a bird. 2. ANATOMY. The outer layer of gray matter—also called the cortex—of the brain's cerebrum. 3. EARTH SCIENCE. The layer of a planet that lies between the crust and the core. [*Mantle* comes from a Latin word meaning "cloak."]

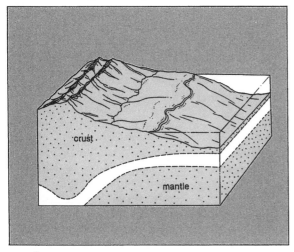

mantle

map A diagram or picture of features on the surface of the earth or of part of it. Map making is called cartography, and maps have been drawn since early times. [*Map* comes from a Latin word meaning "sheet," on which maps of the known world were once drawn.]

marble A hard, metamorphic rock made of recrystallized limestone or dolomite. Natural marble may be white, streaked, or various colors. Marble can be polished to a high degree of shininess. It is used as a building stone or for sculpture. [*Marble* comes from a Greek word meaning "to sparkle."]

Marconi, Guglielmo (1874–1937) An Italian physicist who invented the wireless telegraph. In 1901, in Newfoundland, Canada, he received a radio signal sent from Cornwall, England, across the Atlantic Ocean. That was the beginning of transoceanic radio communication. In 1909, Marconi was awarded the Nobel Prize in physics for his achievements.

Marconi, Guglielmo

marine Concerning the sea or ocean. Marine biology is the study of the living things in the sea.

Mariner Program A United States unmanned space program in the early 1970s that made close flyby observations of the planets Mars, Venus, and Mercury.

marrow The soft tissue in the center of most bones in which red blood cells, many white blood cells, and platelets are made.

Mars The fourth planet from the sun. Mars is about 141 million miles (about 228 million kilometers) from the sun and revolves around the sun in 687 days. Mars is smaller than Earth, about 4,221 miles (about 6,796 kilometers) in diameter. It has two tiny moons, Deimos and Phobos. A Martian day is only about 40 minutes longer than our own. The atmosphere of Mars is very thin and made up mostly of carbon dioxide and nitrogen with only traces of oxygen. No life has been found on Mars, though the possibility of some kind of life on the planet has not been ruled out.

marsh Low, soft land covered by water at most times. Great clumps of plants such as reeds and rushes grow in marshes. Marshes may be created when lakes fill up with sediment.

marsupial Any of an order of mammals characterized by a pouch covering the mammary glands on the abdomen. Kangaroos, koalas, opossums, and wombats are marsupials. Australia has many marsupials; a few are found in North and South America, but none in Africa or Eurasia. [*Marsupial* comes from a Greek word meaning "little bag" or "purse."]

mass The amount of matter in an object, usually measured in grams or kilograms. Mass is not dependent on gravity and is not the same as weight. An object's mass remains the same anywhere, while its weight will change in space or on another planet. An object's mass is a measure of its inertia—its tendency to resist change in its motion. The greater an object's mass, the greater its inertia.

mathematics The science that deals with measurements, shapes, and quantities and how they relate to each other. Mathematics is expressed in numbers and symbols. Arithmetic, algebra, geometry, and calculus are some of the branches of mathematics. [*Mathematics* comes from a Greek word meaning "learning" or "knowledge."]

matrix 1. EARTH SCIENCE. A rock in which minerals, gems, or fossils are embedded. 2. ANATOMY. The part of an organ from which growth occurs, such as the skin (dermis) beneath the fingernail or toenail. 3. BIOLOGY. The material between the cells of a tissue. [*Matrix* comes from a Latin word meaning "mother."]

matter Any substance that has mass and occupies space. Matter usually exists as a solid, liquid, or gas and is made of tiny particles called atoms.

Maxwell, James Clerk (1831–1879) A British physicist who studied the nature of electromagnetism. He devised the important Maxwell equations of the electromagnetic field. These explain the relationships between electricity and magnetism in a particular space. Maxwell was the first to identify light waves as a form of electromagnetic radiation. Maxwell's contributions to science have been compared in significance to those of Newton and Einstein.

Maxwell, James Clerk

measles An infectious childhood disease caused by a virus. It results in a rash of red spots on the skin, fever, and coldlike symptoms. German measles (rubella) is a different disease with similar but milder symptoms. Children are commonly vaccinated as a protection against both diseases.

mechanical energy The energy of a moving object. Anything in motion has mechanical energy. For example, wind has mechanical energy. When wind hits a windmill, the moving particles of air pass mechanical energy along to the blades and they move. The windmill can also be used along with a generator to change mechanical energy into electrical energy.

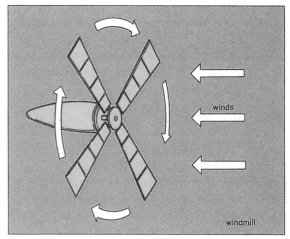
mechanical energy

mechanics The branch of physics that deals with motion and the effect of forces acting on an object. One part of mechanics, called dynamics, is based on Newton's three laws of motion. Another part, called kinetics is used to describe objects in motion.

medicine The science of healing and maintaining health. In past times, medicine was often a matter of magic and superstition. In the last century, so-called Western medicine has been based more on scientific principles. Medicine is often successful in preventing infectious diseases such as smallpox, and diphtheria. It is less successful in treating and curing other illnesses such as heart disease and cancer. [*Medicine* comes from a Latin word meaning "to cure" or "to comfort."]

medium 1. BIOLOGY. A substance in which microorganisms are grown for study or other purposes. In a laboratory, bacteria are often grown in a medium called nutrient agar. Also, an environment in which something lives. Pond life lives in a water medium. 2. PHYSICS. A substance in which something acts or takes effect. Copper is a good medium for conducting electricity.

medulla The inner, or central, part of an organ or structure in an animal or plant. The central part of the kidney is often called the medulla. Also, bone marrow. The medulla oblongata is the lower part of the brain that is connected to the top of the spinal cord. It controls breathing, heartbeat, and other automatic body functions. [*Medulla* comes from a Latin word meaning "pith" or "marrow."]

meiosis In cell biology, the process by which the number of chromosomes in reproductive cells is reduced to half the original number. This usually results in the production of gametes (sperm and egg cells) in animals, and pollen and ovules in higher plants. [*Meiosis* comes from a Greek word meaning "to diminish" or "to lessen."]

melanin A dark coloring material found in the skin, hair, and eyes of humans and many animals. Large amounts of melanin in the skin may help protect against sunburn and other harmful effects of the sun's rays. [*Melanin* comes from a Greek word meaning "black."]

melt To change from a solid to a liquid by heating. When ice is heated, it melts and becomes water. Metals such as iron and zinc melt when they are heated in furnaces.

melting point The temperature at which a solid melts. The melting point of ice at normal atmospheric pressure is 32°F (0°C).

membrane A thin layer of animal or plant tissue. A membrane lines or covers a body or plant parts. Mucous membranes line the nose and throat and other passages. Living cells are enclosed in cell membranes. Food molecules pass into the cell and waste materials are excreted through the cell membrane. [*Membrane* comes from a Latin word meaning "parchment."]

memory 1. BIOLOGY. The ability to store information and experience in the mind and to recall them in certain situations. Little is known of exactly how memories are stored, but recent studies seem to show that chemical changes in the brain are involved with memory. 2. COMPUTING. A device in which information may be stored in a computer, such as a RAM (Random Access Memory) or ROM (Read-Only Memory) chip. Also, the amount of data that a computer can store, such as a one-megabyte (one million bytes) memory.

memory card A removable electronic flash memory data device used to store digital information. Memory cards are used in many kinds of electronic devices including mobile phones, digital cameras, tablets, and laptop or handheld computers. They are small, can be reused, and can hold data without power.

Mendel, Gregor Johann (1822–1884) An Austrian botanist whose experiments with breeding pea plants laid the foundations of the modern science of genetics. Mendel published the results of his experiments in 1865 and 1869, but it was not until after his death that the importance of his work was appreciated.

Mendeleyev, Dmitry Ivanovich (1834–1907) A Russian chemist who formulated the periodic law, which states that the properties of elements vary according to their atomic weight. Later, Henry Moseley, a British physicist (1887–1915), changed the periodic law to state that the properties of elements vary according to their atomic number. The new law resulted in the periodic table of elements, which is still in use today.

Mendeleyev, Dmitry Ivanovich

menstrual cycle The monthly fertility cycle in women of reproductive age, which ends in menstruation, the flow of blood when the lining of the uterus is shed. During the menstrual cycle, changes occur in the level of hormones, body temperature, and in fluid retention. This may result in changes in mood, which can vary from one person to the next. The patterns of the menstrual cycle begin at puberty (called menarche) and end in middle life (called menopause).

mercury A heavy, metallic element that is a silvery liquid at ordinary temperatures. Mercury is used in some kinds of barometers and thermometers, in mercury vapor lamps, and in many other industrial devices. Mercury has an atomic number of 80 and an atomic weight of 200.59. Its chemical symbol is Hg. Once called quicksilver.

Mercury (planet) The planet closest to the sun and the second-smallest planet in the solar system (after Pluto). Mercury is a cratered ball of rock that looks much like our moon. It takes about 88 days for Mercury to complete one orbit around the sun, at an average distance from the sun of about 36 million miles (58 million kilometers).

Mercury Program The first United States space flights, using the one-person *Mercury* capsule. Alan Shepard made the first suborbital flight from Cape Canaveral on May 5, 1961. John Glenn became the first American to go into orbit, on February 20, 1962.

meridian 1. GEOGRAPHY. An imaginary circle that passes through the poles and is at right angles to the equator. 2. ASTRONOMY. Also called the celestial meridian. An imaginary circle that runs overhead in the sky from the horizon due south through the zenith (the point directly overhead) and then down to the horizon due north.

mesa A steep-sided, flat-topped plateau or hill. Mesas are common in the southwestern United States. [*Mesa* is the Spanish word for "table."]

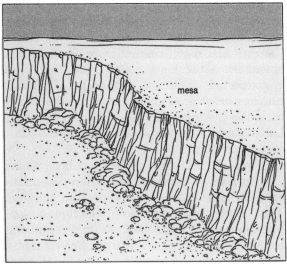
mesa

Mesozoic Era The geological era before the present (Cenozoic) era. It began about 225 million years ago and ended about 65 million years ago. The Mesozoic was the era of dinosaurs, flying reptiles, and early mammals, birds, and flowering plants. It has three periods: the Triassic, Jurassic, and Cretaceous.

metabolism The total of all the chemical processes that maintain life in an organism. Metabolism includes reactions such as the breaking down of foods that yield energy and simple chemicals the body can use for growth and repair. The smallest amount of energy an organism uses at complete rest is called the basal metabolism. [*Metabolism* comes from a Greek word meaning "change."]

metal An element such as iron, copper, tin, aluminum, silver, or gold, that usually is shiny and a good conductor of heat and electricity, and can be hammered into thin sheets or drawn into wires. In chemical reactions, a metal reacts with nonmetals by losing electrons and taking on a positive charge. Some metals—or a metal and a nonmetal—can be melted together to form alloys such as steel (iron and carbon), brass (copper and zinc), and bronze (copper and tin).

metallic Having to do with or being made of a metal or metals.

metallurgy The science and technology of metals. This includes the extraction and refining of metals from their ores, making alloys, and shaping metals, as well as the study of their properties. A scientist who studies metals is called a metallurgist.

metamorphic 1. EARTH SCIENCE. Describes a rock that has been changed in structure by heat, pressure, or water after it was originally formed. Marble is a metamorphic rock formed from limestone. 2. BIOLOGY. Having to do with the change in form by some animals, such as the stages in the life cycle of a frog or a butterfly.

metamorphosis 1. EARTH SCIENCE. The changes that a rock undergoes when it is exposed to pressure, heat, or water for a long

period of time. 2. BIOLOGY. A sharp and rapid change in the form and behavior of an animal during its development from young to adult. Moths and butterflies go through metamorphosis when they change from a larva (a caterpillar) to a pupa in a chrysalis (a cocoon) to an adult winged form.

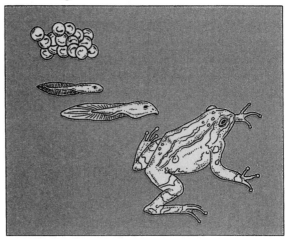
metamorphosis

meteor A mass of rock, or iron and nickel, in space that enters Earth's atmosphere at high speeds. Friction with the particles of air in the atmosphere cause the meteor to glow and usually burn up. In a meteor shower a large number of meteors fall. That occurs when Earth encounters the remains of a comet in space. The Perseid meteor shower occurs in the middle of August each year.

meteorite A piece of rock or metal from space that reaches Earth's surface without burning up completely. Meteorites are either mostly stony (aerolites), metal (siderites), or both (siderolites).

meteoroid A piece of rock or metal in interplanetary space. When it is very small, it is called a micrometeoroid. A meteoroid becomes a meteor when it enters the earth's atmosphere.

meteorology The science that deals with the atmosphere and the weather. A meteorologist is a scientist who studies weather and makes weather forecasts.

meter 1. MATHEMATICS. The basic unit of length in the metric system, equal to about 39.37 inches. 2. ENGINEERING. An instrument—such as a voltmeter, water meter, or gas meter—used to measure and record the amount of something.

metric system A system of measurement based on units of ten. The meter is the unit of length, the gram is the unit of mass, and the liter is the unit of volume. The common prefixes used with any of these are: micro = 1/1,000,000; milli = 1/1,000; centi = 1/100; deci = 1/10; deca = 10; hecto = 100; kilo = 1,000; mega = 1,000,000. For example, a centimeter is 1/100 of a meter and a kilogram is 1,000 grams.

mica Any of a group of minerals that can be split into thin, almost transparent layers. Because mica does not burn or conduct electricity, it is used in many kinds of equipment as an electrical insulator. [*Mica* comes from a Latin word meaning "crumb" or "grain."]

microbe A microscopic living thing such as a bacterium, often associated with disease or with fermentation.

microbiology The branch of biology dealing with the study of microscopic living things including bacteria, protozoa, viruses, fungi, and algae.

microclimate The climate of a very small area such as a lawn or a clump of trees.

micrometer An instrument used to measure very small distances, angles, or objects. Also, a unit of length in the metric system equal to one millionth of a meter. These are pronounced differently: The instrument is a mi-KROM-eter and the unit of length is a MI-kro-ME-ter.

microorganism A living thing such as a bacterium or virus that can be seen only through a light microscope or an electron microscope.

microphone A device that changes sound waves into electrical signals. Telephones and tape recorders contain microphones.

microphotography Photography of very tiny things that can only be seen through a microscope.

microprocessor A complex electrical circuit on a single chip that is used in a computer, calculator, and one of many other electronic instruments.

microscope An optical instrument that uses a lens or lenses to produce enlarged images of small objects that are difficult or impossible to see with the unaided eye. The simplest microscope is a single lens or magnifying glass. A compound microscope has two lenses: The objective lens produces a magnified, inverted image of an object. The image is viewed through the eyepiece, or ocular lens, which magnifies the image even further. Also, electronic or other instruments that are used to magnify the images of very small objects, such as parts of cells. These include electron microscopes, field-ion microscopes, and acoustic microscopes.

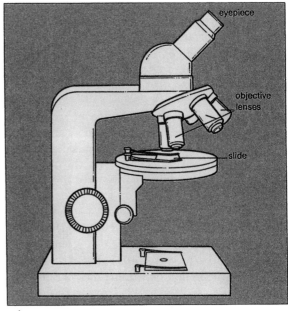

microscope

microscopic Describes something that is too small to be seen without the use of a microscope.

microwave A high-frequency electromagnetic wave used in radar, radio communications, to and from satellites, and for cooking. In microwave ovens, food is heated and cooked by the energy of microwaves.

mid-ocean ridge A series of submarine mountain ranges that stretch around the world through the Atlantic Ocean and across the Pacific and Indian Oceans.

middle ear The air-filled space in the ear between the eardrum and the inner ear. In humans, the middle ear contains three small bones—the malleus (hammer), incus (anvil), and stapes (stirrup)—which amplify sound waves.

midnight sun The sun when it is seen both at night and day above the horizon in the polar regions during summer.

migration The long-distance movement of animals from one location to another. Migration usually takes place with the change of seasons.

mildew The growth of fungi on plants or on objects made of natural materials such as paper, leather, and cotton. Mildew usually occurs in damp places.

mile A unit of length or distance used in many parts of the world. The statute mile is 5,280 feet, 1,760 yards, or about 1,609.3 meters. [*Mile* comes from a Latin word meaning "thousand"; a mile for the ancient Romans was 1,000 paces, or about 4,850 feet (1,478.6 meters).]

milk The white liquid that is secreted by the mammary glands of female mammals. The milk produced in any species of animal provides a complete food for the young of that species. For thousands of years people have used the milk of animals such as cows, goats, sheep, and water buffalo to produce butter, cheese, and other foods.

milk teeth The first set of teeth in humans and other mammals. Milk teeth are replaced in early years by permanent teeth that push through the gums.

Milky Way The hazy-white band of light that arcs across the night sky. The light comes from countless stars that are too far away to be seen separately without a telescope. It is what we see from Earth when we look out at the nearby portions of the Milky Way galaxy.

Milky Way galaxy The galaxy that contains the sun, Earth, and the rest of the solar system. The Milky Way galaxy is made up of more than 100 billion stars and large clouds of gas and dust. Also called just the Galaxy.

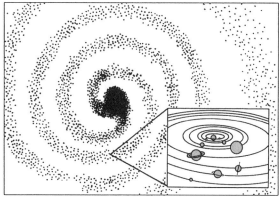

Milky Way galaxy

milli- A prefix that means one thousandth of something, as in millimeter (one thousandth of a meter) or milligram (one thousandth of a gram).

mimicry The close resemblance of an animal or plant to its surroundings or to another animal or plant. For example, harmless insects may have the same markings as harmful or poisonous insects. Predators that have learned to avoid eating harmful insects may avoid any harmless insects that look the same.

mind The part of a human being that thinks, remembers, learns, and feels emotions. All of the mind's activities take place in the brain.

mineral An element or compound found in the ground that does not come from living things and has a definite chemical composition and regular crystal form. Common minerals include quartz, feldspar, and mica. Also, a natural material that can be mined or quarried.

This includes coal, petroleum, and natural gas, even though they come from living things of long ago.

minute A unit of time equal to one sixtieth of an hour, or 60 seconds. Also, a unit of measurement of an angle or the arc of a circle equal to one sixtieth of a degree.

Miocene Epoch The next-to-last epoch of the Tertiary Period of the earth's history. It lasted from about 25 million to 7 million years ago. During the Miocene, large herds of grazing mammals developed.

mirage An optical illusion usually seen in deserts or other hot places. Mirages are caused by light rays being refracted or bent when they pass through air of different densities. Some mirages appear as a sheet of water in the distance. Other mirages appear as objects floating in the air. [*Mirage* is a French word that comes from a Latin word meaning "to reflect."]

mirror A smooth reflecting surface in which images can be seen. Most mirrors are made of glass with a silvered backing that reflects light. In a flat or plane mirror, the image, called a mirror image, is reversed left-to-right but remains right-side up. A concave mirror, such as the inside of a spoon, produces an upside-down, inverted image of distant objects. A convex mirror, such as the outside of a spoon, produces a right-side up image but shows a wider field of view than a flat mirror, so objects appear smaller than they really are.

missile Something that is launched or thrown into the air. Guided missiles are rocket weapons. [*Missile* comes from a Latin word meaning "to throw" or "to send."]

Mississippian Period The fifth period of the Paleozoic Era of the earth's history. Also called the Lower Carboniferous Era. It lasted from about 345 to about 315 million years ago.

mist A cloud of very fine water droplets in the air right above the ground. Mist forms when water vapor in moist air is cooled and condenses. Also, a cloud of very small droplets of any liquid in the air.

mistral A strong, cold wind that blows from the north across the central part of France. It occurs mainly in the winter and is a hazard to transportation and crops.

mitochondria Tiny structures found in cells that contain genetic information and enzymes. Mitochondria produce most of the energy needed by cells.

mitosis The normal process by which the nucleus of a cell, including each chromosome, divides into two, forming two new cells. Each of the new cells contains a nucleus with the same number of chromosomes as the original nucleus. [*Mitosis* comes from a Greek word meaning "thread."]

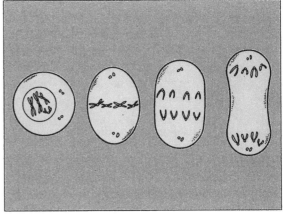

mitosis

mixture A substance made of two or more substances that are not chemically combined. Mixtures can be separated by filtration, distillation, freezing, or other physical means. Air is a mixture of nitrogen, oxygen, and other gases. Seawater is a mixture of water and many salts.

mobile Able to move from one place to another or to flow easily. Most animals are mobile. Mercury is a mobile metal.

modulation The process by which data or

information is added to an electromagnetic wave such as a radio wave. The information changes, or modulates, the electromagnetic wave. The two main kinds are amplitude modulation (A.M.) and frequency modulation (F.M.)

Mohs' scale A scale for measuring the hardness of minerals, with 10 (diamond) the hardest and 1 (talc) the softest. Hardness is determined by trying to use a harder mineral to scratch a softer mineral. The scale was invented by Friedrich Mohs (1773–1839), a German mineralogist.

molar 1. ANATOMY. Any of the large teeth with a broad surface used for grinding found at the back of a mammal's mouth. Humans normally have twelve molars. 2. CHEMISTRY. Pertaining to a measure of the amount of solute dissolved in a solution. It is equivalent to the number of moles (a particular amount of a solute dissolved in one liter of a solution).

mold 1. BIOLOGY. A small, fuzzy-looking fungus that grows on the surface of damp or decaying food or other organic materials. Different molds are greenish-blue, white, or black. 2. GEOLOGY. An impression in a rock or in the earth of a plant, shell, or animal part. 3. ENGINEERING. A cavity used to produce a part of a machine or an object with a particular shape.

molecular weight The sum of the atomic weights of all the atoms in a molecule.

molecule The smallest particle of an element or compound that has all the chemical properties of that substance. A molecule is made up of two or more atoms linked by chemical bonds. A molecule of oxygen is two atoms of hydrogen and one atom of oxygen linked together. [*Molecule* comes from a Latin word meaning "little lump" or "mass."]

mollusk Any member of a large group of animals without backbones. A mollusk has a soft, muscular body and a muscular foot for movement. Most mollusks, such as snails, clams, and mussels, are protected by hard shells, but some, such as slugs, squids, and octopuses, have no shell. [*Mollusk* comes from a Latin word meaning "soft."]

molt To shed skin, feathers, fur, hair, or a hard outside covering. Birds and mammals molt to renew worn-out fur or feathers. Insects, crustaceans, and snakes molt so that they can grow larger within a new covering. [*Molt* comes from a Latin word meaning "to change" or "to mutate."]

molten Made liquid by being heated, such as molten rock, called lava or magma. The temperature at which substances become molten is called their melting point.

momentum A measure of the amount of motion of a moving object. Momentum is equal to the mass of the object multiplied by the velocity at which it is moving. [*Momentum* comes from a Latin word meaning "to move."]

moneran A one-celled living thing that does not have a distinct nucleus. Bacteria and blue-green algae belong to the moneran kingdom. [*Moneran* comes from a Greek work meaning "solitary" or "single."]

monkey Any one of a group of small, long-tailed primates, such as the rhesus, capuchin, or howler species. Monkeys live in tribes and spend at lease part of the time in trees.

monocotyledon Any flowering plant that has one seed leaf (cotyledon). There are many different kinds of these plants including grasses, bamboo, palms, and orchids. They generally have leaves with parallel veins and flower parts in units of three.

monsoon A regular seasonal wind that blows in the tropics. It blows from sea to land during the summer and from land to sea during the winter. Monsoons are caused by seasonal differences of temperature and air pressure between land and sea. [*Monsoon* comes from an Arabic word meaning "seasonal."]

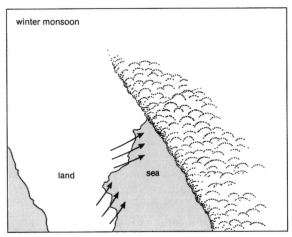

monsoon

month A period of time usually based on the phases of the moon. A calendar month is one of the twelve parts into which a year is divided on the Gregorian or Julian calendar. A lunar month is the time from one new moon to the next new moon, approximately 29.5 days. A sidereal month is the time it takes the moon to make one revolution around Earth in relation to the stars, approximately 27.3 days.

moon Earth's natural satellite, which has diameter of about 2,160 miles (3,475 kilometers) and an average distance from Earth of about 235,000 miles (384,000 kilometers), and orbits Earth in about 27.3 days. The force of the moon's gravitational pull helps cause ocean tides. On the much less massive moon, a person would weigh only a sixth of his or her weight on Earth. The moon is covered with thousands of craters of all sizes, flat plains, mountains, and trenches. It has no air or water, and is very hot in the sunlight and very cold in the dark. Also, a natural satellite of any planet, such as any of Jupiter's moons.

moraine The accumulation of earth and rocks carried and then dropped by a glacier when it melts. A moraine is deposited at the end of a glacier (terminal moraine) or at its sides (lateral moraine).

Morse, Samuel F. B. (1791–1872) An American inventor of the electric telegraph and of Morse code, a combination of dots and dashes representing letters and numbers. It is still occasionally used in radiotelegraphy. Morse's famous message "What hath God wrought!" was sent in 1844.

Morse, Samuel F. B.

mortar A building material made of sand, water, and cement used to bind together bricks and stones. When mortar sets, it is strong and water resistant.

moss Any of a class of very small, soft, green or brown plants that grow low and close together in clumps or carpets that cover damp ground, rocks or tree. Mosses do not have flowers but reproduce by forming spores.

moth An insect that, together with butterflies, belongs to an order called Lepidoptera. An adult moth has four wings and antennas that are sometimes feathery but always without knobs at their ends. Moths fly mainly at night.

motile Describing a microscopic living thing such as a paramecium that is able to move about by itself.

motion Movement. A change in the position of a body, a particle, a machine, or other object. Atoms and molecules are continually in motion.

motor 1. ENGINEERING. A machine that changes one form of energy, such as electrical, into mechanical energy, the energy of motion. Also, an internal-combustion engine—such as those in automobiles and other vehicles or in machines such a power lawn mowers. 2. PHYSIOLOGY. A motor nerve or a motor neuron carries an impulse or message from the central nervous system to a muscle or organ, which results in movement.

mountain A very high hill. An elevation of the earth's surface that stands high above its surroundings. A connected group of mountains is called a mountain range or a mountain chain. The Himalayas, the Alps, the Andes, and the Rockies are big mountain ranges. There are even longer and higher mountain ranges beneath the sea.

mouse An input device that lets you control a computer.

mouth 1. ANATOMY. The opening in the body of an animal or person through which food is taken. In humans and other mammals, the mouth contains teeth and a tongue. Humans produce sounds mostly through their mouths. 2. GEOGRAPHY. The end of a river where it enters into the sea or another body of water. Also, an opening that provides an entrance to a volcano, cave, or other earth feature.

mucus A thick, slimy fluid produced by the cells of the mucous membranes that line the nose, mouth, lungs, intestines, and other parts of the respiratory and digestive systems. Mucus protects the membranes and keeps them moist.

mulch A layer of plant or other material kept on the surface of soil to keep it moist, protect it from erosion, and prevent weeds from growing. Mulches may contain grass clippings, leaves, straw, wood chips, or peat moss. [Mulch comes from German words meaning "something that is soft or beginning to decay."]

multicellular Describing an animal or plant that consists of many cells.

mumps A contagious virus infection, common in childhood, that results in swelling of the salivary glands in the mouth and in front of the ear. An attack of mumps results in future immunity.

muon A subatomic particle. Muons are about 207 times as heavy as electrons. They are the main particles in cosmic radiation on Earth's surface. Muons decay to form high-energy electrons.

muscle The tissue in humans and animals that is capable of changing in size and making the body move when stimulated by nerves. Muscle tissue is of two main kinds: striated and smooth. Striated (striped) tissues form the muscles that are controlled by the brain and voluntarily move a part of the body such as an arm or a leg. Smooth muscles tissues, also called involuntary muscles, are controlled automatically by the autonomic nervous system and we are rarely aware of their movement. Smooth muscle tissue is found in the linings of tubes such as blood vessels and intestines. Cardiac muscle is a third type that combines the features of both striated and smooth muscles, because it is striped but involuntary. It has the ability to contract regularly and be active for extended periods.

mutation A sudden and permanent change in a gene that results in the appearance of new characteristics in offspring. Mutations are usually caused by radiation, chemicals, or some other environmental feature. The changed animal or plant is called a mutant. [*Mutation* comes from a Latin word meaning "to change" or "to modify."]

myopia Nearsightedness. A condition of the eye in which images of close objects are in focus, but images of distant objects are blurred. Suitable lenses in eyeglasses or contact lenses are used to correct myopia.

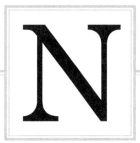

N

nail 1. BIOLOGY. A flat, thin, hard plate that protects the tips of the fingers and toes in vertebrates. Nails are made of a substance called keratin. Some animals have claws or hooves instead of true nails. 2. ENGINEERING. A thin, pointed metal shaft with a flat head at one end. A nail can be hammered into pieces of wood or other materials to join them together.

narcotic A drug that caused a person to sleep or that reduces pain by dulling the nerves. Narcotics are used in medicine in a controlled way. But narcotics can cause poisoning, illness, and death. [*Narcotic* comes from a Greek word meaning "numb."]

NASA *N*ational *A*eronautics and *S*pace *A*dministration. An agency of the United States responsible for new developments in civilian aviation and spaceflight. Its main mission is to pioneer the future in space exploration.

nasal cavity In vertebrates, the part of the breathing passageway in the front of the head that opens into the nostrils. The nasal cavity is lined with a mucous membrane that produces a sticky liquid that warms, moistens, and partly filters dust and germs from the air.

natural Describing an element or substance found in nature; not synthetic, artificial, or made by people. Hydrogen and oxygen are natural elements. Wool and silk are natural fibers. Wood and stone are natural building materials.

natural gas A combustible gas found naturally in underground pockets, usually near petroleum and coal deposits. The gas is pumped into holding tanks and is used for fuel.

natural history The study of animals, plants, minerals, and other things found in nature, often by observing in the field rather than by experimenting in a laboratory. A person who studies the natural history of animals and plants is called a naturalist.

natural science Any science that deals with the physical or natural world. Biology, physics, chemistry, and geology are natural sciences.

natural selection A gradual process in nature by which those animals and plants best suited to their environment tend to survive and pass on their characteristics to future generations. In his writings on evolution, Charles Darwin called the process of natural selection "survival of the fittest."

nautical mile A measurement of distance at sea, approximately 6,076 feet (1,852 meters), about 1.15 statute miles.

navigation The science of finding the location

of a ship, aircraft, or spaceship and directing it from one place to another. In early times, lodestones and compasses were used. Nowadays, radar and satellites are used in navigation.

Neanderthal people A prehistoric race of humans who lived sixty to seventy thousand years ago in Europe and the Middle East. Neanderthal people were hunters and used weapons made of flint and bone. Neanderthals became extinct during the Stone Age, when Cro-Magnon people came upon the scene. [*Neanderthal* is the name of a valley near Düsseldorf, in West Germany, where the remains of Neanderthal people were first discovered in 1856.]

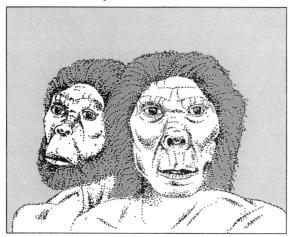

Neanderthal people

neap tide A tide that comes twice a month, in the first and third quarter of the moon. Neap tide occurs when the gravitational pulls of the moon and the sun are at right angles to each other. During neap tide, the difference in height between the daily high tide and daily low tide is the smallest.

nebula A cloud of stars or dust and gases in deep space. Galactic nebulas are clouds of dust in our own galaxy, the Milky Way. They may be dark or the gases may be lit up by surrounding stars. Extragalactic nebulas are galaxies of stars beyond the Milky Way. Some kinds of nebulas may be the birthplaces of stars. [*Nebula* comes from a Latin word meaning "mist" or "fog."]

neck 1. ZOOLOGY, ANATOMY. The part of the body of some animals that connects the head with the shoulders. Also, a narrow part of a bone or organ. 2. GEOLOGY. The eroded remains of a plug of lava that filled the vent of an extinct volcano. 3. GEOGRAPHY. A narrow strip of land such as an isthmus or a peninsula. Also, a narrow body of water such as a strait.

nectar A sweet liquid found in many flowers. Nectar attracts insects and birds to flowers. Bees bring nectar back to their hives and make it into honey.

needle 1. BOTANY. A thin stiff, pointed leaf such as those on a pine or spruce tree. 2. EARTH SCIENCE. A long, pointed crystal of rock or mineral. Also a thin, pointed rock structure caused by erosion.

negative The kind of electrical charge carried by an electron, or the kind of charge present in an object when it has more electrons that protons. The tendency of nonmetallic elements to gain electrons is called negative valence. Also, the part of an electric cell or electric device called a negative pole or a negative electrode.

nekton The larger animals, such as fish and whales, that swim in the open sea. The term is used in contrast to plankton, which are microscopic animals and plants that drift along with sea currents.

neon A rare element that is a colorless, odorless, inert gas. Neon is a small part of the atmosphere. When an electric current is passed through a tube filled with neon, it glows with a bright orange-red color. Neon has an atomic number of 10 and an atomic weight of 20.183. Its chemical symbol is Ne. [*Neon* comes from a Greek word meaning "new."]

Neptune The fourth-largest planet in the solar system, 30,540 miles (49,160 kilometers) across. Neptune is the eighth planet in distance from the sun, but for a short time, until 1999, it was the most distant planet. Thereafter, Pluto became the most distant planet. Neptune orbits the sun every 165 years at an average distance of about 2,794 million miles (4,498 million kilometers) and rotates about once every 16 hours. Neptune is a bluish gas planet circled by two rings, has two large moons called Triton and Nereid, and has at least six other small moons. Much of what we now know about Neptune was discovered by the *Voyager* flyby in 1989.

nerve A fiber or a bundle of cell or tissue fibers that carry electrochemical impulses between the brain and spinal cord and the other parts of the body. Nerves are enclosed in protective, fatty sheaths with their own blood and lymph vessels.

nerve cell A neuron; the kind of cell that makes up nerve tissue. Each nerve cell consists of a central body containing the nucleus, usually one long, threadlike extension called an axon, and one or more shorter threads called dendrites. Nerve impulses travel along a path of nerve cells.

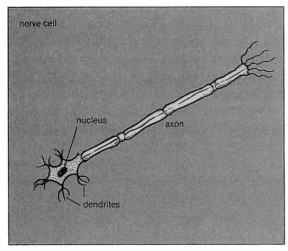

nerve cell

nervous system The system of nerve cells and other nerve tissue in a human or an animal by means of which nerve impulses are received and transmitted from one part of the body to another, and then interpreted. The human and vertebrate nervous systems are divided into two parts. The central nervous system consists of the brain and the spinal cord, which store and process information and send messages to muscles and glands. The peripheral nervous system consists of 12 pairs of cranial nerves and 31 pairs of spinal nerves, which carry messages between the central nervous system and the rest of the body. The autonomic nervous system is usually considered part of the peripheral nervous system. It controls involuntary actions such as heartbeat and digestion. The nervous system keeps humans and animals aware of their surroundings and allows them to respond with appropriate actions.

nest A structure or place used by animals such as some birds, fish, and insects for laying eggs and rearing young. A bird's nest is usually shaped like bowl and constructed out of twigs, straw, leaves, or mud.

neuron A nerve cell.

neutral 1. CHEMISTRY. Describes a chemical that is neither acid nor alkaline. 2. PHYSICS. Neither positive nor negative in electrical charge. A neutral atom has the same number of positively charged protons and negatively charged electrons. 3. BIOLOGY. Neuter. Not developed sexually.

neutralize To make a solution neutral by adding an acid if the solution is basic, or a base if the solution is acidic.

neutrino Any of three kinds of tiny subatomic particles having no electrical charge. The mass of a neutrino is so small that it has not been measured.

neutron A subatomic particle with no electrical charge found in the nucleus of all atoms except hydrogen. A neutron has a mass slightly greater than that of a proton.

neutron star The densely packed remains of a supernova, a collapsed giant star. A neutron star may be only about the size of New York or London yet contain more matter than the sun.

Newton, Sir Isaac (1642–1727) An English scientist who proposed the theory of universal gravitation, formulated his three laws of motion, invented the methods of mathematical calculus, showed that white light is a mixture of other colors (the spectrum), and made many other important discoveries. He is considered by many to be the greatest scientist who ever lived. Newton's achievements are summed up in his monumental book *Philosophiae naturalis principia mathematica* (Mathematical Principles of Natural Philosophy), published in 1687. Written in Latin and with proofs carefully worked out in geometry and principles clearly explained, the *Principia* established the mathematical method by which modern scientists try to understand and explain the laws of nature. The English poet Alexander Pope wrote these lines about him:

Nature and Nature's laws lay hid in night;
God said. 'Let Newton be!' and all was light.

Newton, Sir Isaac

Newton's laws of motion Three basic principles about motion proposed by Sir Isaac Newton. The first law says every object remains at rest or remains in straight-line motion at constant speed unless it is made to change because of an outside force (a push or pull). This is also called the principle of inertia. The second law says the change in motion of an object is directly proportional to the force producing it and in the same direction (the more force used, the faster an object will change its speed or direction). The change is also inversely proportional to the mass of the object (it's easier to change the speed and direction of a light

object than of a heavy one). The third law says for every action there is an equal and opposite reaction. This is also called the principle of action-reaction (if you push on something, you feel a force of the same amount pushing back against you).

nickel A hard, silvery metallic element frequently used in alloys such as stainless steel because of its resistance to corrosion. Nickel has magnetic properties similar to those of iron. It is found in igneous rocks and combined with iron in metallic meteorites. Nickel has an atomic number of 28 and an atomic weight of 58.71. Its chemical symbol is Ni.

nicotine A poisonous, colorless, oily liquid found in tobacco leaves. Even the small amount inhaled during smoking raises blood pressure and increases the rate at which the heart beats. Nicotine can also cause nausea and headache, and interfere with digestion. It is also used as an insecticide.

nimbostratus A dark-gray, low-hanging layer of clouds that often produces long periods of rain or snow.

nimbostratus

nimbus Any rain cloud, especially nimbostratus.

nitrate A salt containing the nitrate group (NO_3^-). Nitrates are found in nature or made from nitric acid. They are used in fertilizers, explosives, and medical drugs.

nitric acid A very strong acid that eats into flesh, clothing, metal, and other substances. Nitric acid is a colorless, fuming liquid when pure. It is used to make plastics, nitrates, explosives, and dyes. Its formula is HNO_3.

nitrogen A colorless, odorless, tasteless gas that makes up about 78% of Earth's atmosphere. Nitrogen does not support burning. It occurs in protein and nucleic acid compounds and is found in all animals and plants. Nitrogen is a chemical element with an atomic number of 7 and an atomic weight of 14.-0067. Its chemical symbol is N.

nitrogen cycle The continuing series of nitrogen exchanges between the air, living things, and the soil. Nitrogen in the air passes into the soil and is changed by nitrogen-fixing bacteria into nitrates or ammonia. The nitrates and ammonia are used to make protein and nucleic acids by green plants, which are then eaten by animals. Decaying plants and animals and animal wastes release nitrogen and ammonia into the atmosphere. It is then available again to be converted into nitrates and ammonia in the soil and used for further plant growth.

nitroglycerine A colorless, oily liquid that is extremely unstable and explosive. Dynamite is made from nitroglycerine and other substances. Nitroglycerine is also placed in tiny capsules and used in medicine to treat pain due to a heart problem known as angina.

Nobel, Alfred Bernhard (1833–1896) A Swedish inventor of dynamite. He left most of his fortune to establish the Nobel Foundation, and this fund has been used since 1901 for awards of Nobel Prizes in the sciences and the arts, and for peace.

noble gas One of a group of chemically inactive or inert gases that are the elements in group 0 of the periodic table. The noble gases are helium, neon, argon, krypton, xenon, and radon. They are colorless, odorless, and tasteless and are found in small amounts in Earth's atmosphere. They glow brightly when an electric current is passed through them.

nocturnal Active during the night. Most bats are nocturnal, as are a number of other animals.

node 1. ANATOMY, ZOOLOGY. A small bump or swelling, such as a lymph node. 2. BOTANY. A joint in the stem of a plant where leaves grow. 3. PHYSICS. In a vibrating object such as a violin string, a point or a place that has little or no vibration. 4. ASTRONOMY. Either of two points where the orbit of a planet or other object in space intersects the part of the sun or the orbit of another celestial body. [*Node* comes from a Latin word meaning "knot."]

nodule 1. EARTH SCIENCE. A small lump of ore or rock that is usually harder than the main rock around it. 2. BOTANY. A small growth or swelling on the roots or stem or other part of a plant. Nodules on the roots of legumes contain nitrogen-fixing bacteria.

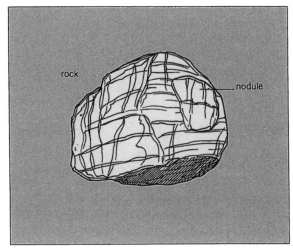

nodule

noise 1. ACOUSTICS. An unwanted sound. Noise is usually a loud sound with a wide range of frequencies that are nonperiodic (as opposed to a periodic musical tone). Too much noise can damage hearing, interfere with speech, and reduce concentration. Noise pollution is increasingly a problem in industrialized countries. 2. ELECTRONICS. Any unwanted or interfering signal or current.

nonconductor A substance that does not freely transmit electricity, heat, sound, or other form of energy. Rubber is a nonconductor of electricity. Also called an insulator.

nonmetal Any chemical element that is not a good conductor of heat or electricity and that has none or few of the chemical and physical properties of a metal. Nonmetals usually gain electrons in chemical reactions. Nitrogen, oxygen, and sulfur are nonmetals.

North Pole The point on Earth's surface that is the northern end of Earth's axis of rotation, 90° north. All directions from the North Pole are south. Also called the geographic North Pole, it lies about 450 miles (750 kilometers) north of Greenland in the middle of the Arctic Ocean.

North Star A fairly bright star, in the handle of the Little Dipper, that is located almost directly over the North Pole. Also called Polaris.

nose 1. ANATOMY. The middle organ in the front of the head just above the mouth. The nose is used for smelling and for warming and filtering the air used in respiration. It contains two openings called nostrils. 2. ZOOLOGY. A similar structure in vertebrate animals.

nostril One of the pair of openings in the nose through which air is inhaled and exhaled.

nova One of a pair of binary stars that suddenly flares up and becomes thousands of times brighter, then gradually fades and becomes dim again. Astronomers think that matter is attracted from one star, builds up on the other star, and explodes, making it look as if a bright new star has suddenly appeared in the night sky.

nuclear energy Also called atomic energy. The energy released when the nucleus of an atom splits into two in a process called nuclear fission. When the nuclei of two atoms join together to make an atom of a different kind, the process is called nuclear fusion.

nuclear magnetic resonance An effect in which the nuclei of atoms interact with an external magnetic field and various kinds of radiation (abbreviated NMR). Recently, an imaging technique, called magnetic resonance imaging (MRI) was developed. It uses NMR in medicine to view internal bodily organs or in physics to view the structures of molecules.

nuclear particle A particle within, or given off by, an atomic nucleus. Nuclear particles include protons, neutrons, and alpha particles.

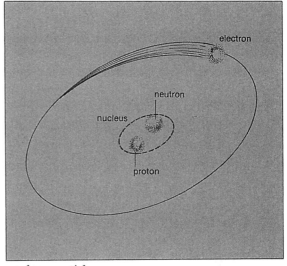

nuclear particle

nuclear physics The study of atomic nuclei, the behavior of subatomic particles, and the energy produced by their reactions.

nuclear reactor A device or machine used to convert the energy released during controlled nuclear reactions into useful forms of energy. Nuclear reactors are used in electricity-generating plants, in research facilities, and to provide power for some ships and submarines. Nuclear reactors need a great amount of insulation and radiation shielding. Accidents at some reactors, such as those at Chernobyl in the Soviet Union in April 1986 and at Three Mile Island, Pennsylvania, in the United States in March 1979, have created great concern about their safe operation.

nucleic acid Any of a group of complex chemicals found in all living cells and viruses. Nucleic acids interact with proteins to control the cell's growth. DNA (deoxyribonucleic acid) and RNA (ribonucleic acid) are two forms of nucleic acid.

nucleolus A small, usually round, body found within the nucleus of a cell. It contains a high concentration of RNA (ribonucleic acid) and is believed to be involved in the production of proteins within the cell.

nucleus 1. CHEMISTRY, PHYSICS. The positively charged central part of an atom consisting of protons and neutrons. The nucleus contains most of the mass of an atom. 2. BIOLOGY. A flattened sphere found in the cells of most organisms, without which the cell cannot grow and divide. It usually consists of chromosomes, nucleoli, nucleic acids, proteins, and a gel surrounded by a membrane.

nut A dry fruit with a tough or leathery shell that contains one seed or kernel, such as a coconut or a walnut. Many kinds of nut kernels are edible.

nutrient A substance that provides food or nourishment for a living organism. Proteins or carbohydrates are nutrients. Also describes anything that is nourishing, for example, a food such as milk or bread.

nutrition The science that deals with the processes by which living things eat food, digest it, and use the nutrients in it. A person who studies nutrition is called a nutritionist.

nylon A tough, strong, lightweight, synthetic substance called a polymer, made into fibers for textiles and ropes, or molded into gears, zippers, and the bodies of some automobile tires, among other uses.

nymph One of the nonadult stages in the development of certain insects such as mayflies. A nymph looks like the adult insect but lacks fully developed wings. [*Nymph* comes from a Greek word meaning "young girl."]

O

oasis An area surrounded by desert where trees and smaller plants grow and water is usually present. Some oases have natural springs, while others are created by means of irrigation.

objective lens A lens or a combination of lenses at the end of a microscope or telescope that is nearest the object. The objective lens forms the image, which is viewed through an eyepiece.

observation The process of watching something very carefully. Observation is an important part of scientific study. Scientists view an event and take notes or make photographic or other records of what they observed.

observatory A building housing a telescope and other instruments designed to study astronomical objects and events. Usually observatories are located on mountaintops or other places where the view is unobstructed and clear. Also,

observatory

a place or building used to observe events in nature, such as a weather or an earthquake observatory.

occluded front A weather condition that is formed when a cold air mass overtakes a warm air mass and pushes it aloft. Precipitation in the form of rain or snow usually accompanies an occluded front.

ocean The large connected body of salt water that covers almost three fourths of Earth's surface. Also, one of the five main regions into which the ocean is divided: Atlantic, Pacific, Indian, Arctic, and Antarctic.

oceanography The science that deals with the oceans and seas. Oceanographers study ocean currents, waves, and tides; life in the sea; the shapes of the ocean basins; and many other ocean features.

ocular 1. ANATOMY, ZOOLOGY. Having to do with the parts and functions of the eye. 2. OPTICS. The eyepiece of a telescope, microscope, or other optical instrument.

ohm A unit of measurement of electrical resistance. One ampere of current flows when one volt is applied across a resistance of one ohm. Ohms are measured by an instrument called an ohmmeter.

Ohm's law   A law that states that the current in amperes in an electric circuit in a conductor or insulator is directly proportional to the electromotive force (emf) in volts and inversely proportional to the resistance in ohms. It is usually expressed as I=E/R where I is the current in amps, E is the emf in volts, and R is the resistance in ohms. Ohm's law does not usually apply to liquids, gases, or semiconductors. The law was formulated in 1827 by Georg Simon Ohm (1787–1854), a German physicist.

oil   Any of several kinds of greasy liquids that burn easily, will not mix with water, but will dissolve in certain solvents such as benzene or ether. There are three main groups of oils: mineral oils, such as petroleum; vegetable and animal oils, such as corn oil and fish oil; and essential or volatile vegetable oils, which evaporate easily, such as turpentine and flower perfumes.

oil pollution   The harmful results of spilling oil into the oceans and other bodies of water. Oil spills can come from tankers that have had accidents or washed their tanks at sea. The oil is often pushed onshore by the winds and the currents. Large amounts of oil pollution at sea kills birds, fish, and sea mammals and causes damage to marine and wildlife habitats. The worst oil pollution ever experienced was the result of the explosion of BP's oil drilling platform *Deepwater Horizon* in the Gulf of Mexico on April 20, 2010. The explosion killed 11 platform operators and resulted in the release of an estimated 5 million barrels of oil. An area damaged by a large oil spill such as that may take many years to recover.

olfactory   Having to do with the sense of smell or the act of smelling. The nose is an olfactory organ.

Oligocene Epoch   The third geological epoch of the Tertiary Period. It began about 37 million years ago and lasted for about 12 million years. During the Oligocene, modern-day horses, pigs, elephants, and carnivores, such as lions and tigers, began to appear. Cats and dogs evolved, and modern grasses also appeared. North America was largely dry, and the Rocky Mountains were eroding.

ommatidium   One of the units making up the compound eye of an insect or crustacean. Some insects, such as bees, have compound eyes that contain thousands of ommatidia. Each ommatidium has its own lens and acts as a simple eye.

omnivore   An animal that usually eats both plant and animal food. Most bears and primates are omnivores.

onyx   A gemstone that is a variety of quartz. It has straight bands of varied colors and takes a high polish.

opaque   Describing a substance that does not allow light rays or other forms of radiation to pass through it. Metals are opaque to light rays. [*Opaque* comes from a Latin word meaning "shaded" or "darkened."]

ophthalmology   The branch of medicine concerned with vision and the eye.

optic nerve   A nerve that sends impulses from the retina in the back of the eye to the brain.

optical illusion   Something that appears to a person to be different from what is really there. There are many different kinds optical illusions. Some are common daily occurrences, such as the way the moon appears to move in the sky as clouds float by in front of it. Other kinds of illusions are used by artists. Perspective is the way in which lines or shading in a picture are used to suggest depth or distance in a flat drawing. Optical illusions may also involve color, brightness and contrast, foreground and background, and changeable figures.

optical instrument   A device that uses lenses and/or mirrors to focus light and produce an image, or to break light into its colors. Cameras, microscopes, spectroscopes, and telescopes are optical instruments.

optics The science of light and vision. Physical optics deals with the nature of light and optical instruments such as the camera and lenses. Biological optics deals with the eye and vision.

orbit (n.) 1. SPACE SCIENCE. The path of Earth or of any other planet round the sun. Also, the path of any celestial body around another celestial body—for example, the path of a moon around a planet. Also, the path of an artificial satellite around Earth or some other celestial body. 2. PHYSICS. In the Bohr model of an atom, the path of an electron around the nucleus. The path of an electron is no longer thought to be similar to the orbit of a planet, and it is now described as an orbital. 3. ANATOMY. The bony cup or socket in vertebrates that contains the eyeball. [*Orbit* comes from a Latin word meaning "wheel" or "circle."]

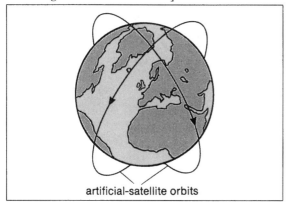

artificial-satellite orbits

orbit

orbit (v.) To move or travel in a regular path around another object.

orbital The mathematical function that describes the motion of an electron around an atom or a molecule. An orbital (an atomic orbital) indicates the region that is the most probable location of an electron in space as well as the likelihood that it will be found there. If there is more than one electron involved, an orbital is sometimes described as an electron cloud.

orbital velocity The speed that must be reached by a spaceship or satellite in order for it to orbit around Earth or another body.

order In biology, a group of organisms that are related to each other. An order is a subdivision of a class and is divided further into suborders and families. Bears belong to the class Mammalia, to the order Carnivora, and to the family Ursidae.

Ordovician Period The second geological period in the Paleozoic Era. It lasted from about 520 to 440 million years ago.

ore Rocks or minerals that are mined and from which metals or other useful materials can be extracted. For example, bauxite is an ore of aluminum.

organ A group of cells or tissues in an animal or plant that performs a particular function. The brain, heart, lungs, kidneys, and stomach are animal organs. The stamen and pistil are plant organs.

organic 1. CHEMISTRY. Describes any compound that contains carbon. Organic compounds, such as proteins or carbohydrates, are found in all living things. 2. BIOLOGY. Coming from or produced by living things. Sugar, coal, and wood are organic substances. Also, anything to do with the organs of an animal or plant. For example, an illness of the heart is called an organic disease.

organism Any living thing. Organisms carry on life processes, which include reproduction and metabolism.

origin 1. BIOLOGY. The source or ancestor of an organism or group of organisms. For example, the origin of birds probably was reptiles. 2. ANATOMY. The larger end of a muscle that is attached or anchored to a bone that does not move when the muscle contracts.

ornithology The scientific study of birds.

oscillate To move from side to side or back and forth in a regular motion. When a tight rubber band is plucked, it oscillates and makes a sound. The electrons in a household alternating-current circuit oscillate fifty or sixty times a second.

oscilloscope An instrument that shows the behavior of electric circuits on the screen of a cathode ray tube (CRT). Sound, radio waves, and even brain waves or heartbeats can also be changed into electrical signals and displayed on an oscilloscope.

osmosis The movement of molecules of solvent through a semipermeable membrane that separates two solutions. The movement tends to make the two solutions equally concentrated. Osmosis is the main way in which water-soluble nutrients pass in and out of animals and plant cells. [*Osmosis* comes from a Greek word meaning "to thrust" or "to push."]

ossicle A small bone or bony part. Also, any of the three small bones found in the middle ear.

Otto, Nikolaus August (1832–1891) A German engineer who developed and built the first four-stroke cycle of an internal-combustion engine in 1876. It rapidly supplanted the externally powered steam engine. The four-stroke cycle (intake, compression, power, exhaust) is used in the engines of most gasoline-driven automobiles and other vehicles.

ounce A unit of weight equal to 1/16 of a pound in common or avoirdupois weight, and 1/12 of a pound in troy weight. One ounce is equal to about 28.35 grams.

outcrop A vein of rock, mineral, or bedrock appearing at the earth's surface.

outer ear The external part of the ear; the part that can be seen at the side of the head.

outer space The space beyond Earth's atmosphere and between the planets. Also, the space beyond the solar system.

output 1. MECHANICS. The work or energy produced by a machine. 2. ELECTRONICS. The electri-

cal signal or power given off by an electronic device such as a transistor. 3. COMPUTERS. The information delivered by a computer as a result of the processing instructions and input data given to it.

ovary The female organ of reproduction. In animals the ovary produces egg cells; in flowering plants, the ovary produces ovules, which become seeds when fertilized. A fruit is a ripened plant ovary.

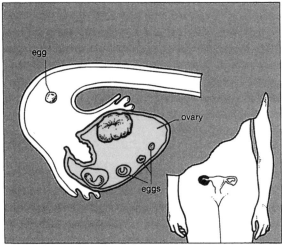

ovary

oviparous Describes an animal that reproduces by laying eggs that hatch outside the female's body. Birds, amphibians, and most kinds of reptiles, fish, and insects are oviparous.

ovule The part of the plant in which the egg forms. An ovule develops into a seed after fertilization.

ovum The female gamete, or egg cell, produced in the ovary. A fertilized ovum is called a zygote. After many cell divisions, a zygote becomes an embryo.

oxidation The chemical act of combining with oxygen that results in the formation of an oxide. Rusting, in which iron combines with oxygen to form iron oxide, is a common form of slow oxidation. The burning of wood or fuel oil are common forms of rapid oxidation. Oxidation-reduction is a chemical reaction in which atoms or ions transfer electrons to other atoms or ions.

oxide A chemical compound of oxygen and another element.

oxidize To combine with oxygen as in oxidation. When substances burn or rust, they oxidize.

oxygen A gaseous element that makes up about one fifth of Earth's atmosphere and is colorless, odorless, and tasteless. Oxygen combines chemically with many other elements to form oxides. It is one of the most abundant elements on Earth and is present in combined form in water, carbon dioxide, animal and plant cells, and many minerals. Animals, plants, and most other organisms need oxygen to live. Oxygen is produced as a pure gas by green plants in a chemical reaction called photosynthesis. Oxygen has an atomic number of 8 and an atomic weight of 15.99. Its chemical symbol is O.

ozone A molecular form of oxygen that has three atoms per molecule (O_3) instead of the usual two (O_2). Ozone has a sharp odor and is produced by electricity moving through air. You can sometimes smell ozone after a lightning storm. Ozone is produced commercially for use in water purification and as a bleaching agent. [*Ozone* comes from a Greek word meaning "smell."]

ozone layer The ozone layer, or ozonosphere, is a region of concentrated ozone in the outer stratosphere. It acts as the principal shield against dangerous ultraviolet radiation from the sun. The ozone layer was being damaged by the propellant gases in aerosol sprays and other chemicals released in certain kinds of manufacturing. Scientists said that the increase in ultraviolet rays reaching the earth would increase the occurrence of cancer and have other serious health consequences for people. An international treaty called the Montreal Protocol was passed in 1989 and was designed to protect the ozone layer by phasing out the substances that were harming the ozone layer. The ozone layer has improved since then but the problem will not be resolved totally for many years.

P

pacemaker 1. ANATOMY. A group of specialized heart tissues that send out impulses to regulate the heartbeat. In humans, the pacemaker is located near the top of the wall of the right atrium. 2. MEDICINE. An electronic device used to regulate the heartbeat when the natural pacemaker is not working properly. The pacemaker is usually implanted in the body under the skin.

pahoehoe Lava that has hardened into a ropy, shiny surface. Pahoehoe is often found in Hawaii. [*Pahoehoe* (pa-HO-ee-ho-ee) is the Hawaiian word for this kind of lava; it also means "satin."]

pain The feeling of hurt in humans and in animals that have highly developed nervous systems. Pain is a warning of imminent danger, and often causes an immediate reaction so that the person or animal can avoid further injury. For example, the instant a person feels pain when touching a flame or a hot object, he or she will jerk his or her arm away. Pain sensations are received by nerve endings found mainly in the skin. Some parts of the skin, such as the fingertips, have many more nerve receptors than other parts, such as the back of the hand. The level at which pain begins to be felt is called the pain threshold, and it varies from one individual to another. [*Pain* comes from the Latin word for "penalty" or "punishment."]

palate The roof of the mouth. The bony part in front is called the hard palate; the fleshy part in back is called the soft palate. The palate separates the mouth from the nose. The soft palate closes off the air passages in the nose and throat during swallowing and speech.

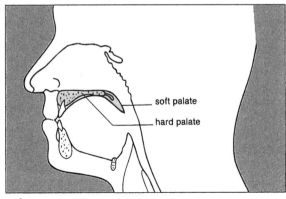

palate

Paleocene Epoch The earliest geological epoch of the Tertiary Period. It began about 65 million years ago and lasted for about 10 million years. During the Paleocene, shallow inland seas withdrew and filled in with land. The continent of Europe emerged. The Rockies and other mountain ranges were formed. Greenland split off from North America. Most common modern plants and birds were present. Many different kinds of primates appeared. In North America and Europe the climate was warm and humid.

paleontology The scientific study of the remains of living things (fossils) of past times. Scientists who study fossils are called paleontologists.

Paleozoic Era The geological era that began 570 million years ago and lasted for 345 million years. During the Paleozoic, fish, insects, amphibians, and reptiles developed. The era also saw the growth of huge forests of fernlike trees and gradual shrinking of the oceans. [*Paleozoic* comes from Greek words meaning "ancient life."]

pancreas A large gland located behind the stomach in vertebrates. It secretes pancreatic juice into the small intestine and insulin into the blood. Pancreatic juice contains several chemicals called enzymes that aid in the digestion of food. Insulin is a hormone that regulates the use of sugar in the body. [*Pancreas,* because it is made of glandular flesh, comes from Greek words meaning "entirely flesh."]

parachute A foldable, umbrella-shaped device used to slow the movement of objects through the air. Parachutes are usually made of nylon or some other lightweight material. When a parachute is opened, usually by pulling a ripcord, it fills with air and produces a great deal of drag. The drag slows the descent of humans or objects dropped from airplanes. Parachutes are also used to slow space capsules or rocket planes on their return to Earth. [*Parachute* is a French word meaning "something that shields you from falling."]

parallax 1. OPTICS. The change in the observed position of an object when it is viewed or photographed from different locations. You can see parallax changes in the position of nearby objects against more distant objects by holding up a finger about a foot in front of your face and closing each of your eyes in turn. Parallax is used in surveying to determine the distances of objects. 2. ASTRONOMY. When viewed from two different points on Earth, or from two different points in Earth's orbit, the change in the position of closer celestial objects against more

distant ones. Parallax is used to measure the distances of planets and closer stars.

paralysis A loss of feeling and control of a muscle. Paralysis may be temporary or permanent, and may result from a disease or injury of the brain, spinal cord, nerves, or muscles.

parasite An organism that lives in or on another organism, called a host, from which it gets food and to which it is often harmful. Many kinds of worms, such as tapeworms, are parasites. Some parasites, such as lice, ticks, and fleas, spread disease. Plants may also be parasites. Mistletoe is a parasite of oak trees.

parotid gland One of the glands that make saliva. The glands are found on both sides of the mouth in front of the ears.

parsec In astronomy, a unit of distance. One parsec is equal to about 3.26 light-years, more than 200,000 times the distance of Earth to the sun. Parsec comes from the words "*par*allax" and a measure of an arc called a "*sec*ond."

particle In physics, an extremely tiny part or unit of matter, such as a molecule or an atom. Inside atoms are even smaller particles, such as protons, neutrons, and electrons. Also, a small piece of material that may be barely visible to the unaided eye, such as a particle of dust or a particle of soil.

Pascal's law In physics, the principle that pressure applied to a fluid is transmitted equally in all directions. The law is named for its discoverer, Blaise Pascal (1623–1662), a French mathematician, physicist, and philosopher. The international unit of pressure is named the pascal, abbreviated Pa.

Pasteur, Louis (1822–1895) A French microbiologist and chemist who discovered the importance of microorganisms (tiny living things) in fermentation and disease. Pasteur developed a method for preventing wine from turning to vinegar and milk from going sour. He proposed that germs (bacteria) cause disease and popularized the idea that medical instruments should be sterilized before use. Pasteur also developed a form of vaccination using dead disease germs that gave future immunity against anthrax and rabies. In his study of rabies, Pasteur concluded that it was caused by a germ too small to be seen with a microscope. We now call this type of germ a virus.

Pasteur, Louis

pasteurization The process of killing germs by heating to a controlled temperature, especially used with milk. The milk becomes safe to drink and will keep for longer periods of time without souring. Named after Louis Pasteur, its inventor.

patella The kneecap. A small, disk-shaped bone in the front of the knee joint of humans and most other mammals. [*Patella* comes from the Latin word meaning "small dish" or "plate."]

Pauling, Linus Carl (1901–1994) An American chemist and physicist who received the 1954 Nobel Prize in chemistry for his work on the chemical bond. In 1962, Pauling received the Nobel Peace Prize for his support of nuclear disarmament.

Pavlov, Ivan (1849–1936) A Russian physiologist who received the Nobel Prize in 1904 for his work on digestion. Pavlov is best known for his work on conditioning of behavior in animals. In a series of experiments, Pavlov rang a bell just before feeding dogs. He found that after a while the dogs began to salivate just on hearing the bell, even when no food was present. This response is called a conditioned reflex.

paw The foot of a four-legged animal—such as a dog or a cat—that has nails or claws.

peak The top of a mountain. Also, the highest part of something, such as an engine's peak performance or the peak value of an alternating current.

peat A dark brown, partly decayed plant material found in layers in marshy or boggy areas. Peat is sometimes cut, dried, and used as a fuel in home furnaces. When peat is buried in the earth under pressure for millions of years, it may form coal.

pectoral Having to do with the chest. The pectoral girdle is a group of bones that join the chest bone to the backbone.

pelvis Part of the skeleton in humans and other animals that walk erect. The pelvis is a cavity surrounded by the bones that form the pelvic girdle. The leg bones are joined to the lower end of the pelvis. [*Pelvis* is a Latin word meaning "shallow bowl" or "basin."]

pendulum A weight hung by a rod or chain from a fixed point in a way that allows the weight to swing back and forth freely. When the

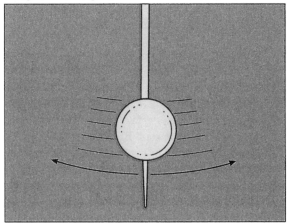

pendulum

weight is pulled to one side and then released, it swings in a path called an arc. As the arc gets smaller and smaller, the time of each swing remains the same because it is determined by only the length of the rod or chain, not the small push or pull that sets it in motion. Because of their regular rhythm, pendulums were used to help measure time in large gear-driven clocks. The pendulum was kept swinging by the clock mechanism. [*Pendulum* comes from the Latin word meaning "to hang."]

penicillin An antibiotic substance produced by certain kinds of blue-green fungi (molds). Penicillin interferes with the growth of bacteria and is used to treat pneumonia and other diseases. The effects of penicillin were discovered by Sir Alexander Fleming in 1928. Along with Sir Howard Florey and Ernst Chain, Fleming received the 1945 Nobel Prize for medicine.

peninsula A large strip of land almost completely surrounded by water but joined to a larger mass of land at one end.

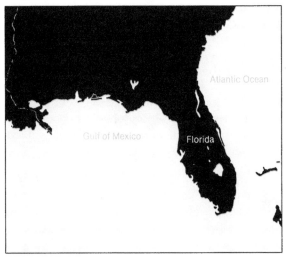

peninsula

penis The male sexual organ of mammals and certain other animals. The penis introduces sperm cells into the female reproductive tract. In mammals, urine passes down a narrow tube in the penis from the bladder to the outside. [*Penis* is a Latin word meaning "tail."]

Pennsylvania Period The sixth period of the Paleozoic Era, lasting from about 315 to 280 million years ago. The Pennsylvanian, named for the state of Pennsylvania, was part of the Carboniferous Period, the "Age of Coal," when huge swampy forests lived and died. Layer upon layer of plant and animal material that accumulated at that time became the coal, oil, and natural gas deposits that exist today. Also called the upper Carboniferous Period.

perennial Any kind of plant whose roots or underground parts continue to grow for two or more years. Some perennials, such as most grasses, daffodils, and peonies, die down to ground level during the winter, then regrow each spring. Other perennials, such as trees and shrubs, have woody stems that thicken each year and leaves that may or may not drop off during the winter. These woody perennials may grow for a hundred years or longer.

perigee The point closest to Earth in the moon's or any artificial Earth satellite's orbit.

perihelion The point closest to the sun in a planet's, asteroid's, or comet's orbit.

period 1. ASTRONOMY. The time it takes one celestial body, such as a planet, to make a complete revolution around another body, such as the sun. Also the time between recurrences of a regularly occurring event, such as the brightest part of the cycle of a variable star or the phases of the moon. 2. EARTH SCIENCE. One of the sections into which the geological time scale is divided. A period is part of an era and may be divided into epochs. 3. PHYSICS. The time for a completion of a cycle, such as the motion of a wave or the swing of a pendulum. 4. CHEMISTRY. The horizontal arrangement of elements in the periodic table.

periodic Describing something that repeats itself over regular intervals, such as a wave cycle.

periodic table A table of the elements in the order of their atomic numbers, arranged in horizontal rows and vertical columns of related groups. Each row, or period, contains elements with the same number of electron shells. Each column, or period, contains elements that have similar chemical properties because their outermost electron shells contain the same number of electrons. In 1869, Dmitry Ivanovich Mendelyev published the first reasonably complete periodic table based on his discovery that the properties of elements vary periodically with increasing atomic weight. Gaps in the table corresponded to elements then unknown. Using the table, Mendelyev accurately predicted the properties of these elements even before they were discovered. The table is added to as new and heavier elements are made in laboratories. Currently, there are 115 known elements though they are not in sequence.

peripheral nervous system The part of the nervous system of vertebrates that is made up of the nerves in the body outside the brain and spinal cord (the central nervous system).

periscope An optical instrument made of mirrors or reflecting prisms at both ends of a long tube to allow an observer to see over or around objects. A submarine periscope permits an observer to see above the surface of the ocean while most of the boat is still submerged. [*Periscope* comes from Greek words meaning "to look around."]

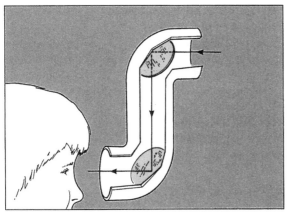
periscope

peristalsis Wavelike, involuntary muscle movements in the alimentary canal that cause food to be mixed and moved onward through the digestive tract.

permeability 1. CHEMISTRY. The property of a substance, such as a membrane, that allows the passage or diffusion of gases or liquids through it. 2. PHYSICS. The property of a substance, such as iron, to change or concentrate the lines of force of a magnetic field.

Permian Period The last period in the Paleozoic Era, lasting from about 280 to 225 million years ago; during this period there was widespread volcanic activity and mountain building. Trilobites and many other ancient sea invertebrates became extinct, and new species of reptiles appeared and spread across the land.

perpetual motion machine A machine that runs continually. A "perpetual motion machine of the first kind" would be one that runs without any energy being supplied. However, because a running machine produces energy, but energy cannot be created from nothing (according to the law of conservation of energy), such a machine is an impossibility. A "perpetual motion machine of the second kind" is one that, once set in motion, will work forever without any more energy being added. Though this kind of machine has been a goal of inventors for many years, it too is impossible because some of the energy is always being lost through friction; if more energy is not added, the machine will eventually stop.

perspiration Sweat. A watery liquid produced by the sweat glands in the skin. The amount of perspiration increases when the body is hot from exercise, fever, or intense emotions. Perspiration evaporating from the skin helps to lower the body temperature.

pesticide A substance that controls or kills harmful or destructive animals or plants. Pesticides include insecticides, miticides, herbicides, and fungicides. A major problem of insecticide use is the possibility of harm to the environment.

petal A part of a flower that often looks like a colored leaf. Some flowers, such as buttercups or tulips, have only a few petals; others, such as daisies or chrysanthemums, have many petals. [*Petal* comes from a Greek word meaning "outspread."]

petrified wood Wood that has been replaced by minerals and turned into fossil rock by a process called petrification. Water containing dissolved minerals soaks into the wood. Over many years, the wood dissolves and the minerals harden, producing a copy of the tree in stone. There is a petrified forest of these trees in Arizona.

petrochemical Any chemical made from petroleum or natural gas. The list includes gasoline, kerosene, diesel fuel, detergents, fertilizers, and a host of others.

petroleum Crude oil or natural gas. A complex mixture of chemicals called hydrocarbons found in nature. Liquid petroleum is a dark, oily substance that is used in industry as fuel and as a source of other chemicals. It was formed over long periods of time, probably from the bodies of millions of tiny plants and animals that accumulated on the bottom of seas and lakes and were covered by layers of sand and clay. Petroleum is brought to the surface through wells and then refined into many different petrochemicals.

pH A measure of the acidity or alkalinity of a solution in terms of the concentration of hydrogen ions in the solution. The pH scale ranges from 0, the most acid, to 14, the most alkaline. A neutral substance, such as pure water, has a pH of 7. [The term *pH* was introduced in 1909 by the Danish chemist Søren Sørensen; it is the abbreviation for *potenz,* the German word for "power," and H, the chemical symbol for hydrogen.]

pharmacology The science that deals with the study of drugs and their preparation, uses, and effects. A person who prepares drugs for medicinal uses is called a druggist or a pharmacist. A scientist who studies the properties, uses, and effects of drugs is called a pharmacologist.

pharynx The passageway at the back of the mouth through which food and air enter the throat. It extends from the nasal cavities to the trachea (which leads to the lungs) and to the esophagus (which leads to the stomach). [*Pharynx* comes from the Greek word meaning "throat."]

phase 1. ASTRONOMY. The apparent change in shape in the lighted part of the moon or of Venus or Mercury. There are four main phases of the moon: new moon, first quarter, full moon, and third quarter. 2. BIOLOGY. A stage in the growth or development of a living thing. For example, a caterpillar is the larval phase in the development of a butterfly or moth. 3. CHEMISTRY. Any of the three forms or states of matter: solid, liquid, or gas. Phase changes usually involve the gain or loss of heat. 4. PHYSICS. A particular stage or point in a cycle or a regular series of changes, such as a wave movement. Waves that are moving together in unison are said to be "in phase." Waves that are moving at different times or in different directions are said to be "out of phase."

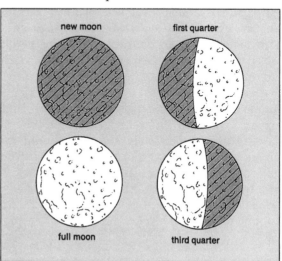

phase

pheromone One of many kinds of chemical substances given off by certain animals that stimulate a specific response in other animals of the same species. Pheromones are common in mammals and in many insects such as bees, ants, and butterflies. [*Pheromone* comes from Greek words meaning "to convey" and "to set in motion."]

phloem The vascular tissue in plants through which dissolved nutrients flow from the leaves to the stems and roots. Maple syrup is drawn from the sap flowing through the phloem of sugar maple trees. [*Phloem* comes from the Greek word meaning "smooth bark" or "husk."]

phosphate A kind of salt coming from or related to phosphoric acid. Phosphates are present in bones and are necessary for growth. Plants get phosphates from the soil. Phosphates are also found in rocks and are used in dyes, fertilizers, and medicines, and are still found in some detergents.

phosphor A chemical substance that gives off light when exposed or energized by ultraviolet rays, X-rays, or certain other kinds of energy. Phosphors are present inside television picture tubes and fluorescent light tubes.

phosphorescence The act of shining or giving off light without noticeable heat. Some substances can remain phosphorescent for hours after they have received certain kinds of radiant energy.

phosphorus A nonmetallic element that exists in several different forms. Phosphorus is very active chemically and is essential for living things. Plants take in phosphorus from phosphates in the soil. Animals get phosphorus from the plants or other animals they eat. Phosphorus has an atomic number of 15, an atomic weight of 30.974 and a chemical symbol of P.

photoelectric effect The process by which certain substances give off electrons when exposed to light. A photoelectric cell (which uses the photoelectric effect) varies the flow of current with the amount of light that it receives. Photoelectric cells are used to detect light, as in electric eyes; to measure light, as in light meters in cameras; and as power sources in solar cells in many different devices. Albert Einstein received the Nobel Prize for physics in 1921 for his explanation of the photoelectric effect.

photography The process of using light-sensitive materials or digital devices to make a permanent visible image (a photograph) of an object. Traditional photographs depended upon the light sensitivity of silver halide deposited in a thin layer of gelatin on paper, glass, or film. When exposed to light in a camera or other photographic instrument, an undeveloped image forms in the silver. The image is made visible in development with a chemical solution and then made permanent by fixing with another solution. Depending upon the kind of photograph, the image may be negative (where light and dark are reversed) or positive (which looks like the original view photographed). Newer photographs use digital cameras and/or computers and printers to make the photograph.

The history of photography dates from the early work of Louis Daguerre and others in the mid-nineteenth century. In 1889, photography came into popular use after George Eastman marketed the Kodak camera, which used flexible transparent film. Motion-picture photography dates from 1890, when Thomas Edison built a device to expose Eastman's roll film in a continuous strip. Digital cameras and video camcorders use electronic means to capture an image and display it on a screen or print a photo on paper.

photomicography Extreme close-ups of things that can be seen with the bare eye.

photon The basic unit or quantum of light or other electromagnetic energy. In many ways the photon behaves like a particle moving with the velocity of light. A ray of light can be thought of as a stream of photons.

photosynthesis The process by which green plants, using the energy of sunlight, combine water and carbon dioxide in the presence of chlorophyll and enzymes to manufacture carbohydrates and thus maintain life. Oxygen is released as a by-product. Most of the oxygen in Earth's atmosphere comes from photosynthesis. Animals depend upon photosynthesis because they breathe oxygen and either eat plants or eat other animals that eat plants.

phototropism The tendency of a plant to grow toward or away from light falling on it. Leaves and stems grow toward the source of light and are called positively phototropic. Some kinds of roots grow away from light and are called negatively phototropic.

phylum A main grouping in the animal or plant kingdoms. For example, animals with a spinal cord belong to the phylum Chordata. Some botanists prefer to use the term division instead of phylum when they refer to the plant kingdom. [*Phylum* comes from the Greek word for "tribe" or "clan."]

physical change A change in the size or form of a substance without its becoming a new substance. For example, when water turns to ice or water vapor, it undergoes a physical change as opposed to a chemical change, as when water is broken down into hydrogen and oxygen by an electric current.

physics The science that deals with the properties and relationships of energy and matter. This includes the study of motion, light, heat, sound, electricity, magnetism, radiation, and atomic energy. Physics is divided into many different branches, including mechanics, thermodynamics, optics, electronics, acoustics, quantum theory, relativity, and nuclear physics. A scientist who studies physics is called a physicist. [*Physics*, the title of Aristotle's treatise on the phenomena of nature, comes from the Greek word for "nature" or "growth."]

physiology The science that deals with the way living things or their parts function, including the study of cells, tissues, organs, and systems. Physiology is important in medicine.

pigment A natural substance that gives color to the tissues of animals or plants. The color of a person's eyes or hair is due to the pigment in them. [*Pigment* comes from the Latin word meaning "to paint" or "to tint."]

pile In construction, a strong beam made of steel, wood, or concrete that is sunk into the ground to support a building or some other heavy structure.

pinion 1. ZOOLOGY. The end joint of a bird's wing. 2. MECHANICS. A toothed wheel used in gear systems.

pinion

pinna 1. ANATOMY. The visible part of the ear, consisting of skin and cartilage. The pinnae act to collect and funnel sounds into the ear passages. Some animals, such as deer, can move their pinnae in different directions to catch sounds. 2. ZOOLOGY. A feather or a part of a bird's wing. Also, a fin, flipper, or similar part of an animal. 3. BOTANY. A leaflet. One of the parts of a kind of leaf that has a series of leaflets on each side of a stalk, such as a fern.

pipette A slender pipe or tube, usually made of glass, used for measuring small amounts of a liquid and/or transferring the liquid from one container to another.

pistil A flower's female reproductive part

that produces seeds. A pistil usually includes an ovary, a style, and a stigma.

piston A solid metal disk that moves up and down in a tightly fitting hollow cylinder within an engine or pump. The piston is equipped with circular rings that fit the cylinder even more snugly. A piston transmits motion or exerts pressure. [*Piston* comes from a Latin word meaning "to pound" or "to crunch."]

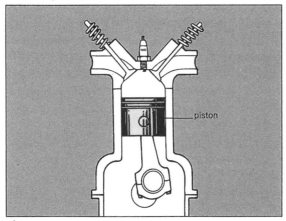

piston

pitch 1. CHEMISTRY. A black, sticky material produced from the distillation of coal or petroleum. Pitch is waterproof and is sometimes used for roofing and road building. 2. ACOUSTICS. The property of a sound that is produced by the number of its vibrations per second (frequency). A violin's thinner strings can produce higher sounds than a cello's thicker strings. 3. AERONAUTICS. The angle at which the propeller blade of an airplane meets the air. Also, the angle of an airplane, satellite, or rocket relative to its lateral (side-to-side) axis.

pith 1. BOTANY. The central core of soft, spongy tissue in the stems of some flowering plants and a few trees. Also, a similar tissue in other parts of some plants, such as the soft lining beneath the skin of an orange or lemon. 2. ZOOLOGY. The soft tissue that forms the core of a feather or a hair.

pituitary gland A small, disk-shaped organ located at the base of the brain in humans and most other vertebrates. The pituitary gland secretes hormones that promote growth, activate the action of other glands, and regulate many body functions. The pituitary is one of the most important glands in the body.

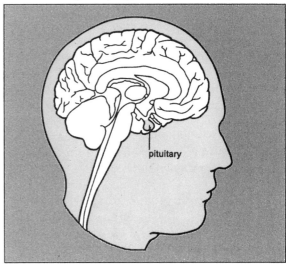

pituitary gland

pixel *Picture el*ement. One of thousands of tiny dots or groups of tiny pieces or picture elements found on a display such as a television screen. A pixel glows when struck by a beam of electrons coming from an electron gun in the display. In a color display, each pixel consists of three or four tinier dots such as red, green, blue, and black. Mixed together, the pixels present the image we see in a color TV or computer screen.

placenta 1. EMBRYOLOGY. In pregnant females of most mammals, including humans, a special organ with many blood vessels by which the fetus is attached to the wall of the uterus. Through an umbilical card, the placenta sends oxygen and food materials to the fetus and receives carbon dioxide and other waste material from it. The placenta is expelled from the uterus after the birth of the baby and is then called the afterbirth. 2. BOTANY. In flowering plants, the part of the ovary to which the ovules are attached.

placer A deposit of sand or gravel in a streambed or riverbed that contains gold, diamonds, or other valuable minerals. Placer mining, which includes panning for gold, is the process of extracting these minerals. [*Placer* comes from the Spanish-American word meaning "sandbank."]

plague Also called bubonic plague or Black Death. A highly infectious disease caused by a bacterium carried by fleas on rats. In the middle of the fourteenth century, half the population of Europe was killed by the Black Death. Nowadays, bubonic plague still occasionally occurs on a small scale in areas of overcrowding and poverty. [*Plague* comes from the Greek word meaning "wound" or "stroke," especially one that results in a calamity.]

plain A large span of level, or nearly level, land.

Planck, Max (1858–1947) A German physicist who proposed the quantum theory. This theory and Einstein's theory of relativity were the most important ideas in physics in the twentieth century. Planck proposed that energy, like matter, cannot be broken forever into smaller and smaller units. He named the smallest possible unit of energy a quantum. Planck was awarded the 1918 Nobel Prize for physics.

Planck, Max

planet One of the major objects that revolve around the sun in nearly circular paths called orbits. Scientist now use three ways to describe a planet: 1. It must orbit the sun. 2. It must be big enough for gravity to squeeze the planet into a round ball. 3. The planet must clear other smaller rocky or icy bodies out of its way when it orbits around the sun. We presently know of eight planets in our solar system: Mercury, Venus, Earth, Mars, Jupiter, Saturn, Uranus and Neptune. Since 2006, Pluto is no longer called a planet since it does not clear bodies as it is orbiting the sun. Pluto is now called a dwarf planet. A dwarf planet only has to be round and orbit the sun. Pluto is the largest of a group of dwarf planets that exist far beyond the orbit of Neptune. Other stars besides our sun have planets revolving around them. We call these "exoplanets" to distinguish them from planets in our own solar system. [*Planet* comes from the Greek word meaning "wanderer" or someone who goes astray."]

planet

planetarium A domed theater of the stars. In the middle of the planetarium is an apparatus that projects lights that simulate the nighttime sky onto the inside of the dome. The planetarium can show the movements and positions of the sun, moon, planets, and stars for any time in the past or future.

plankton Tiny animals and plants that live in the sea. Plankton plants float or drift in the water and are carried along by the currents. Most plant plankton, such as microalgae or diatoms, are found at or near the surface where light can reach. Animal plankton such as protozoans or tiny crustaceans may be found at the surface or at great depths. Plankton are the basic food for many large sea animals such as fish and even the blue whale, the biggest animal on Earth.

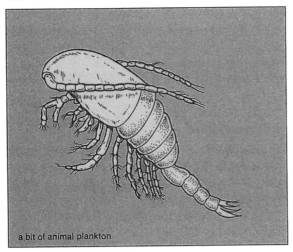

a bit of animal plankton

plankton

plant A many-celled living thing that usually makes its own food from carbon dioxide and water using light energy during a process called photosynthesis. Plants have thick cell walls that contain cellulose and are the primary source of food for all other living things. Plants include familiar living things such as trees, bushes, grasses, vines, ferns, mosses, and green algae. The scientific study of plants is called botany. Nearly 300,000 different species of plants have been identified. At one time all living things were considered to belong to either the plant or the animal kingdom. The major difference between the two kingdoms was thought to be that plants can manufacture their own food while animals cannot, and plants cannot move about while animals can. But even this simple distinction is not always true; some kinds of one-celled living things seem to have the characteristics of both plants and animals. For example, a euglena, a one-celled organism, moves about in water but also contains chlorophyll and manufactures its own food. Today, most scientists consider plants to be only those more complex many-celled living things that can perform photosynthesis. Widely in use today is a five-kingdom system of classification: animals, plants, fungi, protists, and monerans. A euglena is now considered a protist.

plaque A thin film of bacteria and carbohydrates that forms on teeth. Unless removed by brushing or cleaning, plaque hardens into a substance called tartar. Plaque is also the first step in the development of cavities in the teeth. Also, a patch of a fiberlike tissue or fatty deposit that sometimes forms on the inside of an artery. Arterial plaque can restrict or stop the flow of blood in the heart, brain, or other vital places and may cause injury or even death.

plasma 1. BIOLOGY. The clear, colorless part of the blood in which the blood cells and platelets flow. Plasma is mostly water but also contains dissolved salts, proteins, other food nutrients, clotting materials, and other substances. Plasma can be stored for long periods by freezing or drying and is often used in blood transfusions instead of whole blood. 2. PHYSICS. A gas made up of electrically charged particles with an almost equal number of free electrons and positive ions. It forms under the high pressures and temperatures found within our sun and other stars. Most of the matter in the universe is thought to be in the form of plasma. 3. TELEVISION. A type of flat panel display used in some kinds of large screen TVs. [*Plasma* is a Greek word meaning "something that is formed or molded."]

plastic 1. PHYSICS. Able to be shaped or formed by pressure. Glass is plastic at temperatures of over 750°F (400°C). 2. CHEMISTRY. A material made from certain kinds of chemicals found in petroleum that is used throughout industry and in the home. Acrylics, nylon, polyethylene, and polyurethane are plastics.

plate (n.) 1. BIOLOGY. A hard part of the skin in certain animals, such as turtles and some other reptiles and some fish. 2. GEOLOGY. One of the huge blocks, several miles long, that make up the crust of the earth. 3. TECHNOLOGY. A thin sheet of metal, such as steel plate.

plate (v.) To cover one metal with a thin sheet of another metal, such as silver or gold plate over a less valuable metal.

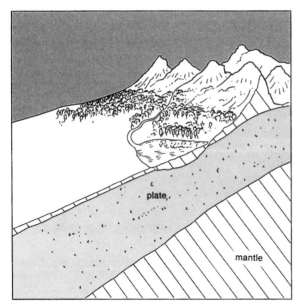

plate (n.)

plate tectonics   The theory that the earth's crust is made up of huge plates that are slowly moving. The continents and oceans ride on the plates. Earthquakes and volcanoes most often occur where one plate pushes against another.

plateau   A large, fairly level area on a mountain or at a high altitude.

platelet   One of many tiny disks that float in the blood plasma and help the blood to clot. Platelets have no nucleus and are produced in the bone marrow.

platinum   A heavy, silvery-white metallic element. Platinum has a high melting point and does not easily react with acids or many other substances. It is very expensive and is used as a catalyst and in dentistry. It is also used in fine jewelry and in some chemical and industrial equipment. Platinum has an atomic number of 78, an atomic weight of 195.09, and a chemical symbol of Pt. [*Platinum* comes from the Spanish word meaning "silver" which this metal resembles.]

Pleistocene Epoch   The epoch just before modern times, from about 2 million to 10,000 years ago. The Ice Age occurred during the Pleistocene. [*Pleistocene* comes from Greek words meaning "newest" or "most recent."]

Pliocene Epoch   The final epoch of the Tertiary Period, lasting from about 7 to 2 million years ago. The first humanlike apes appeared during this time. [*Pliocene* comes from Greek words meaning "newer" or "more recent."]

plumage   A bird's feathers.

plumule   In plants, the growing tip of the embryo of a seed. The plant stem grows from the plumule.

Pluto   The ninth planet and usually the most distant from the sun. It was discovered in 1930 by Clyde Tombaugh, an America astronomer. Pluto takes about 249 years to orbit the sun at an average distance of 3,666 million miles (5,902 million kilometers). Only about 1,430 million miles (2,300 million kilometers) across, Pluto is smaller than our own moon, yet it has a moon of its own called Charon. Pluto is named after the ancient Greek god of the underworld; Charon is named for the boatman in Greek myth who ferried the dead across the river Styx to that underworld.

plutonium   An artificial radioactive element produced from uranium, used as fuel in nuclear reactors and in an atomic bomb. It is highly dangerous, and exposure to even small amounts can cause illness and death. Plutonium has an atomic number of 94, an atomic weight, in its most stable form, of 244, and a chemical symbol of Pu.

pneumatic   Containing air or functioning by using air or some other gas. A pneumatic drill is powered by compressed air.

pod   1. BOTANY. The casing that holds seeds in some kinds of plants, such as peas or beans. 2. ZOOLOGY. A group of whales or seals.

polar   1. GEOGRAPHY. Having to do with Earth's North or South poles. For example, a polar orbit is an orbit of a satellite that passes over Earth's poles. 2. PHYSICS. Having to do with the poles of a magnet or a battery.

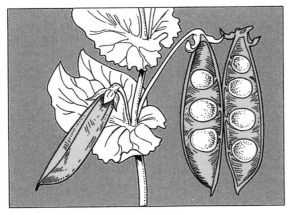

pod

pole 1. GEOGRAPHY, ASTRONOMY. Either end of Earth's axis, or of the axis of any spinning star, planet, or moon. 2. PHYSICS. Either end of a magnet where the magnetic forces are concentrated. Also, either of the two terminals of a battery or electric cell. 3. BIOLOGY. Either of the opposite ends of a living cell or a cell nucleus, especially an egg cell.

poliomyelitis A viral disease, often called polio or infantile paralysis, that causes muscle paralysis as a result of damage to nerves of the spinal cord. Polio can be prevented by a vaccine first developed by Jonas Salk in 1952–1954 and by a different kind developed by Albert Sabin in 1955. [*Poliomyelitis* comes from Greek words meaning "gray" and "marrow."]

pollen Tiny, yellowish grains produced by the male parts of flowering or cone-bearing plants. Each grain of pollen contains a male reproductive cell. At shedding times, such enormous amounts of pollen are produced in evergreen forests that the air may become a yellow haze. [*Pollen* is a Latin word meaning "powder" or "finely ground flour."]

pollination The act of spreading pollen for fertilization. In flowering plants, pollination takes place when pollen grains from the male anther are carried to the female stigma.

Pollination can be carried out by the wind, which blows the pollen grains from one flower to another, or by insects, or other animals, which accidentally carry the pollen grains on their bodies as they gather nectar or simply brush past. Self-pollination occurs when pollen from an anther is deposited on a stigma in the same flower.

pollute To spoil, dirty, or poison the natural environment by introducing toxic substances into the air, water, or soil. Oil spills from tankers or offshore drilling pollute the oceans. A material that pollutes is called a pollutant.

pollution The result of polluting a part of the environment. Open-air burning of refuse and exhaust fumes from automobiles, combustion engines, and oil refineries result in the pollution of air. Disposal of garbage at sea results in the pollution of ocean waters.

polymer A substance composed of very large molecules (macromolecules) built up by the linking together of many identical smaller molecules. Proteins, nucleic acids, starch, and cellulose are natural polymers. Nylon, polyethylene, polystyrene, and many other plastics are synthetic polymers. [*Polymer* comes from the Greek words for "many" and "parts."]

polyp 1. ZOOLOGY. A kind of small water animal attached at the bottom of its column-shaped body, with a mouth and small food-gathering tentacles at the other end. Polyps often grow in colonies and include corals, sea anemones, and hydras. 2. MEDICINE. A small outgrowth from the surface of a body part such as the vocal cords or the colon.

pond A body of fresh water that is smaller than a lake and shallow enough for sunlight to reach to the bottom.

population The number of organisms that live in a particular area or region. In the year 2010, the human world population is estimated to be nearly seven billion people; about four times what it was at the beginning of the twentieth century. Also, a group of organisms of the same kind. Also, the number of items or objects in a particular group, such as the population of stars in a galaxy.

pore 1. BIOLOGY. In surface tissues of living things, a tiny opening to the outside. Sweat passes through pores in human skin. Water vapor, carbon dioxide, and oxygen pass through pores called stomata on the undersides of leaves. 2. GEOLOGY. A small opening or space in rocks or soil that allows water to pass through. 3. ASTRONOMY. A tiny sunspot. [*Pore* comes from the Greek word meaning "passage" or "opening."]

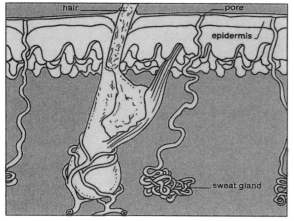

pore

porous Full of pores. Liquids and gases can pass through porous materials such as sandy soils or sponges.

positive 1. PHYSICS, CHEMISTRY. Describing a kind of electricity. When a substance loses electrons, it becomes charged with positive electricity. Also, describing the pole or electrode of an electric cell or battery toward which electrons flow. 2. BIOLOGY. In plants or animals, describing motion or growth toward light, water, or some other stimulus. For example, plant growth toward light is called positive phototropism.

positron A tiny particle that has the same mass as an electron but a positive instead of a negative charge. Positrons are found in cosmic rays.

potassium A soft, silvery-white metallic element that is chemically very active and easily combines with nonmetals. The seventh most abundant element on the earth, potassium is needed for plant growth and is present in plant fertilizers and found in many kinds of rocks. Potassium has an atomic number of 19 and an atomic weight of 39.102. Its chemical symbol is K.

potential energy The energy present in an object because of its position or condition. A coiled spring and a rock on a mountain have potential energy. When the spring is released o the rock falls, the potential energy becomes kinetic energy, the energy of movement.

power 1. PHYSICS. In everyday terms, a force that can do work, such as the power of an engine to move an automobile or the power of the wind to turn a windmill. In physics, the rate at which work is done. Power is measured in work per unit of time, such as foot-pounds per minute or horsepower-hour. The metric system uses the watt, kilowatt, or megawatt as a unit of power. 2. OPTICS. The degree of magnification of a lens in a telescope, microscope, or other optical instrument. With a ten-power telescope, an object is magnified ten times.

prairie A broad, flat grassy plain with few trees. Prairies are found in the Midwestern United States and Canada. In Europe and Asia, similar grasslands are called steppes. In South America, particularly Argentina, they are called pampas. [*Prairie* comes from an Old French word meaning "tract of meadowland."]

precipitation 1. METEOROLOGY. In the atmosphere, the process by which water vapor turns into water or ice in the form of rain, snow, hail, sleet, dew, fog, or mist. Also, the water or ice that comes down as rain, snow, or hail, and the amount that is precipitated. For example, precipitation in many parts of the interior United States averages about 30 inches per year. 2. CHEMISTRY. The process by which a substance is separated out of a solution and settled to the bottom as a solid; the newly separated solid is called a precipitate. [*Precipitation* comes from a Latin word meaning "fall" or "headlong descent."]

predator An animal that hunts or preys upon other animals for food. Big cats, hawks, and sharks are predators.

pregnancy The time (usually weeks or months) that a mammal mother carries an embryo growing inside her uterus. In humans, there is a nine-month pregnancy period from fertilization to birth. In elephants, pregnancy lasts 20 to 22 months. Also, the condition of carrying an embryo within the uterus.

prehistoric animals Animals, such as dinosaurs, that lived and then became extinct before humans appeared on the earth. Large numbers of these animals are preserved in fossils.

prehistoric people Early humans who lived and became extinct 7,000 or more years ago. These date back several million years at least and include *Pithecanthropus erectus* and Neanderthal and Cro-Magnon peoples. Modern-day humans are called *Homo sapiens*.

pressure A continual weight or force acting on a surface. It is measured in units of force per unit of area. For example, the pressure of the atmosphere at sea level is about 14.7 pounds per square inch. In the ocean depths thousands of feet down, the pressure of seawater is more than eight tons per square inch.

prevailing wind A wind that usually blows from one direction. In the temperate zones between latitudes 30° and 60°, the prevailing westerlies blow from the southwest in the Northern Hemisphere and from the northwest in the Southern Hemisphere.

prey Animals that are hunted and eaten as food by other animals called predators.

Priestly, Joseph (1733–1804) A British chemist who discovered oxygen in 1774. He later discovered ammonia, carbon dioxide, and hydrogen sulfide. Priestly also found that green plants need sunlight and give off oxygen.

Priestly, Joseph

primary color Any one of three colors that when mixed together in different amounts can produce any other color. For paints or other pigments, the primary colors are red, yellow, and blue. A heavy mixture of all three produces near black. For light, the primary colors are red, green, and blue. A mixture of all three produces white light.

primate Any member of a group of mammals that includes humans, apes, monkeys, and lemurs. Primates have large brains and forward-facing eyes. Humans are the only primates that have developed a written method of communication. [*Primate* comes from the Latin word meaning "highest" or "supreme."]

prism In optics, a solid piece of glass or other transparent material, usually with triangular ends and three sides that are each parallelograms. A prism is usually used to bend rays of light so that white light is split—refracted—into the colors of the spectrum. It is also used for internal reflection, as in telescopes.

probe ASTRONOMY. A spacecraft designed to escape Earth's gravity and explore and photograph other planets, their moons, and other elements of outer space. The *Voyager* probes took photos of Jupiter, Saturn, Uranus, and

Neptune. Also, any detector placed or sent to gather information in a spot that is difficult to reach.

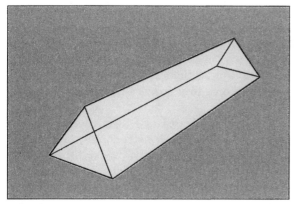

prism

proboscis An elephant's trunk or the long, flexible snout of another mammal, such as the tapir. Also the tubelike mouth part of an insect, such as the mosquito, used for piercing or sucking, or a similar organ found in many worms, usually opening above the mouth.

process (n.) 1. BIOLOGY. A natural sequence of changes leading to some particular stage, such as the process of digestion or the process of decay. 2. ANATOMY. A projecting part or outgrowth on a human or animal, such as a bird's beak or the bony spinal column on a human's back. 3. MANUFACTURING. A sequence of actions that produces useful objects or substances, such as the process of steelmaking.

process (v.) In computing, to manipulate data, or perform calculations that produce a result.

projectile An object that is thrown or shot into the air or space. Bullets, rockets, and pitched baseballs are projectiles.

prokaryote Living organisms that lack a cell nucleus, such as bacteria and cyanobacteria. Most are one-celled. They differ from eukaryotes, which have a cell nucleus.

prominence A jet of gases that erupts from the sun, sometimes to a height of hundreds of thousands of miles. [*Prominence* comes from the Latin word for "something that projects or sticks out."]

propagate 1. BOTANY. To reproduce plants either by seeds (sexually) or by cuttings or vegetative means (asexually). 2. PHYSICS. To transmit motion, light, sound, or some other form of energy through a medium such as air or water. [*Propogate* comes from the Latin word meaning "to breed" or "to enlarge."]

propeller A mechanical device that produces motion in some kinds of airplanes or ships. A propeller consists of two or more twisted blades that rotate around a central hub. As the propeller spins, air or water is pushed in one direction, pushing the craft in the opposite direction. [*Propeller* comes from a Latin word meaning "to thrust forward."]

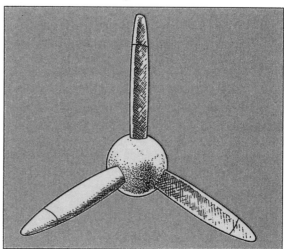

propeller

propulsion A driving force that pushes an object. In jet propulsion, hot gases forced out the back of an airplane or boat push the craft forward.

protein Any one of a group of complex organic substances necessary for life and growth and containing carbon, hydrogen, oxygen, nitrogen, and usually sulfur. Proteins are composed of large molecules called polypeptides that contain many different amino acids, and are found in all living things. Muscle and blood are rich in protein. Foods such as meat, milk, beans, and fish are high in protein. [*Protein* comes from the Greek word for "primary."]

protist A member of a kingdom, protists, that includes most of the one-celled organisms with visible nuclei. Protists include protozoans such as amoebas, slime molds, and blue-green algae. [*Protist* comes from a Greek word meaning "the earliest" or "very first."]

proton A particle in the nucleus of an atom that has a positive charge and a mass about 1,836 times that of an electron. The number of protons in the nucleus determines the element the atom forms and its atomic number. For example, an atom with 1 proton in its nucleus is a hydrogen atom with an atomic number of 1; an atom with 8 protons is an oxygen atom with an atomic number of 8.

protoplasm The clear, jellylike material that makes up all living cells and includes the nucleus and the cytoplasm. Protoplasm is a mixture of proteins, fats, mineral, and other substances suspended in water.

protozoan Any of a group of microscopic, one-celled organisms that reproduce by fission or budding. There are tens of thousands of different kinds of protozoa. Great numbers live in the oceans and in freshwater lakes and ponds. Others live in the soil or are carried by the air. Still others are parasites and live in other organisms, where they cause illnesses such as malaria, sleeping sickness, and amoebic dysentery. Many protozoans can move by beating numerous tiny, hairlike cilia, by flailing one or more whiplike flagellum, or by pulling themselves in one direction or another.

Ptolemy *or* **Claudius Ptolemaeus** (second century A.D.) A Greek astronomer, mathematician, and geographer. His most famous book is the *Almagest,* which tried to explain the motions of the stars and planets with Earth as the center of the universe. Ptolemy's geocentric theory held sway in Western science until Copernicus proposed his heliocentric theory (holding that the sun was the center of the solar system) in the sixteenth century.

Ptolemy or Claudius Ptolemaeus

pulley A simple machine consisting of a grooved wheel mounted on a block with a rope or chain passing over it. A pulley can be used to change the direction of a force and lift a load. A system of several pulleys working together can be used to lift heavy weights with a small amount of effort.

pulsar Pulsating radio star. A pulsar is a rapidly spinning neutron star that seems to send out short, rapid pulses of radio waves and other radiant energy. First discovered in 1967, pulsars have been found in all parts of the sky.

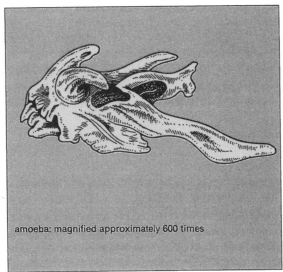

amoeba: magnified approximately 600 times

protozoan

pulley

A pulsar in the Crab Nebula seems to flash on and off 30 times a second. Actually, a pulsar sends out energy constantly but directionally. As a pulsar rotates, the beam sweeps across Earth like a lighthouse beacon. Thus we see it as pulses.

pulse   1. PHYSIOLOGY. A regular beating in the arteries caused by the rush of blood after each contraction of the heart. The pulse can be felt in arteries near the skin such as those in the neck, ankles, or wrists. A normal pulse rate in a human at rest is about 60 to 80 beats a minute. Exercise, fever, and anxiety increase the pulse rate. 2. PHYSICS. A short burst of energy such as a pulse of electricity or a pulse of radio or sound waves.

pump   A mechanism for forcing fluids from one place to another. The heart acts as a pump that forces blood around the body. A fuel pump in an automobile forces gasoline from the tank into the cylinders.

pupa   A stage in the development of many insects, such as butterflies and moths. The pupa is the stage between the larva and the adult. Most pupas do not eat or move and seem to be resting, enclosed in a cocoon or a tough casing of hardened body material. At the end of this stage, the pupa case splits and a greatly changed adult insect emerges. [*Pupa* is a Latin word meaning "girl" or "doll."]

pupil   An opening in the center of the front of the eye. It is circular in humans and many other vertebrate animals, although in some it is a vertical (cats) or horizontal (sheep) slit. The pupil appears as a black spot in the middle of the iris. Light enters the eye through the pupil and is focused by the lens onto the retina at the back of the eye. The size of the pupil is determined by the amount of light and regulated by expansion and contraction of the iris.

pure   Not mixed with other substance or materials: pure water or pure cotton, for example. Also, sciences that are concerned with theories rather than with practical applications: pure physics as opposed to engineering. In the breeding of animals or plants, breeding true to some characteristics of the parents. Those kinds of offspring are called purebred.

purify   To remove pollutants or other unwanted substances.

pus   A thick, yellowish substance consisting of dead and living bacteria and white blood cells, blood plasma, and other body materials. Pus forms in boils, sores, and other infected body tissues.

putrefy   To rot or decay; to break down organic matter by the action of bacteria and fungi. This process sometimes produces foul odors. Putrefaction is the result of putrefying.

pyrite   A common metallic ore in which a metal is combined with sulfur. Iron pyrite is a yellowish, shiny substance sometimes called fool's gold because it is often mistaken for real gold by inexperienced rock collectors. [*Pyrite* comes from a Greek word meaning "flintstones," which produce sparks when struck, and is also related to the Greek word for "fire."]

quadruped An animal with four feet such as a horse, dog, cat, or lizard.

quantum The smallest amount of electromagnetic or radiant energy that can exist. The idea of a quantum was first proposed by Max Planck. The size of a quantum depends upon the kind of energy involved. A quantum of radiant energy is called a photon.

quantum mechanics The branch of physics that deals with the structure of the atom and the motion of atomic particles such as electrons and nuclei within atoms. It is also concerned with the interaction between matter and radiation. Because quantum mechanics treats physical events that we cannot directly observe, its concepts are unknown in everyday experience. For example, quantum mechanics describes certain kinds of energy as having the characteristics of both waves and particles. The three scientists most closely associated with the fundamental ideas of quantum mechanics are Max Planck, Erwin Schrödinger, and Werner Heisenberg.

quark One of a theoretical group of subatomic particles, each having an electric charge less than that of an electron. The concept of quarks was put forth by American physicists Murray Gell-Mann and Richard Feynman, who also suggested the name. Gell-Mann received the Nobel Prize for physics in 1969. Feynman was awarded the Nobel Prize for physics in 1965.

quarry (n.) 1. EARTH SCIENCE. A place where rocks and minerals are dug out from the earth. 2. BIOLOGY. An animal hunted by another animal; prey.

quarry (v.) To dig out rocks or minerals from the earth.

quartz A very hard mineral commonly found in sand and in many kinds of rock, such as granite, and sandstone. Quartz can vary in color and appearance from white and opaque to colorless and transparent. In the crystalline form, called rock crystal, quartz crystals are six sided and come to a point. Agate, jasper, onyx, and amethyst are different forms of quartz.

quasar Also called QSO, *Q*uasi-*S*tellar *O*bject. One of a number of distant celestial objects larger than stars but smaller than galaxies. Quasars give off blue light and powerful radio waves. Even though quasars seem to be much smaller than galaxies, they give off thousands of times more energy. Some scientists think that quasars are associated with black holes.

Quaternary Period The present geological period, marked by the appearance of human beings here on Earth. It began about 2 million years ago. It is divided into the Pleistocene (or Glacial) Epoch and the Holocene (or Recent) Epoch, which began about 10,000 years ago. [*Quarternary* comes from the Latin word meaning "four."]

queen An adult egg-laying female in a colony of social insects such as bees, ants, or termites. There is usually only one queen in a colony.

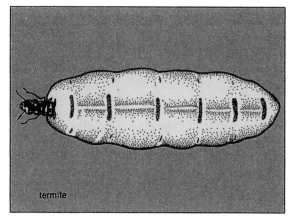

queen

R

rabies A viral disease of mammals that results from the bite of an animal, often a dog or some wild animal. Death after several weeks almost always results unless medical treatment is started early. Injections of an antirabies vaccine may help to prevent the onset of the disease. Infected domestic and trapped wild animals are destroyed. Many countries try to stop the spread of rabies across their borders by having strict laws controlling the entrance of dogs and other animals. Licensing laws often require rabies shots for pets. [*Rabies* comes from the Latin word meaning "frenzy" or "madness."]

radar *R*adio *D*etection *and R*anging. An instrument system used to detect objects at long range and to determine their distance, direction, and speed. Radar works by timing the interval between the emission and return of pulses of radio waves that are bounced off objects such as planes, ships, or storm clouds.

radiant Giving off energy in the form of rays or waves. The sun is a radiant body: It radiates heat and light.

radiation The giving off of energy in the form of rays or waves. The radiation of light and heat by the sun warms the planets. Also, the kind of energy radiated in the form of rays or waves. Heat, light, and radio waves are types of radiation. Also, a stream of particles or waves given off by the atoms and molecules in a radioactive substance such as uranium. This kind of nuclear radiation includes alpha and beta particles, gamma rays, and neutrons. Nuclear radiation is often harmful to living tissue.

radiator 1. PHYSICS. Anything that gives off radiant energy, such as a light bulb, the sun, or a radioactive substance. Also, a device used to give off heat. In some automobiles, the radiator is part of the cooling system that draws heat away from the engine.

radical An atom or group of atoms acting as a unit in chemical reactions.

radicle A part of a plant seed that develops into the root. It is the first to grow when the seed germinates.

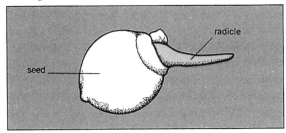

radicle

radio A communications device that sends out and receives electromagnetic waves known as radio waves. In radio broadcasting, a powerful central transmitter sends out signals to many individual receivers. Because there are so many different users on radio communications—airplanes, shops, police, commercial broadcasters, and individuals—the use of the radio frequencies is controlled by governments.

radio astronomy The branch of astronomy that deals with detecting objects in space that give off radio waves. Radio astronomy enables observers to investigate quasars, pulsars, the hydrogen gas clouds of the Milky Way, and distant galaxies beyond the reach of optical telescopes.

radio telescope The basic instrument of radio astronomy. It usually consists of a sensitive receiver and a large antenna or a group of antennas that collect and focus radio waves coming from objects in outer space. A radio telescope can show objects in space that are difficult to see by optical means, much as an infrared scope can picture an object difficult to see in the dark.

radio telescope

radio wave A form of electromagnetic energy used in radio and television communication.

Radio waves travel at the speed of light, but have a much longer wavelength and can pass through dense clouds and many materials that are often opaque to light.

radioactive decay The continual, natural breakup of the nuclei of the atoms in a radioactive substance. The decay is accompanied by the release of energetic particles or penetrating gamma rays. The rate and amount of radioactive decay depends upon the substance.

radioactivity The property of certain elements, such as radium and uranium, to give off radiation in the form of alpha and beta particles and gamma rays. It occurs as a result of radioactive decay and in fission.

radiocarbon dating A method of determining the age of a preserved prehistoric organic object. It is based on computing the relative amounts of radioactive and nonradioactive carbon the object contains. Radiocarbon dating depends upon the fact that once an organic object is no longer part of the natural carbon cycle, it stops absorbing and giving off any carbon, but the radioactive isotopes of carbon in it continue to decay and in time decrease in strength. Also called carbon dating.

radioisotope A radioactive form of an element, especially that artificially produced for use in medicine, for sterilizing foods, and for controlling insect pests. Also called radioactive isotope.

radium A rare radioactive metallic element found in very small amounts in uranium ores. Radium is very unstable and gives off energetic particles and gamma rays as it undergoes radioactive decay. Because of the radiation, radium is dangerous to handle. A piece of radium is always one or two degrees hotter that its surroundings. Radium has an atomic number of 88, an atomic weight of 226, and its chemical symbol is Ra.

radon An element that occurs as an odorless, tasteless, invisible gas given off in the natural radioactive decay of substances in certain kinds of rock and soil. Radon is believed to the cause of some cases of lung cancer. When it seeps into the basements of houses in some areas, it tends to concentrate there because it is heavier than air. To guard against the potential health problems caused by radon, particular homes need to be checked by local authorities. Radon has an atomic number of 86, an atomic weight of 222, and chemical symbol of Rn.

rain Precipitation that falls from clouds in drops of liquid water. Rain forms from the condensation of water vapor in the atmosphere.

rain forest A large, dense forest of mostly evergreen trees found in regions where rainfall is very heavy during the year. Most rain forests grow in tropical areas, but some are found in temperate zones, such as the northwest coast of the United States. A rain forest has tall trees and heavy foliage, so little sunlight penetrates to the forest floor. Rain forests usually have a great variety of plant and animal life. A tropical rain forest is sometimes called a jungle. In some countries, the rain forests are being cut down or burned at an alarming rate. Many scientists believe that the destruction of the rain forests will have serious effects on Earth's atmosphere and climate.

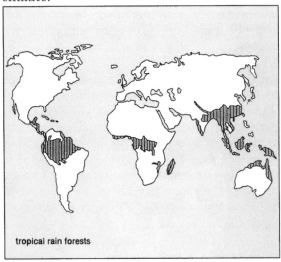

tropical rain forests

rain forest

rain shadow An area of low rainfall on the downwind or sheltered side of a mountain or mountain chain. The upwind or exposed side of the mountain has greater rainfall. Sometimes rain shadows cause deserts to form.

rainbow A curve or arc of the colors of the spectrum sometimes seen in the sky or in mist or spray. Rainbows are seen when the sun shines from behind the observer onto raindrops or water drops. The colors of a rainbow are red, orange, yellow, green, blue, indigo, and violet.

RAM *R*andom *A*ccess *M*emory. RAM is a temporary computer memory. It can be electronically "written" within the computer, used, and rewritten over and over again. Most computers use a kind of RAM that loses its information when the power is turned off. Various magnetic disks or other memory devices are used to store information permanently.

range A line or chain of mountains, such as the Rocky Mountains or the Alps.

rare earth element Any of a group of metallic elements that have similar properties and are found in group IIIB of the periodic table. The rare earth elements, such as scandium and yttrium, are actually not rare, just difficult to extract. They are used in making glass and ceramics, in alloys, and to make phosphors in cathode-ray tubes.

ray 1. PHYSICS. A line or beam of light, heat, X-ray, or other form of radiant energy. 2. ASTRONOMY. One of the bright streaks seen coming out from some craters on the moon, such as the giant crater Tycho. 3. BIOLOGY. A part of a plant or animal that resembles a ray, such as an arm of a starfish or a petal on a ray-flower head such as a daisy. 4. ZOOLOGY. One of a group of large, flat fish that live in ocean waters, such as a stingray, a skate, or an electric ray.

react To undergo or cause a chemical change. Also, to produce a chemical change. Most acids react with metals.

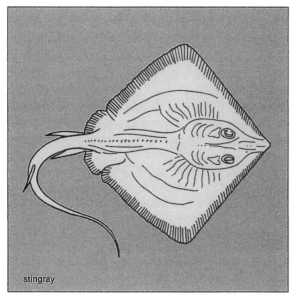
stingray

ray

reaction 1. CHEMISTRY. A change in the arrangement of elements or molecules that occurs when different substances are put together. Also called a chemical change or a chemical reaction. For example, when an acid is combined with a metal, hydrogen and a salt are formed. 2. PHYSICS. An equal and opposite force that an object exerts against a force acting upon it. For example, when a bullet is fired from a gun, the gun recoils in the opposite direction from the bullet. 3. NUCLEAR PHYSICS. A process, such as nuclear fission or nuclear fusion, in which the nucleus of an atom undergoes a change. Also called a nuclear reaction. 4. BIOLOGY. The response of a nerve or muscle to a stimulus. For example, the pupil of the eye contracts when it is exposed to a bright light. Also, the response of the body to a test, such as a test for sensitivity to pollen.

reactor In nuclear physics, an apparatus for the controlled release of atomic energy. A reactor is the core of an atomic power plant. Also called a nuclear reactor.

reagent A substance involved in a chemical reaction used to detect the presence of other substances. For example, iodine turns blue-black in the presence of starch, so it is used as a reagent to test for the presence of starch in food.

receiver A device, such as a television or radio, that picks up radio waves and translates them to sound or pictures.

receptor In the nervous system of an animal, a cell, or a group of cells that is sensitive to stimuli. For example, receptors in the skin are sensitive to touch, pain, and temperature. Receptors in the eye are sensitive to color and light.

recombinant DNA In molecular biology, genetic material that is produced in laboratories by breaking up and then recombining DNA molecules from different organisms. The recombinant DNA is then introduced into another cell, where it is used to do a particular job, such as supplying important genetic information. Recombinant DNA research is often called gene splicing.

rectum The last section of the alimentary canal. It is a short tube that stores solid wastes until they are expelled from the body through an opening called the anus. [*Rectum* is a Latin word meaning "straight," which describes its form in the intestine.]

recycling The recovery and reuse of products that are otherwise thrown away. For example, materials such as used paper, scrap metal, and glass bottles can be recycled and made into usable paper, metal, and glass products. Recycling is important in the conservation of natural resources as well as in solving some of the problems of pollution in the environment.

red blood cell A disk-shaped cell found in the blood. It contains a reddish substance called hemoglobin that carries oxygen from the lungs (or from the gills in fish) to tissues all over the body. Hemoglobin is made in the bone marrow. There are many million of red blood cells in a drop of blood. Also called an erythrocyte.

red dwarf star A star that is smaller, cooler, and usually fainter than our sun.

red giant star A huge star that is bright but

has a cooler surface temperature than most other stars. Red giants may be hundreds of times larger than our sun.

red shift A change in the light of stars and galaxies toward the red end of the spectrum. The red shift shows movement away from the observer. The light from nearly all galaxies shows a red shift. This makes scientists believe that the galaxies are moving way from each other and that the farthest galaxies are receding fastest, providing support for the theory that the universe is expanding.

Redi, Francesco (1627–1697) An Italian biologist who showed that maggots develop in spoiled meat from eggs laid there by flies, not from the decaying meat itself.

reduction A chemical reaction that removes oxygen from a compound. Also, a chemical reaction in which an atom or ion gains one or more electrons.

reef A barely submerged ridge of rock or coral in the ocean. A reef may be visible above the water at low tide. [*Reef* may come from a Dutch or German word with the same meaning, probably related to "rib."]

reef

refinery A factory where raw materials such

as petroleum or cane sugar are cleaned and purified.

refining The process of removing impurities from metal ores, petroleum, or other materials.

reflection The bouncing back of energy waves—such as light, heat, electricity, or sound—from a surface. If the surface is smooth, the reflection is called regular. Rough surfaces have irregular reflections. An optically smooth surface such as a mirror appears shiny, while an optically rough surface such as brick appears dull. A reflected sound wave is called an echo.

reflex An involuntary action in direct response to a nerve stimulation. Sneezing, yawning, jerking the knee, and shivering are all examples of simple reflexes. [*Reflex* comes from a Latin word meaning "to turn back" or "to reverse."]

refract To bend light, heat, or sound waves from a straight path. A curved lens refracts light passing through it.

refraction The bending or turning of light rays, sound or heat waves, or streams of electrons when they pass at an angle from one medium (such as air) into another of different density (such as glass or water). Light striking a flat transparent material (such as clear glass) at an angle other than a right angle is also refracted. Light coming from an object in water is refracted when it passes out of the water into the air. A glass prism produces a spectrum of colors from white light because each color refracts to a different angle when it passes through the slanted surfaces of the prism.

refractor A refracting telescope, one in which light passes, and is focused, through an objective lens, and the image is magnified by another lens called the eyepiece.

refrigeration The removal of heat from an enclosure. Refrigeration is used for food preservation as well as for making ice and cooling objects. Cooling food slows the action of enzymes and bacteria that results in food spoilage.

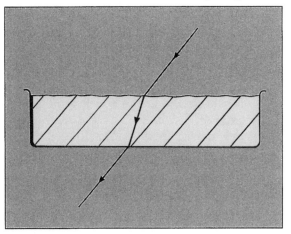

refraction

regeneration 1. BIOLOGY. The regrowth of a lost or damaged part of an organism. Most mammals can regenerate only scar tissue to heal wounds. But many kinds of lizards can regenerate lost tails, while some more primitive animals such as worms, sponges, and sea stars can regenerate the rest of the body from a single part. 2. ELECTRONICS. An increase in the strength of an electric signal, brought about by sending back part of the output current into the circuit again.

region 1. GEOGRAPHY. A large area of the earth's surface that has particular properties. For example, a desert region is dry and a tropical region is hot. So a tropical desert region is hot and dry. 2. ECOLOGY. A part of the earth defined according to the kind of life that inhabits the region. For example, a region of grasslands. 3. ANATOMY. An area of the body, such as the region of the heart or the region of the kneecap. 4. OCEANOGRAPHY. A part of the sea defined according to depth such as the abyssal region, the deepest part of the ocean. 5. EARTH SCIENCE. A part of the atmosphere defined according to altitude, such as the stratospheric region.

relative humidity The ratio between the amount of water vapor present in the air and the amount of water vapor the air can contain at that temperature. For example, if the air contains half of the water vapor it can hold at a certain temperature, the relative humidity is 50%. When the relative humidity is 100%, the air is said to be saturated.

relativity The theories of Albert Einstein that deal with matter, space, motion, and time. The theories are mathematical and very complex, and they can only be described here rather than explained. According to Einstein's special theory of relativity (1905), only the velocity of light in a vacuum is the same when measured from anywhere by any observer; everything else—matter, space, motion, and time—can be determined only relative to something else. For example, Einstein's theory would explain why time runs more slowly for a moving object; a moving object is shortened in the direction of its motion; an object has greater mass when it is moving than when it is at rest.

These effects are too small to be noticed in the everyday world but can be readily measured at velocities close to the speed of light (186,000 miles per second). Einstein also proposed the bold idea that all energy has a corresponding mass. That led to his famous equation $E = mc^2$, in which E stands for energy, m stands for mass, and c is the velocity of light.

REM *R*apid *E*ye *M*ovement. Describing a phase of sleep (called REM sleep) that is accompanied by the jerky eye movements associated with dreaming and by restlessness. Usually there are five or six REM sleep phases during a sleep period.

rem *R*oentgen *E*quivalent *M*an. A unit used in measuring absorbed doses of radiation.

remote control The control of an electronic device or a machine from a distance. Television receivers and radio cassette recorders often come with remote controls that function by using infrared light signals.

renal Having to do with the kidneys.

renewable energy A source of energy that can be used continuously without eventually being used up. Wind power, water power, and solar energy are examples of renewable energy.

reproduce To produce offspring. One function of living things is to reproduce.

reproduction The process by which living things produce other living things similar to themselves. In sexual reproduction, offspring are produced by the fusion of male and female sex cells (gametes). Asexual reproduction occurs when new organisms develop from a cell or cells of a single parent without fusion, in a process such as budding or fission. Asexual reproduction takes place mostly in plants and protists.

reptile One of a class of cold-blooded vertebrates that breathe with lungs and have dry, scaly, or horny skin. Most reptiles are land animals and lay eggs covered by a tough membrane. Snakes, lizards, alligators, crocodiles, and turtles are reptiles. Fossil remains of reptiles, such as dinosaurs are found in rocks dating back to 280 million years ago. [*Reptile* comes from a Latin word meaning "to creep" or " slink."]

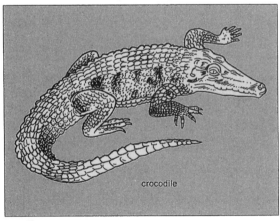

crocodile

reptile

repulsion A force that causes objects to move away from other objects. For example, electrically charged particles exert forces of repulsion against other particles with the same charge. Also used to describe the way like poles of a magnet push away from each other.

research Scientific investigation to solve a problem, test a theory or hypothesis, or invent a new machine or way of doing something. Research can entail just looking for something new about the world without any definite goal in mind.

reservoir 1. EARTH SCIENCE. A large natural or artificial lake or tank in which water is stored before being used. 2. MECHANICS. A place in a piece of machinery in which some kind of fluid is stored. 3. BIOLOGY. A part of an animal or plant in which some kind of fluid is collected or stored. 4. MEDICINE. An individual who carries a disease, germ, or virus from which infection can spread but to which he or she is immune.

resin A sticky yellow or brown substance that oozes from cuts in the bark of some kinds of bushes and trees such as pines and spruces. Resin is used to make products in medicine, paints, varnishes, plastics, and adhesives. Heating pine resin yields turpentine and a yellow substance called rosin. Amber is a kind of fossilized resin that is cut into gems and used in jewelry.

resistance A force that acts against another force, preventing or slowing down motion. Also, in electric circuits, the property of a substance that opposes the flow of electricity. The standard unit of resistance is the ohm.

resistor A device used in electrical or electronic equipment, such as a television receiver or computer, to control the flow of current. A variable resistor can be used to change the volume in a radio or the brightness of a light bulb.

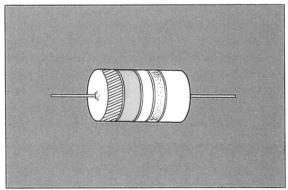

resistor

resonance In physics, a condition in which the natural frequency of oscillations (back-and-forth changes) of an object are matched in frequency by an outside source of oscillation energy. Resonance results in a great increase in the size of the oscillations. For example, if a glass container begins to resonate at its natural frequency with an outside sound of the same frequency, the glass may vibrate violently enough to break. Resonance may also occur in electrical, magnetic, mechanical, optical, atomic, and other systems. Devices such as magnetic resonance imaging (MRI) medical instruments use nuclear magnetic resonance.

resource recovery The process of obtaining materials or energy from solid wastes such as garbage.

respiration 1. BIOLOGY. The process by which an organism or a cell obtains oxygen from air or water and uses it for the oxidation of food to provide usable energy and excess carbon dioxide and water. Respiration is constantly going on in every living cell and organism. 2. PHYSIOLOGY. The act of breathing air. In land vertebrates, breathing replaces the used air in the air sacs of the lungs with fresh air from the outside. In fish, respiration takes place through the gills. In one-celled organisms, respiration takes place over the whole cell area.

respiratory system The group of organs, tissues, and tubes by which air enters and leaves the body and oxygen and carbon dioxide are exchanged. In humans and other land animals that have backbones, the respiratory system includes the nasal cavities, pharynx, larynx, trachea, and lungs

retina A light-sensitive layer of cells at the back of the eyeball. It contains two kinds of nerve endings: rods and cones. In humans, cones make up the central part of the retina and are responsible for color vision and fine details, while the rods are more sensitive to light. The retina's inner surface is part of the optic nerve.

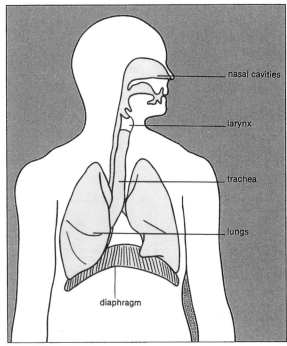

respiratory system

revolution 1. ASTRONOMY. The motion of one object in space around another. Earth makes on revolution around the sun in a year. 2. PHYSICS. Turning around an axis or a center. An automobile engine makes several thousand revolutions per minute.

revolve To move in a circle or an orbit. The moon revolves around Earth.

Rh factor A kind of protein found on the surface of the red blood cells of most humans. Persons who have the factor are known as Rh-positive; those who do not are known as Rh-negative. If a person who is Rh-negative receives a transfusion of Rh-positive blood, the blood will clot and the person may die. *Rh* comes from *Rhesus* monkeys, in whose blood the factor was first discovered.

rhizome An underground stem of some kinds of plants that grows horizontally and has scaly leaves and buds. A rhizome produces new plants by sending out roots below and leafy shoots above. It stores food that will be used by the new plants the following growing season. Often called a rootstock. Some plants that have rhizomes are irises, ferns, and many kinds of grasses. [*Rhizome* comes from a Greek word for "root."]

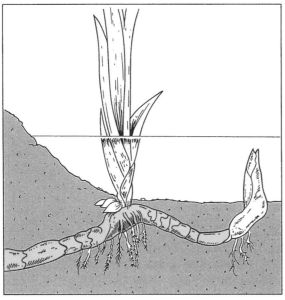

rhizome

rhyolite A common volcanic rock containing quartz and feldspar. Rhyolite is often banded and generally light colored.

rib One of the curved bones that enclose and protect the heart and lungs in vertebrates. The enclosure is called the rib cage. In humans, there are 24 ribs. They are attached in pairs to the backbone and the sternum.

Richter scale A scale used to indicate the magnitude or strength of earthquakes. An earthquake of magnitude 4 is barely felt as a rumble. An earthquake of magnitude 5 has ground motions ten times as large and will crack building walls and dislodge heavy objects. Above magnitude 7, earthquakes do major damage to buildings. Above magnitude 8, there is complete destruction. The Richter scale was named after Charles F. Richter (1900–1985), the American seismologist who devised it. These days the Richter Magnitude Scale has largely been supplanted by the moment magnitude scale (MMS). Even though the ways in which the strength of quakes are determined is

different, the MMS uses fairly similar values as defined by the Richter scale. So far the largest earthquake ever recorded was assigned a magnitude of 9.5 on the MMS (Chile, 1960).

rickets A vitamin-D-deficiency disease in children causing soft bones and slow growth.

ridge 1. EARTH SCIENCE. A long, narrow chain of hills or mountains. 2. METEOROLOGY. A zone of high barometric pressure.

rift valley A valley formed by the lowering of land between roughly parallel faults in the earth's crust. East Africa has a number of long, narrow rift valleys, including the Great Rift Valley. Rift valleys often contain many long, narrow lakes.

Ring Nebula A famous nebula that looks like a smoke ring in the constellation Lyra.

ringworm A common, contagious disease of the skin, hair, or nails caused by a fungus. Ringworm appears on the skin as a ring-shaped, reddish patch. Athlete's foot is ringworm on the toes.

rip current A strong, narrow surface current that flows rapidly away at right angles from the shore. Also called a riptide.

river A long, natural body of water that flows in a channel into the ocean, a lake, or another river. The sources of rivers are springs, lakes or glaciers. Rivers flow rapidly at the source, more slowly in the middle part of the course, and sluggishly at the river mouth.

RNA *Ribo*Nucleic*A*cid. A genetic substance present in all living cells and many viruses. RNA and DNA are the complex chemical agents that contain the "plans" to make new cell materials.

robot An automatic machine that carries out complex tasks in industry, replacing humans. Robots are often used in activities that are dangerous to humans, such as handling hot or radioactive materials. The study of robots is called robotics. [*Robot* was first used by the Czech dramatist Karel Čapek in his 1920 play *R.U.R.;* it comes from the Czech word for "labor."]

rock   The material that makes up the outer part, or crust, of the earth. Most kinds of rock are hard but some, such as talc, clay, and volcanic ash, are soft. Rocks are usually mixtures of minerals: For example, granite is composed of the minerals quartz, feldspar, mica, and hornblende. But some rocks are mainly made of single materials: Marble consists of the mineral calcite. Rocks are usually classified into three groups according to the way they were formed. Igneous rock is formed when molten lava or magma from beneath the earth's surface cools and solidifies. Granite, rhyolite, and obsidian are examples of igneous rocks. Sedimentary rock is formed from the breaking down and settling of other rocks and of inorganic remains, such as shells, of organisms. The sediments are deposited in layers. Over time they are pressed together and harden into sedimentary rocks such as sandstone, shale, and breccia. Metamorphic rocks are produced by heat and pressure affecting other rocks. Slate, for example, is a metamorphic rock that was once shale. Marble, gneiss, schist, and quartzite are all examples of metamorphic rocks.

rocket   A device that moves by usually burning fuel and expelling the resulting hot gases from one end. The rocket moves in the opposite direction from the escaping gases, an example of Newton's third law of motion: For every action there is an equal and opposite reaction. Rockets can be used on the earth or in outer space.

rod   1. BIOLOGY. One of the tiny sense organs in the retina of the eye of humans and most vertebrates. Rods are sensitive to dim light. 2. NUCLEAR PHYSICS. A metal bar that contains a neutron-absorbing material such as boron. Rods in nuclear reactors are used to control and regulate the speed of the reaction.

rodent   One of a group of small mammals that have two long, chisel-edged teeth used for gnawing. These incisor teeth continue to grow throughout the animal's life, but they are also always being worn down through use. Rats, mice, guinea pigs, beavers, and porcupines are rodents. Rodents eat many of the same things that humans eat, and some have become pests because they eat food people store away. [*Rodent* comes from the Latin word meaning "to gnaw" or "to chew."]

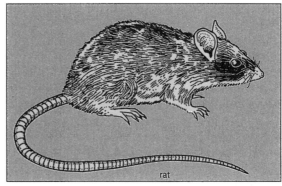
rodent

Roentgen, Wilhelm   (1845–1923) A German scientist who in 1901 received the first Nobel Prize in physics for his discovery of X-rays. The roentgen is the international unit of the intensity of X-rays and gamma rays.

Roentgen, Wilhelm

root   1. BOTANY. The part of a plant that grows downward into the ground or air or water. Roots hold the plant in place, absorb water, and in some plants are used to store food materials. 2. ANATOMY. A part of an organ that is buried in tissue, such as the root of a tooth or a hair root.

root hair A tiny hairlike part of a root through which water and minerals from the surroundings are absorbed.

rot To decay or decompose because of the action of bacteria and other microorganisms.

rotate To turn around the center or on an axis. The sun, Earth, and the planets all rotate. [*Rotate* comes from a Latin word for "wheel."]

rotation The act of turning on an axis. Also, the time needed for one such movement. Earth's period of rotation is one day.

roughage The coarser parts of some foods, such as bran and the skins of fruits and vegetables, that stimulate the passage of food through the intestines. Roughage is also called fiber.

rubber An elastic substance made from the juices of certain tropical trees or synthetically by chemical means. Rubber will not let air or water pass through it. It is used to make tires, rubber thread, foam rubber, hoses, insulation, shoes, and many other things.

rubidium A soft, silvery-white metallic element. Rubidium ignites when exposed to air and reacts violently with water. It is used in making electron tubes, special kinds of glass, and ceramics. Rubidium has an atomic number of 37 and an atomic weight of 85.47. Its chemical symbol is Rb.

ruby A clear, very hard precious gem. It is a variety of the mineral corundum. [*Ruby* comes from the Latin word meaning "red."]

rudder A moveable, flat surface at the tail of an airplane or ship that is used for steering.

ruminant An animal that regurgitates and rechews its food. Cows, sheep, deer, and camels are ruminants. [*Ruminant* comes from the Latin word meaning the enlarged "gullet" where some mammals store food while digesting it.]

rust 1. CHEMISTRY. A reddish-brown coating that forms on iron or steel when they are exposed to air and moisture. Rust is mainly ferric oxide. It is a form of corrosion. 2. BOTANY. A fungus disease of certain plants. Rust fungus usually appears as reddish spots on leaves or stems of affected plants.

Rutherford, Ernest (1871–1937) A New Zealand-born English physicist who studied the rays given off by uranium and found two kinds, which he named alpha particles and beta rays. In 1903, along with another scientist, Frederick Soddy, Rutherford posited that atoms of certain substances, such as uranium and radium, give off alpha particles and beta rays and thus change into elements of lesser atomic weight. He later showed alpha particles to be positively charged helium atoms that had been stripped of their electrons. These emissions constitute radioactive decay. In 1908, he was awarded the Nobel Prize for chemistry. In 1911, Rutherford published his theory of the atom, in which he stated that the mass of the atom is located in its center, or nucleus, and the electrons revolve around the nucleus as planets revolve around the sun. Two years later, Niels Bohr based his theory of the atom upon Rutherford's work.

Rutherford, Ernest

S

Sabin, Albert Bruce (1906–1993) A United States medical scientist who developed a live-virus vaccine against polio that is now often used instead of the Salk vaccine.

Sabin, Albert Bruce

sac A baglike part of an animal or plant. Tiny air sacs in the lungs of mammals allow oxygen to get into the blood.

Sachs, Julius von (1832–1897) A German botanist regarded as the founder of experimental plant research. Sachs discovered plant tropisms, the existence of plant chloroplasts, and details of seed germination.

saline Salty or containing a salt. Seawater is saline.

saliva A colorless, watery fluid secreted by the salivary glands into the mouth. Saliva keeps the mouth moist and helps in chewing and in moistening food, making it easier to swallow. Saliva in humans and certain animals also contains a digestive enzyme that begins the breakdown of carbohydrates.

Salk, Jonas Edward (1914–1995) A United States medical scientist who developed the first killed-virus vaccine that was successful against polio and was used for mass inoculations starting in 1954. It was later largely replaced by the Sabin live-virus vaccine.

salt 1. The common name of sodium chloride (NaCl), a white substance found commonly in the earth (called rock salt) or dissolved in seawater. For many years, particularly before refrigeration, people used salt as a seasoning and also as a preservative for foods because it killed bacteria. Salt is also used to preserve hides in leather making. 2. CHEMISTRY. Any compound formed when the hydrogen in an acid is replaced by a metal or a group of elements called a positive ion. A salt is also formed as a precipitate in water when an acid and a base neutralize each other. Many minerals are salts of one kind or another.

salt dome A globular structure of sedimentary rocks forced upward by an underground mass of salt that has become buoyant beneath the underlying rocks. Salt domes often form natural traps for petroleum deposits. Today, domes are put to uses such as storing liquid petroleum gas or nuclear materials

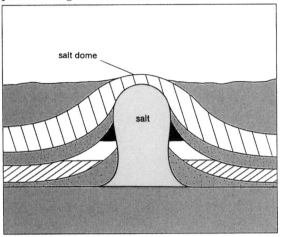

salt dome

salt flats The dried-up bed of a salty stretch of water such as a salt lake. Best known are the Bonneville flats in Utah.

sand A material found naturally in the earth consisting of grains of worn-down rock, often quartz or feldspar. Sand grains can be of various sizes but are larger that silt particles and smaller than gravel. Sand can be many different colors, depending on its chemical composition. Sand is mostly silicon dioxide.

sandstone A sedimentary rock formed by grains of sand bonded together by minerals such as silica, iron oxide, or calcium carbonate.

sandstorm A strong wind, usually in a desert, that carries along clouds of sand.

sap A fluid that moves through the phloem and xylem tissues of trees and other kinds of plants. Sap contains minerals, gases, and other substances dissolved in water. Maple syrup is made from the sap of sugar maple trees.

sapling A young tree.

sapphire A clear, hard, bright-blue semi-precious gem that is a variety of the mineral corundum, aluminum oxide.

saprophytes Fungi, bacteria, or plants that live on nonliving organic matter. The mold that lives on bread or the bacterium that sours milk is saprophytic. [*Saprophyte* comes from Greek words meaning "rotten" or "stinking" and "plant."]

satellite A body orbiting around a planet, especially around one of the nine planets of our solar system. Earth has one natural satellite, the moon. Also any object launched into an orbit around Earth or any other body in space; an artificial satellite. [*Satellite* comes from a Latin word meaning "escort" or "bodyguard."]

saturated 1. CHEMISTRY. Unable to absorb any more of or combine any further with a second substance. Air that holds all the water vapor it can at a given temperature is said to be saturated. 2. PHYSICS. In electronics, something charged to its full extent.

saturated fat A kind of fat that remains hard at room temperature. It is found mostly in butter, cheese, and other milk products. There is some evidence that large amounts of saturated fats in a diet can lead to hardening of the arteries and heart disease, though the exact way this happens is not known.

Saturn The second largest planet and the sixth in order from the sun. Saturn orbits the sun once every 29.5 years at an average distance of 887 million miles (1,428 million kilometers) and spins on its axis once in 10 hours and 39 minutes. Its diameter is 74.977 miles (120,712 kilometers). A gas planet made up mainly of hydrogen and helium, Saturn's rapid spin tends to flatten out the poles while causing a bulge at its equator. Astronomers see large white spots (or clouds) on Saturn which they believe are storms. Saturn has an beautiful ring system formed by a thousand individual rings. The rings appear to be particles and chunks of water ice and dust. There are gaps between some rings, while other rings appear to be braided together. Astronomers believe the rings developed from the break-up of naturally occurring moons. Saturn still has at least 52 moons.

saurian Describing any member of the group of reptiles that includes lizards but not snakes. Also, any similar reptile, such as a dinosaur.

anole lizard

saurian

savanna A tropical or subtropical region of grasslands found in South America and Africa, usually with scattered trees or shrubs. In South America these regions are called pampas. [*Savanna* comes from a Caribbean word meaning "grasslands."]

scabies An infectious skin disease caused by a tiny mite, a relative of spiders and scorpions. The mite burrows under the skin and lays eggs, making the skin very itchy. [*Scabies* comes from a Latin word meaning "to scratch."]

scale 1. ZOOLOGY. One of the thin, flat, hard plates that cover the bodies of many fishes, snakes, and lizards. Also, a part like this in other animals, such as one of the tiny scales on the wings of moths and butterflies. 2. BOTANY. One of the parts of a plant that overlap a bud to cover and protect it. 3. CHEMISTRY. An oxide that forms on metals when heated in air. 4. PHYSICS. *a.* A series of marks along an instrument used for measuring weight, temperature, or some other variable. Also an instrument marked in that way. *b.* The size of a map, chart, or model compared to the thing it represents. For example, a map of the city may have a scale in which one inch on the map represents one mile.

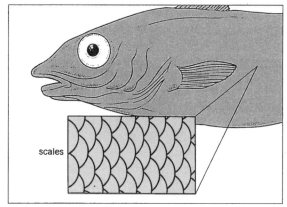

scales

scale

scalp The soft skin over the top and back of the human skull. It is usually covered with hair.

scarp A steep slope or ridge of a cliff.

scatter To change the direction of moving particles or energy waves.

scavenger An animal that usually feeds on the remains of other animals it has not killed. Hyenas and vultures are scavengers.

Schiaparelli, Giovanni Virginio (1835–1910) An Italian astronomer best known for calling the markings on the surface of Mars *canali* (channels). This was incorrectly translated into English as "canals," which implied that they had been "constructed" by Martians. The controversy over the Martian "canals" lasted for a century. Space probes such as *Viking* have now shown that there are no canals on Mars, only natural markings.

schist Any of a common group of metamorphic rocks, usually composed mainly of mica that split easily into layers.

science A body of knowledge and understanding of the physical and natural world. Also a branch of that knowledge as a separate body of knowledge; for example, the science of biology or the science of physics. [*Science* comes from a Latin word for "knowledge" or "understanding."]

scientific method A way of investigating questions by pursuing facts and fitting them into current theories or creating new theories to fit new facts. It is sometimes simplified to include several steps: identifying a problem, making observations, stating a hypothesis, collecting data to prove or disprove the hypothesis, and drawing a conclusion. But scientists do not follow all of these steps in this order or even do all these things. Scientists explore science in many different ways.

scientist A person involved in the study of science.

sclera In humans, the tough, whitish outer covering of the eyeball to which the eye muscles are attached. [*Sclera* comes from a Greek word for "hard" or "stiff."]

scoria A porous, cinderlike rock. Scoria forms from lava that trapped bubbles of steam within it as it hardened. Also slag. [*Scoria* comes from a Greek word for "manure" or "dung."]

screw An inclined plane wrapped around a cylinder. It usually fits into or makes a threaded hole and is used as a fastener.

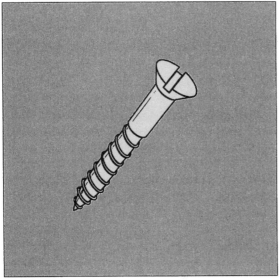

screw

scurvy A disease of the skin caused by a deficiency of Vitamin C. Vitamin C is found in fresh fruits and vegetables, in particular, citrus fruits. In the past, sailors sometimes suffered from scurvy because fresh fruits or vegetables were not available for months at a time.

sea The ocean, the great mass of saltwater that covers almost three fourths of Earth's surface. Also, a large body of water, somewhat smaller than an ocean, usually surrounded almost entirely by land, such as the Mediterranean Sea.

sea level The surface of the sea halfway between high and low tides. Sea level is used to compare the heights or depths of mountains, hills, plains, valleys, and the ocean depths.

Seaborg, Glenn Theodore (1912–1999) A United States chemist and physicist who shared the 1951 Nobel Prize for chemistry (with Edwin M. McMillan) for research on transuranium elements. He and his group of scientists discovered the elements plutonium, americium, curium, berkelium, californium, einsteinium, fermium, mendelevium, and nobelium.

Seaborg, Glenn Theodore

season A regularly recurring period or division of the year, especially spring, summer, autumn, and winter. Each season in a particular place has a certain general kind of weather or climate. In many temperate zones for example, summer is usually warm and fairly dry while winter is usually cold and wet. Astronomically, each season begins at either a solstice or an equinox, but the actual climate changes may take place earlier or later each year. Some tropical parts of the world seem to have only two seasons: a rainy season and a dry season. [*Season* comes from a Latin word that describes the act of planting or sowing.]

seaweed Any of many different kinds of plants that grow in the sea. Most kinds of seaweed are saltwater algae. Seaweed can be red, brown, green, or a combination of colors.

sebaceous gland One of the many glands in the skin. In mammals, it secretes oil into the hair follicles.

second A unit of measurement of time equal to 1/86,400 part of a solar day (1/60 of a minute, 1/3600 pf an hour). A second is now officially measured using atomic radiation. This is accurate to one second in 5,000 years, several hundred times more accurate than astronomical measurements or mechanical instruments. [*Second* comes from a Latin word for things that follow each other in sequence.]

secretion A substance that is formed by a gland or cell from materials supplied by the blood. Secretions perform specific functions or have certain effects. For example, saliva is a secretion formed by the salivary glands in the mouth. Body secretions include tears, sweat, mucus, and bile and other digestive juices. Other kinds of secretions called hormones are formed by ductless glands and carried to the blood. [*Secretion* comes from a Latin word meaning "to separate or remove."]

section A slice of tissue or mineral cut thin so that light can pass through it and it can be easily examined under a microscope. [*Section* comes from a Latin word meaning "to cut or divide."]

sediment Earth, silt, rocks, and other natural materials that have been deposited by water, wind, or ice. [*Sediment* comes from the Latin word meaning "to settle" or "to sink."]

sedimentary Describing a kind of rock formed by mineral particles, bits of older rocks, and other kinds of natural materials depos-

ited over time by oceans, rivers, or glaciers. Sandstone and shale are two common kinds of sedimentary rock.

sedimentation The process of depositing minerals and other natural materials

seed (n.) The ripened, fertilized ovule of a plant from which a new plant may grow under the right conditions of warmth and moisture. A seed consists of an embryo; a tough, protective seed coat; and stored food. Also, the seedlike part of certain fruits such as strawberries and raspberries.

seed (v.) To scatter crystals or chemicals. Silver iodine or dry ice is seeded into a cloud in an attempt to produce rain.

seed plant Any of a large group of plants that bears seeds and has either flowers or cones. Roses and daffodils are flowering seed plants; pines and firs are cone-bearing seed plants.

seedling A young plant grown from a seed. Also, a young tree less than three feet tall.

segment In biology, one of the sections or parts into which an organism is divided. Segments are easily seen in earthworms and insects.

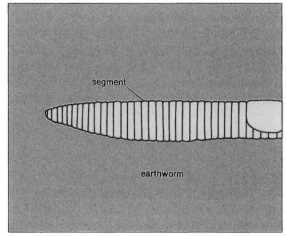

segment

seismic Having to do with earthquakes or other movements of the earth's crust. Seismic waves are waves of motion in the ground produced by earthquakes. [*Seismic* comes from a Greek word meaning "to shake."]

seismograph An instrument used to record seismic waves in the earth's crust, especially those from an earthquake.

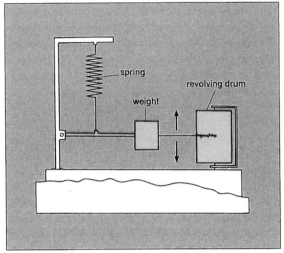

seismograph

seismology The scientific study of earthquakes and other movements of the earth's crust.

selenium An element that exists in several different forms. It is used to make photocells, solar cells, and semiconductors. Selenium has an atomic number of 34 and an atomic weight of 78.96. Its chemical symbol is Se.

semen The fluid, normally containing sperm cells, that is produced in the male reproductive organs. [*Semen* is a Latin word meaning "a seed" or "something that is planted."]

semicircular canal Any one of three curved tubes, filled with fluid and lined with hairs and nerve endings, found in the inner ear. The semicircular canals help to maintain balance by monitoring head movements and relaying the information along nerves to the brain.

semiconductor A substance such as silicon or germanium whose electrical conductivity is less than that of metals and greater than that of insulators. Semiconductors are the basic materials of transistors and integrated circuits, which are the building blocks of modern computers and many other electronic devices.

semipermeable Allowing some material to pass through but not others; usually applied to thin layers of tissue or protoplasm, such as membranes. Sometimes called a selective membrane or differentially permeable. Cell membranes are semipermeable.

Semmelweiss, Ignaz Philip (1818–1865) A Hungarian physician who first insisted that doctors in hospitals wash their hands before they examine patients.

sense Any of the ways in which stimuli from outside or inside an organism are received and recognized by the organism. Sight, touch, hearing, taste, and smell are the principal senses in most animals. [*Sense* comes from a Latin word meaning "to recognize something or become aware of it."]

sensitive Able to respond to stimulus from some outside source. The eye is sensitive to light. The skin is sensitive to touch and temperature. Plant roots are sensitive to gravity and water; plant leaves are sensitive to light.

sensor A device that receives or detects an object or a stimulus such as heat, light, or sound. Sensors are used in automatic fire alarms, automatic doors, heart monitors, and a host of other applications.

sensory Having to do with sensations or the senses. The eyes, ears, and nose are sensory organs. A sensory nerve picks up sensations and sends a message to a nerve center such as the spinal cord or the brain.

sepal One of the leaflike parts of a flower. Sepals are usually green; they cover and protect the unopened bud.

septic Infected by or containing bacteria or viruses or something that causes infection. A septic tank is a sewage disposal container in which wastes are decomposed by bacteria.

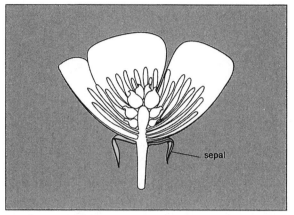

sepal

septum A dividing wall or partition that separates cavities or tissues in an organism. The ventricles of the heart are separated by a septum. Between the nostrils is a septum. [*Septum* is a Latin word meaning "a barrier or partition."]

series 1. CHEMISTRY. A group of similar or related compounds. Also, a group of elements in a period in the periodic table of elements. 2. PHYSICS. A type of electric circuit that has a single conducting path and all of whose parts are joined one after another. 3. BIOLOGY. A sequence of events that happen one after another, such as the changes that occur during the life cycle of an insect as it changes from egg to larva to pupa to adult. [*Series* is a Latin word meaning "a line or procession."]

serum 1. The clear, pale-yellow liquid that separates from blood as it clots. Serum is the plasma of the blood minus the clotting factors, which were used up as the blood clotted. 2. A liquid substance used to prevent or cure a disease, usually made from the blood of an animal that has been made immune to the disease; for example, tetanus antitoxin is a serum. 3. Any watery substance found in an animal or plant.

sewage Liquid and semisolid waste materials from factories and houses. Sewage is carried away through drains and sewers, usually treated to eliminate harmful substances, and then discharged into the ground, rivers, lakes, or oceans. Dumping large amounts of untreated sewage into rivers or lakes pollutes the water.

sex 1. Either of the two divisions, male and female, into which most species of animals are divided on the basis of their reproductive functions. 2. Either of similar divisions in some species of plants having male or female organs and functions. 3. The uniting of a sperm and an egg.

sex-linked characteristics A trait, such as color blindness or hemophilia, which is caused by genes located on the chromosomes that determine sex.

sextant An instrument used to determine the altitude of the sun or of a star above the horizon. A sextant is used in navigation to plot the position of a ship. [*Sextant* comes from a Latin word meaning "six"; the arc of a sextant is one sixth of a circle.]

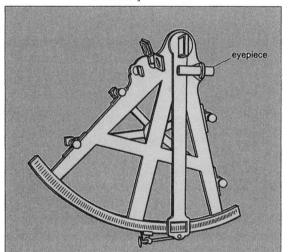

sextant

sexual reproduction A kind of biological reproduction in which animals or plants produce offspring of their species by the union of male and female sex cells called gametes, which results in a combined cell called a zygote.

shadow The dark shape cast by an object when it blocks light falling on a surface. The dark, central part of the shadow is called the umbra; the surrounding area of partial shadow is called the penumbra.

shale A soft, fine-grained sedimentary rock formed from hardened particles of clay, mud, or silt. Shale is the most common kind of rock found beneath the sea. It is formed in thin layers that split easily. Depending upon their sources and composition, shales can be black, red, or other colors. Under extremes of pressure over long periods of time, shale turns into slate.

Shapley, Harlow (1885–1972) A United States astronomer who made the first reasonably accurate estimate of the structure and size of the Milky Way galaxy.

Shapley, Harlow

shelf In earth science, a ledge of land or rock, especially a submerged ledge such as the continental shelf.

shell 1. ZOOLOGY. The hard or leathery outer covering of certain animals, such as clams and other mollusks, beetles and other insects, lobsters and other crustaceans, and some other animals such as turtles. Also, the hard outside covering of some eggs. 2. BOTANY. The hard outside covering of a nut or seed. 3. GEOLOGY. A hard, thin layer of rock such as the earth's crust. 4. PHYSICS, CHEMISTRY. The patterns of electrons that surround the nucleus of an atom. Electrons are grouped in various "shells" around the nucleus. Each shell holds a certain maximum number of electrons.

shellfish A water animal with a shell, especially a mollusk such as a clam or a crustacean such as a lobster that is used for food. A shellfish is not really a fish, because it lacks a backbone.

shellfish

shoal 1. GEOLOGY. A sandbank or ledge of rock that makes the water shallow and that can be seen at low tide. 2. ZOOLOGY. A large number of fish swimming together in a group, also called a school.

shock 1. A medical condition that sometimes results from an injury. Heavy blood loss, a severe burn with plasma loss, or heart failure can result in the symptoms of shock, which include low blood pressure, faintness, clammy skin, and mental confusion. 2. The effect of an electric current passing through the body.

shock wave A sudden violent compression disturbance, especially in air or water, produced by a sudden change in pressure, such as an explosion or an aircraft moving at a supersonic speed.

shooting star A common term for a meteor, especially one seen plummeting through the night sky. The term is inaccurate because a meteor is a chunk of rock blazing as a result of friction with Earth's atmosphere—it is not a star.

shore The place where land and water meet.

short circuit An accidental defect in an electrical circuit that occurs when the current flows along a path of low resistance. This may result in a very high current flow that can melt wires or set fire to flammable substances nearby. A fuse or circuit breaker present in the system will automatically disconnect the electric power when a short circuit occurs.

short wave A radio signal of shorter wavelength than those used in commercial radio broadcasting. Short-wave frequencies are used for a variety of purposes, including two-way "citizen's band" radio.

shrub A woody perennial plant smaller than a tree, usually with many stems starting near the ground. Shrubs are common in forests and along streams and ponds, and are often planted around houses.

shutter In photography, a device that opens and closes rapidly, allowing light to fall for an instant on a light sensitive electronic sensor or film in a camera that captures an image.

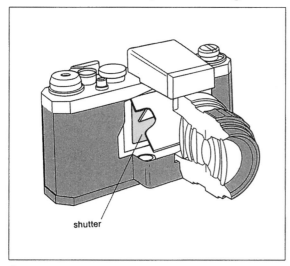
shutter

shutter

sial The granitelike rock that makes up the upper portion of the earth's crust. Sial gets its name from the *si*licon and *al*uminum compounds of which it is made.

Siamese twins Twins that are physically joined at some part of their bodies at birth. Surgery can separate such twins if no vital organ is shared.

sidereal time Time measured by the relationship of stars to Earth. A sidereal day is one rotation of Earth in reference to any star and is about four minutes shorter than a solar day, which is more commonly used.

siderite 1. GEOLOGY. A brown or grayish-green iron-bearing mineral often found in sedimentary rocks. Siderite is a major iron ore. 2. ASTRONOMY. A meteor made of stone and iron. [*Siderite* comes from a Greek word meaning "iron."]

sight The sense by which animals can detect or identify objects or lights with the eye. Also, the process by which the position, shape, color, and brightness of something is perceived.

silica Silicon dioxide. Quartz and sand are composed of silica. A very common mineral, silica is used to make glass, ceramics, concrete, and other industrial products.

silicon A common chemical element that usually occurs as a compound with oxygen. Next to oxygen, silicon is the most abundant element in the earth's crust. Crystals of silicon are used to make electronic parts (including computer chips), solar cells, and integrated circuits of all kinds. Silicon has an atomic number of 14 and an atomic weight of 28.086. Its chemical symbol is Si.

silicone Any of a group of substances used for lubricants, rubberlike plastics, insulators, and other industrial purposes. Silicones are synthetic compounds containing silicon, carbon, hydrogen, and oxygen. They are resistant to water and stable when heated.

silk A fine, soft natural fiber produced by insects and spiders to make cocoons and webs. Silk made into textiles comes from the cocoons of the silkworm, the larval stage of a kind of moth.

silt Fine particles of soil that are larger than clay and smaller than sand and are carried by moving water and deposited as a part of sediment.

Silurian Period The third period of the Paleozoic era, about 440 to 400 million years ago. The Silurian was characterized by the development of early invertebrate land animals and the first land plants. Armored, jawless fish were common in the seas, and trilobites declined in number. The lamprey and the hagfish trace their ancestry back to the jawless fish of the Silurian Period.

silver A shiny, white metallic element that is soft, very malleable, and very ductile. Silver is an excellent conductor of heat and electricity. It is used in electrical circuits, dental alloys, and storage batteries, and for ornaments, tableware, and jewelry. Silver salts are used in photographic film. Silver occurs in nature as a pure metal and in ores combined with copper, lead, or zinc. Silver has an atomic number of 47 and an atomic weight of 107.868. Its chemical symbol is Ag.

sima The basaltic rocks that form the lower part of the earth's crust. Sima forms the rocks at the bottom of the oceans, below the sial layer. It is mainly composed of the *si*lica and *ma*gnesium for which it is named.

sink (n.) In physics, a means of removing energy or a substance from a place. The polar caps are heat sinks because they absorb heat from the surrounding atmosphere.

sink (v.) 1. To go beneath the surface of a liquid or quicksand. 2. To drill a hole or a well in the ground.

sinkhole In geology, any hole or funnel-shaped cavity in the ground. A sinkhole forms when groundwater or rain dissolves underground limestone, causing a collapse at the surface.

sinus 1. ANATOMY. A small cavity or hollow in bone, especially an air cavity that opens into the nose in the bony skull of a mammal. 2. BOTANY. A curve or margin between two lobes of a leaf.

siphon 1. PHYSICS, CHEMISTRY. A bent tube of glass or plastic that uses atmospheric pressure to transfer fluids from one container into a lower container. When the surfaces of the fluid are the same level in both containers, the flow stops. 2. ZOOLOGY. A tube-shaped organ in certain shellfish that draws in and expels water. The water washes over the animal's gills, bringing fresh oxygen.

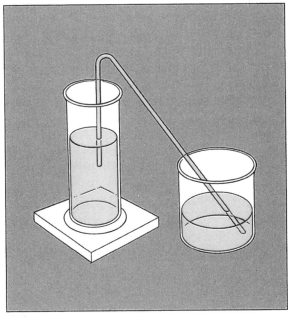

siphon

Sirius The brightest star (not a planet) in the night sky. Sometimes called the Dog Star, it is located in the constellation Canis Major (the Big Dog). Sirius is really a double star, the larger of which is twice the size of the sun. The smaller of the two (called "the Pup") is a small, dim star that was the first to be recognized as a white dwarf star.

sirocco A very hot, dry wind that blows from the northern coast of Africa across the Mediterranean, picking up moisture and blowing warm and moist air across southern Europe. [*Sirocco* is an Italian word derived from the Arabic word meaning "east" which was where the wind was believed to come from.]

skeleton 1. In vertebrates, an internal bony framework that supports and protects the soft organs and tissues of the body. Also called an endoskeleton. 2. In some invertebrates, as external hard covering such as the shell of a mollusk or the chitin covering of crustaceans. Also called an exoskeleton. [*Skeleton* comes from a Greek word meaning "withered" or "dried up."]

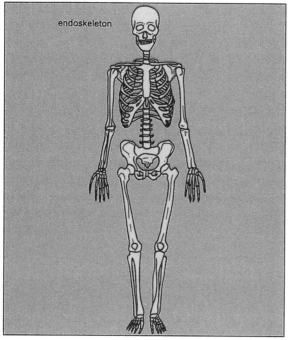

skeleton

skin The soft and flexible tissue covering of a human or animal body. The skin often bears scales, hair, or feathers. It consists of an outer layer of waterproof cells called the epidermis and a thicker, inner layer called the dermis. The skin is the largest organ in the body and contains many different kinds of glands, nerve endings, and blood vessels

skull The bony framework of the head in humans and other vertebrates. The skull encloses and protects the brain. It has small openings for blood vessels, nerves, the spinal cord, and other facial structures. In humans, the skull is usually divided into three main sections: the cranium, the face, and the lower jaw or mandible.

slag The waste that is formed as the upper, molten layer when metal ores are refined in a furnace. Some solidified slag is used to build roads; other kinds are used as fertilizer and as insulating materials.

slate A dark, bluish-gray rock that splits easily into thin, smooth layers or plates. Slate is a hard rock that is used to make roofing tiles and for other construction uses. Slate is formed when shale is subjected to great pressure.

sleet Small ice pellets formed when rain drops freeze before they hit the ground. A mixture of rain and snow is also often called sleet.

small intestine The part of the digestive system between the stomach and the large intestine, in which digestion is completed by the action of enzymes, and food nutrients are absorbed into the blood. In humans, the small intestine is a narrow, coiled tube about 20 feet long and consists or three sections: the duodenum, the jejunum, and the ileum.

smell The sense by which animals can detect or identify a substance by its scent or odor. In humans and other mammals, the nose is the organ of smell. Certain animals such as lions and wolves depend mainly upon the sense of smell to locate their prey and otherwise orient themselves to their surroundings. Humans depend more upon the sense of sight to locate objects.

smelting A process of obtaining a metal from its ore by heating the ore with coke—a form of carbon—or other materials to a high temperature in a furnace.

smog A kind of air pollution formed by a combination of smoke, chemicals, and fog. Smog is usually found in cities or industrial areas where there are many automobiles and factories. Smog is a combination of *smo*ke and f*og*.

snake A legless reptile with a narrow body that may be as short as a finger or as long as a bus. Like other reptiles, snakes have backbones and scaly skins and are cold-blooded. Snakes need warm surroundings in order to be active. For this reason, snakes live mainly in warm areas of the world or in places that are warm for part of the year. Most snakes line on land, but some live in the oceans or in lakes and ponds.

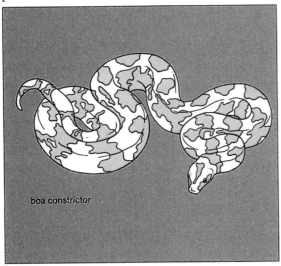

snake

snow Soft, white ice crystals that form from water vapor in the air and then fall to the ground as snowflakes. Snow often spreads as a layer over the ground and may last for minutes, days or longer depending upon the air temperature. Fresh snow is full of air and is a good insulator, protecting plants from severe cold.

snowflake A crystal of snow. Snowflakes may take many different shapes of great beauty. Large snowflakes are formed by the combination of smaller flakes, usually at temperatures at or near freezing. Snowflakes are usually six sided because of the arrangement of hydrogen and oxygen atoms in the crystal. Small flakes form at colder temperatures. On the ground, snowflakes lose their structure and become grainy.

soap A substance that dissolves in water and is used as a cleaning agent. Soap cleans because one end of its molecule attaches to grease and dirt particles and the other end of the molecule makes the dirt particles soluble

in water. Rinsing with water loosens the dirt and washes it away. Soap is made by heating a fat or oil with an alkali such as caustic soda. Soap has been used for hundreds of years, first as a medicine and since the second century as a cleaner.

soapstone A kind of soft metamorphic rock composed mainly of the mineral talc.

social Living in a group or colony in an organized way. Bees, ants, and termites are social insects. Wolves and prairie dogs are social animals. Humans are also social.

socket 1. ANATOMY. In vertebrates, a hollow place into which a part of the body fits and, usually, moves. Eyes and teeth are set into sockets. The hip joint is a ball of bone set into a socket in another bone. 2. ENGINEERING. A hollow part into which something fits, such as an electric socket into which the prongs of a plug fit.

soda Any of various chemicals containing sodium, such as baking soda (sodium bicarbonate).

sodium A soft, chemically active, silvery-white metallic element. Sodium occurs naturally only in compounds. Sodium is the sixth most common element found on Earth, most often found in sodium chloride, which is common table salt. Sodium has an atomic number of 11 and an atomic weight of 22.9898. Its chemical symbol is Na.

soft water Water that contains few dissolved minerals such as magnesium or calcium salts and easily lathers with soap.

software The nonhardware elements used in electronic computing, particularly the programs.

soil The thin, top part of the earth's crust, composed of rock and mineral particles and, in the upper layers, mixed with decaying animal and plant matter called humus. Growing plants take water and minerals from the soil. Soil is essential to much of the life found on Earth. Soils are affected by climate and weather, by the organisms that live in them, by groundwater, by age, and by other factors. Between the topsoil and the bedrock is a layer called the subsoil, which generally has little or no humus and is not very good for plant growth. There are many different types of soils, ranging from heavy clay soils with little humus to light sandy soils with large amounts of organic materials.

solar   Having to do with or coming from the sun.

solar cell   A device used to change the sun's radiant energy into electrical energy. Solar sells are used to power artificial satellites and to provide some energy for electric cars. Solar cells are now being used to heat homes and provide hot water.

solar energy   The energy given off by the sun in the form of electromagnetic radiation. Solar energy heats the Earth and makes it livable. Solar energy is usually collected by solar panels that transform the sun's light energy into electrical energy that is then used to power electrical devices of all kinds. Only a tiny fraction of the available solar energy falling on Earth is being used.

solar system   The sun and all the planets, moons, comets, asteroids, and other objects that revolve around it. The solar system is bound together in space by the sun's enormous gravitational force.

solenoid   A coil of wire surrounding a movable iron core. When a current passes through the wire, it becomes a magnet and the core moves, opening or closing an electric circuit. Solenoids are used in circuit breakers, electric starter motors, and electric buzzers and bells. [*Solenoid* comes from a Greek word meaning "a tube or hollow pipe."]

solid   One of the three physical states of matter; the others are liquid and gas. Solids have a definite size and shape that can be changed by a force. Most inorganic solids have a crystalline structure and can be melted by heat to a definite temperature, at which they become liquids; a liquid becomes a solid when it freezes. Some solids, such as glass, melt over a wide temperature range and are not crystalline. Others, such as "dry ice" (solid carbon dioxide), go directly from the solid to the gaseous state, a process called subliming.

solid-state physics   A branch of science that deals with the properties of solid materials. Most often, this term refers to the study of transistors and other semiconductor electronic devices. Recently, another term for this has come into use: condensed-matter physics.

solidify   To make or become a solid. Water will solidify into ice when cooled below its freezing point.

solstice   The time of year when the sun reaches its most northerly or southerly position in the sky. In the Northern Hemisphere the summer solstice, June 21 or 22, is the longest day of the year, and the winter solstice, December 21 or 22, is the shortest. In the Southern Hemisphere, the dates are the same but the solstices are reversed. [*Solstice* comes from Latin words meaning "sun" and "standstill."]

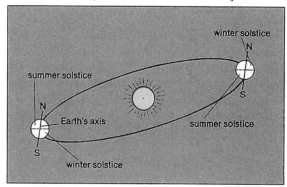

solstice

soluble   Describing a substance that can be dissolved. Sugar is soluble in water.

solute   A substance that is dissolved, usually in water or another liquid, to form a solution. Salt is a solute in seawater.

sonar *S*ound *N*avigation *A*nd *R*anging. An echo technique used at sea for detecting and determining the position of underwater objects such as submarines, shoals of fish or the ocean bottom. Sonar works by sending out a high-pitched sound pulse and then timing the returning echo.

sonic Having to do with sound waves.

sound 1. PHYSIOLOGY. The sensation produced in hearing organs by vibrations traveling through the air, water, or some other substance. 2. PHYSICS. Mechanical (movement) vibrations that travel through the air or some other substance. Sound can be detected by an instrument, or by an observer who hears the sensation it produces. All sounds are produced by a vibrating object of some kind. Sound travels in waves as it moves through a substance. There is no sound in outer space.

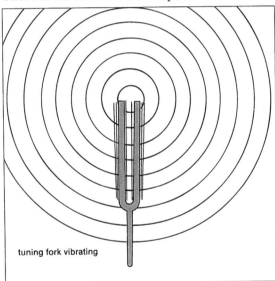

tuning fork vibrating

sound

South Pole The point on Earth's surface that is the southern end of the Earth's axis, 90° south. All directions from the South Pole are north. Also called the south geographic pole, it lies in the middle of the continent of Antarctica. The south magnetic pole is the point on the Earth's surface toward which the southern end of a compass points. It is about 1,500 miles north of the south geographic pole.

south pole In physics, the pole of a magnet that points to the south magnetic pole of Earth. Also called the south-seeking pole of a magnet.

space 1. ASTRONOMY. The part of the universe that lies beyond Earth's atmosphere. In the solar system, it may be called interplanetary space; beyond the solar system, it may be called interstellar space, and between galaxies it may be called intergalactic space. 2. PHYSICS. The three-dimensional volume in which matter exists.

space shuttle The United States space program that features an orbiting spacecraft that carries the crew and payload. The spacecraft is lifted into orbit by external rockets, which are then shed. After its mission, the spacecraft reenters the atmosphere and lands like a glider. It is then used again for further flights. The external rockets are also recovered and reused.

spacecraft Any craft designed to travel in space. An artificial satellite or an orbiter is a spacecraft that orbits Earth. A space probe or spaceship is a spacecraft that travels into interplanetary or interstellar space.

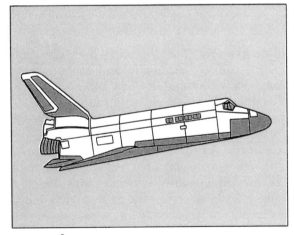

spacecraft

Spallanzani, Lazzaro (1729–1799) An Italian biologist who disproved the theory that life appeared spontaneously from decaying substances (spontaneous generation). In a series of experiments, Spallanzani showed that spontaneous generation of organisms does not take place in bottles of food materials that were boiled and then tightly closed. He suggested preserving food by boiling it and then sealing it in airtight containers.

spam Unsolicited advertising or other messages that are sent to many people on their e-mail accounts as well as instant messaging and text messaging on cellular telephones. Often called junk mail, spam messages have grown to become a major problem all over the world.

spark 1. An electric discharge into a gas such as air. Spark plugs produce sparks that ignite the fuel in a gasoline engine. Lightning is a huge spark. 2. A glowing particle of material thrown out by a fire.

spawn 1. ZOOLOGY. The eggs of aquatic animals such as fish, frogs, and salamanders that are laid directly into water. Also, the young newly hatched from these eggs. 2. BOTANY. The tangled clump of underground threads, also called mycelium, from which mushrooms grow. [*Spawn* comes from a Latin word meaning "to spill" or "to pour out."]

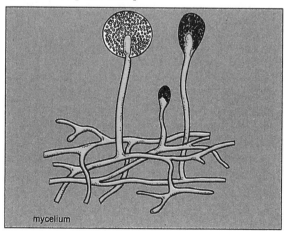

spawn

species The basic unit of the classification of living things, a division of a genus. A species is a group of similar organisms that can interbreed in nature and produce fully fertile offspring. A species usually cannot interbreed successfully with another species. Wheat and rice are species of grass. Tigers and lions are species of cats.

specific gravity The ratio of the weight of an object to the weight of the same volume of water. Substances with a specific gravity of less than one will float in water; those with a specific gravity that is greater than one will sink.

specimen 1. One of a group of objects taken as an example to show what others in the group are like. For example, a geologist might collect specimens of the different rocks in an area. 2. A small sample of something to be tested or examined. For example, doctors take a specimen of blood to help determine the health of a patient. [*Specimen* is a Latin word meaning "model" or "example" of something.]

spectroscopy The scientific technique that deals with the production and examination of the spectrum of a ray of light from any star or any incandescent source. Spectroscopy is used to determine the composition of the source of the ray. It is an essential tool for astronomers, chemists, and physicists.

spectrum 1. The band of colors seen when a beam of light is broken up as it passes through a prism or by some other means. The main colors of the spectrum of white light are red, orange, yellow, green, blue, indigo, and violet. A rainbow, which is produced when light passes through water droplets in the air, has all the

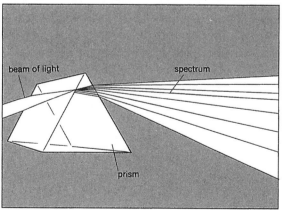

spectrum

colors of the spectrum. 2. The whole range of electromagnetic waves, including gamma rays, light rays, radio waves, and X-rays. [*Spectrum* comes from a Latin word meaning "to see" or "to observe."]

speech The ability to speak. Humans are the only creatures we know can communicate complex ideas through speech.

speech recognition The process of converting spoken words as captured by a microphone or cell phone to a set of electronic commands or text. Speech recognition programs or applications include using voice commands such as "call home" or "navigate to an address."

speed The rate at which something moves, measured in units of distance per intervals of time, such as miles or kilometers per hour and feet or meters per second.

sperm A male reproductive cell, also called a spermatozoon. A sperm cell is usually microscopic and is able to move by means of a whiplike tail called a flagellum. [*Sperm* comes from a Greek word meaning "seed."]

spider One of a class of small animals with a body divided into two parts (head and thorax), four pairs of jointed legs, usually eight simple eyes, and no antennae. Most spiders live on land and usually spin webs to catch insects for food.

spinal column The backbone; also called spine, or vertebral column. A flexible column of small bones (vertebrae) in the body of a human or other vertebrate. The spinal column stretches along the center of the back and tendons in the back. It encloses and protects the spinal cord.

spinal cord An important part of the nervous system in vertebrates. A thick, white bundle of nerve tissues running through the spinal column and connecting the brain to pairs of nerves that branch off through openings between the vertebrae to various parts of the body. The spinal cord is important in reflex actions.

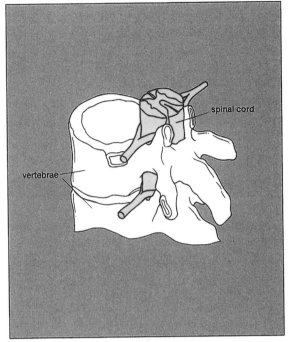

spinal cord

spinneret An organ by which spiders and some kinds of insect larvae such as silkworms spin threads for webs or cocoons.

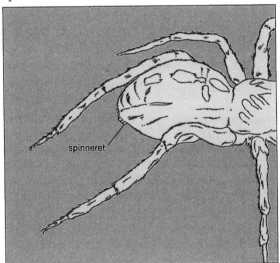

spinneret

spleen An organ near the stomach or intestines in humans and most vertebrates. The spleen stores blood, breaks down old red blood cells, and helps filter foreign substances from the blood.

spore A tiny reproductive body, usually one-celled, produced in great numbers particularly by flowerless plants such as ferns and algae, and by molds and other fungi, and also by some kinds of protozoa. Under the right conditions, a single spore is capable of growing into a new organism, much as a seed can. Spores are hardy and can often survive for many years. Spores are the reproductive agents of asexual (one-parent) reproduction; seeds contain both male and female gametes. [*Spore* comes from a Greek word meaning "planting or scattering seed."]

spring 1. ASTRONOMY. The three-month-long season between the vernal equinox and the summer solstice. Spring is often the season of flowering and new growth in plants, and the birth of young in animals. 2. GEOLOGY. The source of a stream flowing naturally out of the ground. 3. PHYSICS, TECHNOLOGY. An elastic device usually made of either a coiled metal strip, called a spiral spring, or a curved bar, called a leaf spring. A compressed spring will return to its original shape or position when the pressure acting on it is removed. Springs are used in mechanical clocks and watches, car suspensions, spring scales, and many other mechanical devices.

spring tide The very high and very low ocean tide combination that comes twice a month, at the time of the new moon and the full moon. At spring tide the sun, moon, and Earth are lined up with each other.

spur 1. EARTH SCIENCE. A high ridge of land that extends at an angle from a mountain or mountain range. 2. BOTANY. A slender, usually hollow, petal found in some plants such as columbine. Also, a short branch or shoot of a tree. 3. ZOOLOGY. A sharp spike on the legs of some kinds of birds.

stability 1. PHYSICS. The property of being balanced and not easily upset or knocked over. Stability is important in chairs, tables, and automobiles. 2. CHEMISTRY, PHYSICS. A property of a compound of being not easily broken down or combined with other compounds. Water has great stability; hydrochloric acid does not.

stable 1. PHYSICS. Able to remain in the same condition unless changed by some outside force. A stable automobile stays on the road even when making sharp turns. A stable element does not show radioactive decay. 2. CHEMISTRY. A substance that is not easily decomposed.

stalactite A rocky structure, shaped like an icicle that grows downward from the roof of a limestone cave. Stalactites are formed by steeping water that contains calcium carbonate (lime). As each drop of water evaporates, the lime remains behind, and a solid accumulation of limestone grows larger and larger. If the water drips down before it evaporates, it contributes to a stalagmite below.

stalagmite A rocky structure, often shaped like a cone, which grows upward from the floor of a limestone cave. A stalagmite forms when limestone-bearing water dripping from a stalactite strikes the floor and then evaporates, leaving a tiny deposit of lime. Each drop leaves another deposit and the stalagmite grows upward, sometimes joining the stalactite above to form a solid column from floor to ceiling.

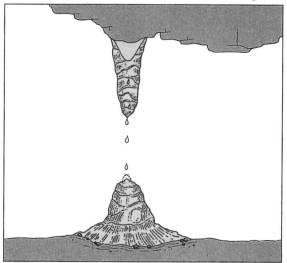

stalagmite

stalk 1. BOTANY. The main part of the plant that grows upward from the root. Also, a similar plant structure that usually supports a leaf or a flower. 2. ZOOLOGY. A stemlike structure that supports an animal organ. The eyes of lobsters and crabs are on stalks.

stamen The male part of a flower that produces pollen. A stamen is a slender stalk with an anther (a pollen sac) at its top. The stamen is usually surrounded by the petals of the flower.

standard time The time that is adopted in a country or in a state or region of a country. Although the lines are adjusted to accommodate political divisions such as state borders, in general, standard time is figured from the nearest line of longitude that is exactly divisible by 15 degrees, east or west of Greenwich, England. Each 15 degrees marks a time difference of one hour, for a total of 24 standard time zones around the world. In a few places, the standard time differs from other places nearby by ½ hour.

star A large, luminous body in space made up of very hot, glowing gases, mainly hydrogen and helium. The sun is the closest star to Earth. Other stars appear only as tiny pinpoints of light in the night sky because they are so distant from us.

starch A food substance with no taste or small that is found in potatoes, grains, beans, and other vegetables. Starch is a complex carbohydrate.

state The condition of a substance, such as the physical state of matter: solid, liquid, or gas.

static (adj.) 1. A discharge of electrical energy in the atmosphere—such as lightning—that interferes with radio or television reception. 2. An electric charge, caused by friction, which builds up on the surface of an object. You can feel the discharge of static electricity when you touch a metal object after walking across a nylon rug. [*Static* comes from a Greek word meaning "standstill" or "rest."]

steam Water in the form of a vapor or gas.

Boiling water produces steam. When the molecules of water vapor cool and join together to produce water droplets, steam becomes visible.

steam engine The first important heat engine used in industry and transport. First invented by Thomas Newcomen in 1712 and improved upon by James Watt in 1796, the steam engine uses steam under pressure to drive a piston that turns a wheel. In the twentieth century, the steam engine has been largely displaced by the internal combustion engine.

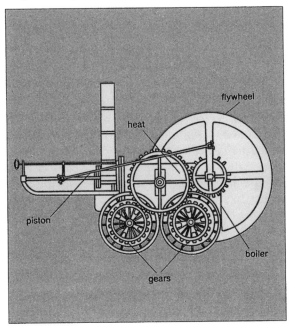

steam engine

steel A metal alloy of iron with small amounts of carbon and traces of other elements. Steel is used in the manufacture of cars, construction materials, machinery, tools, and many other things. Steel is far stronger than iron, and steel manufacturing is one of the world's chief industries.

stellar Having to do with a star or stars.

stem The main stalk of a tree, shrub, or other plant that bears leaves. The stem supports the branches, flowers, and fruits. The stem carries water and dissolved nutrients up from the roots to other parts of the plant, and carries food substances downward from the leaves. Also, a similar part of a plant that grows underground.

stem cell A kind of undifferentiated cell that is able to change into a specialized cell such as skin, muscle or bone cell. Stem cells are found in all kinds of multi-celled living things. In adults, stem cells act to repair damage to the other cells in the body. In human embryos, stem cells transform into other kinds of cells during growth. Stem cells can now be grown and are used in medicine in various ways.

steppe A large stretch of treeless grasslands, similar to the prairies of North America, that is found in Europe and Asia. [*Steppe* is a Russian word for this kind of terrain.]

sterile 1. BIOLOGY. Free of bacteria and other microorganisms. 2. PHYSIOLOGY, BOTANY. Not able to produce offspring.

sterilization 1. BIOLOGY. A technique used to kill or remove all microorganisms by heating or treatment with chemicals. 2. PHYSIOLOGY, BOTANY. Making an animal or plant incapable of reproduction.

sternum In most vertebrates other than snakes and fishes, a long bone or bones extending along the front midline of the trunk and connecting with the ribs.

stethoscope An instrument used in medicine for listening to the heartbeat, lungs, and

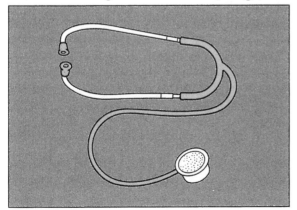

stethoscope

other sounds from within the body. [*Stethoscope* comes from a Greek word meaning "the chest" and "to examine and observe."]

stigma The part of a pistil in a flower that receives the pollen grains during pollination. [*Stigma* is a Greek word meaning "a tattoo" or "a mark made by a brand."]

stimulate 1. BIOLOGY. To cause an animal or plant to respond to stimulation of a sense organ or receptor. For example, light stimulates a green plant to grow towards it. Also, to make a living thing, or a part of a living thing, more active by changing its surroundings in some way. For example, a muscle contracts when stimulated by electricity or pressure. 2. PHYSICS. To use energy to induce a change in a physical system. For example, lasers operate by stimulated emission of radiation.

stimulus Something that excites or causes a living organism, or part of an organism, to respond—that is, to do something, such as to move or grow in a particular direction. [*Stimulus* is a Latin word meaning something that stings or pricks, causing continual discomfort.]

sting 1. ZOOLOGY. A sharp, pointed part of an insect or other animal that pricks and injects a poison or some irritating substance. Bees and hornets have stings. Also called a stinger. 2. BOTANY. A fine, stiff hair found on certain plants, such as the nettle, that contains a substance that causes irritation when touched.

stoma One of the many tiny openings found in the outer cell layer on the undersides of leaves and some plant stems. Also called stomate; the plural is stomata. [*Stoma* comes from a Greek word meaning "mouth."]

stomach A hollow organ that is part of the digestive system in vertebrates. It serves as a receptacle for food and a place where digestion begins. In humans, the stomach is a large, muscular part of the alimentary canal between the gullet and the small intestine. The lining of the stomach contains glands that secrete gastric juices and hydrochloric acid, which begins to digest food. In invertebrates, any part of the body able to digest food.

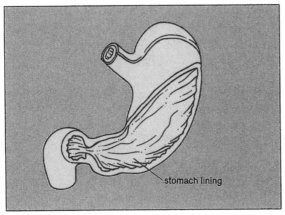

stomach

stone 1. GEOLOGY. A small piece or fragment of a rock. In industry, stones are the pieces of rocks, such as limestone or granite, used to construct roads and buildings. In gemology, a stone is a precious or semiprecious jewel. 2. BOTANY. A hard seed of a soft, pulpy fruit such as a peach or a plum.

storm A strong wind, generally accompanied by rain, snow, or hail, and often by lightning and thunder.

strait A narrow channel connecting two large bodies of water, such as the Strait of Magellan,

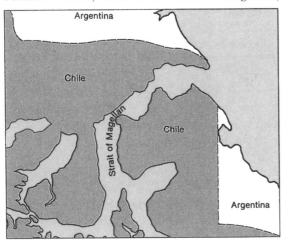

strait

which connects the Atlantic and Pacific Oceans. [*Strait* comes from a Latin word meaning "narrow" or "tightly bound."]

stratosphere The region of the atmosphere in which there is almost no temperature variation and winds blow horizontally, and that lies above the troposphere and below a region called the mesosphere. The stratosphere is between about 12 and 15 miles above sea level. [*Stratosphere* comes from a Latin word meaning "something that is spread out" and a Greek word meaning "a ball or globe."]

stratum 1. A layer of sedimentary rock that is mostly the same kind throughout. The plural is strata. 2. A horizontal region of the atmosphere or of the sea.

stratus A low-lying layer of clouds that spread over a large area, cover the sky, and make a gray day.

stream 1. A natural flow of water along a channel or a bed; a small river or a large brook. 2. A strong, steady current of water within the ocean, such as the Gulf Stream in the North Atlantic Ocean. 2. Any current or flow, such as the bloodstream or a stream of air or electricity, or a prevailing wind such as the jet stream.

streamlined Describing a vehicle such as an aircraft, ship, or automobile that has been designed to move smoothly through a fluid, such as air or water.

streptococcus A type of bacterium responsible for many common ailments, including, in humans, sore throat, tonsillitis, and scarlet fever. [*Streptococcus* comes from Greek words for "twisted" or "chained" and "berry."]

stress The application of forces, such as tension, that tend to cause an object to change its shape or size. Stress is expressed in force per unit of area, such as pounds per square inch or grams per square centimeter. Strain is the alteration of the form of an object caused by stress.

structure 1. BIOLOGY. The arrangement of organs, tissues, and cells of a whole organism; for example, the structure of an insect in its adult stage is different from the structure of the same insect in its larval stage. Also, the arrangement of a part of an organism that has a function, such as the structure of the eye. 2. GEOLOGY. The features and properties of rocks that are the result of faults, or fractures, or due to the type of rock stratum. 3. CHEMISTRY. The way in which the atoms of a molecule are attached to each other, called the chemical structure.

style The long, slim part of a flower pistil, with the ovary at its base and the stigma at its top.

subatomic particle Any of the tiny packets of energy/matter that make up atoms or are produced in nuclear reactions. All atoms and all matter are composed of these elementary particles. The first such particle to be discovered was the electron, and then in 1932 the proton and the neutron were identified. Since then a host of other subatomic particles have been discovered, including many kinds of fermions, quarks, leptons, and bosons.

submarine (adj.) Having to do with the region below the surface of the sea.

submarine (n.) A vessel that is able to travel underwater.

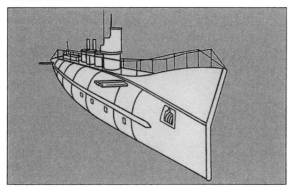

submarine (n.)

subsoil The layer of the soil that lies just under the surface or topsoil. Because it lacks nutrients, subsoil is not good for growing plants.

substance In chemistry, any element or compound. A substance has properties that make it different from other substances, such as its atomic weight or molecular weight and its melting and boiling points. All samples of a substance are the same chemically. Iron, oxygen, and water are all substances.

sucrose Ordinary table sugar made from sugar cane or sugar beets. Sometimes called cane sugar.

sugar A sweet, soluble carbohydrate manufactured by photosynthesis in green plants. There are many different sugars, including sucrose, glucose, and lactose. Table sugar is sucrose.

sulfa A light-yellow, nonmetallic element. Sulfur is highly flammable and burns in air with a blue flame, producing sulfur dioxide, a gas with a strong odor of rotten eggs. Sulfur occurs in nature mainly in volcanic regions in both pure form and in sulfate and sulfide ores. It is used extensively in industry for making matches and gunpowder, for making sulfuric acid, for vulcanizing rubber, as a preservative and bleach, and also in medicine. Sulfur has an atomic number of 16 and an atomic weight of 32.064. Its chemical symbol is S.

sulfa drug Any of several antibiotics first used in 1932 for treating bacterial infections. Sulfa drugs are made in the laboratory, mostly from a substance called sulfanilamide. Their use was a major step forward in medicine, though today they have been replaced by more effective antibiotics.

summer The three-month-long season between spring and autumn. Summer begins in the Northern Hemisphere with the summer solstice on or about June 21, the time when the sun at noon appears highest overhead and farthest north from the horizon; at the same time the Southern Hemisphere experiences the winter solstice, when the sun is lowest in the sky at noon.

sun The star around which the Earth and

the other planets, moons, asteroids, and all the other members of the solar system revolve. The sun is the brightest celestial object and supplies the Earth with heat and light. The sun is a ball of boiling hot gases, mainly hydrogen and helium, with a temperature of millions of degrees at its core. It is like an endless hydrogen bomb explosion with enough fuel to continue shining for another 5 billion years. About 93 million miles (149 million kilometers) from the Earth, the sun is approximately 865,000 miles (1.4 million kilometers) across. That is nearly 600 times bigger than all the planets in the solar system put together. Also, any star like the sun. The other stars seem so much dimmer than the sun because they are so much farther away.

sundial A simple kind of clock that dates back to ancient times. It tells local time according to the shadow cast by an indicator, called gnomon, onto a sunlit dial.

sundial

sunspot One of the dark patches seen on the sun's surface by astronomers from time to time. Sun spots are giant electrical storms on the sun that appear in varying numbers over an eleven-year period called the sunspot cycle. Large numbers of sunspots disturb Earth's magnetic field and interfere with radio, television, and other communications.

superconductivity The ability of some metals and metal alloys to conduct electric currents with virtually no resistance at varying low temperatures near absolute zero. Metals such as lead and aluminum or certain alloys of tin that have this property are called superconductors.

supernova A star that suddenly bursts and flares up, becomes millions of times brighter than it was, and then dies. A supernova gives off as much energy in one day as the sun does in a million years. The most recent supernova blazed into view in February 1987. In our galaxy, supernovas occur only once every few hundred years.

surface tension A property of the surface of a liquid that makes the surface pull together to take up the smallest possible area. It is caused by the attraction of molecules in a liquid. It makes a liquid surface behave as if it has an elastic film stretched over it.

surge In physics, a sudden increase in the flow of electricity or some other form of energy, such as the rush of water when a dam breaks.

surveying The measuring of distance and features on the surface of the earth. Surveying is important in making maps, fixing boundaries, and planning for dams, buildings, and other construction projects.

measuring an elevation

surveying

survival of the fittest In biology, an expression often used as a summary of the Darwinian theory of natural selection. It states that those organisms that are best adapted to their environment are most likely to live long enough to have offspring. For example, rabbits that can run faster than other rabbits are more likely to avoid predators and thus reach reproductive age. Their offspring that inherit the trait will continue the line of fast runners.

suspension   In chemistry, a mixture in which tiny particles of a solid are dispersed through a liquid and settle out slowly. A shaken mixture of chalk dust and water is an example of a suspension.

swamp   A low-lying area of land permanently saturated with water. Swamps usually develop in places where the surface is flat and there is poor natural drainage or where a lake has become filled with plants.

swarm   A large number of insects, such as locusts, flying or moving together in a group. When bees leave a hive with a queen to form a new colony, they are said to swarm.

sweat   In humans, the colorless, salty moisture secreted by the sweat glands through tiny openings in the skin called pores. Sweat helps to keep the body cool by evaporation. Also called perspiration.

symbiosis   In biology, a long association or living together of two organisms of different species. When both organisms benefit, such as nitrogen-fixing bacteria and bean plants, the relationship is called mutualism. When one benefits at the expense of the other, such as the parasites that cause malaria, the relationship is called parasitism. When one benefits and the other is unaffected, such as the remora fish's attaching itself to a shark, the relationship is called commensalism. [*Symbiosis* is a Greek word meaning "companionship" or "partnership."]

symbol   In chemistry, a letter or a group of letters and numbers that represent an element, atom, compound, or molecule. For example, the symbol H stands for the name of the element hydrogen, and also for one atom of the element.

symmetry   The exact matching of shapes on opposite sides of an abject. An object that is symmetrical has parts that are mirror images of each other.

synapse   The place at which a nerve impulse passes from the axon of one nerve cell across a tiny gap to the dendrite of another. [*Synapse* comes from a Greek word meaning "a junction" or "a point of contact."]

synthetic   In chemistry, something made by artificial means in a factory or laboratory, as opposed to a substance found in nature. For example, polyester is a synthetic fiber; wool is a natural fiber. [*Synthetic* comes from a Greek word for something that is composed or constructed of several other things.]

system   1. BIOLOGY. A group of organs, tissues, or cells that serves or performs some body function, such as the circulatory or digestive system. 2. ASTRONOMY. A group of related objects in space, such as the solar system. 3. PHYSICS, CHEMISTRY. A substance or a group of substances that can be studied together, such as compounds containing carbon. 4. GEOLOGY. Layers or groups of rocks formed during a single geological period. 5. ENGINEERING. A network of parts or components that performs a certain function, such as a computer system.

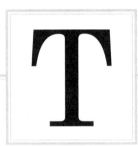

tachometer An instrument used to measure the number of rotations per unit of time (for example, revolutions per minute, or RPM) of a shaft, such as the crankshaft of an automobile engine. [*Tachometer* comes from Greek words meaning "speed" and "measure."]

tactile Having to do with the sense of touch. Tactile nerve endings in the skin are sensitive to pressure, pain, or temperature.

tadpole The young of a frog or toad in the larval stage. Tadpoles live in water and have gills, a long tail, and no legs. Through metamorphosis, tadpoles lose their gills and tails and develop lungs and legs, which allow them to live on land.

taiga A swampy region of evergreen forests found in Siberia between the tundra and the steppes. Also, similar forested land areas in China and North America. [*Taiga* is the Russian word for these dense forests.]

tail 1. ZOOLOGY. The thin, bony hind part of an animal that extends backward beyond the trunk or main part of the body. Also, the feathers that come from the rump of a bird. A bird's tail acts like a rudder during flight. 2. ASTRONOMY. A luminous stream of particles that are swept off the head of a comet when it comes near the sun. A comet's tail always points away from the sun.

talc A common, smooth mineral used in making talcum powder, blackboard chalk, cosmetics, and other substances. Talc is the softest mineral known.

talon The sharp, curved claw of a bird such as an eagle or hawk.

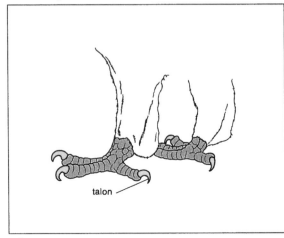

talon

talus A mass of loose rocky debris at the base of a cliff or mountain. Talus is the result of erosion of the rocks of the cliff or mountain above.

tape 1. A narrow band or strip of plastic coated with magnetic particles used to store audio and video signals, such as in audio and video cassettes. Magnetic tape is also used to store computer information. 2. A narrow, flexible band of paper, cloth, metal, plastic, or other material. Tapes have many uses, including sticking things together.

tar A dark, thick, sticky liquid obtained by heating coal or wood. When tar is cold, it becomes solid. It is used to waterproof and preserve wood and other materials that come into contact with the ground or are exposed to weather. Tar is also mixed with gravel to surface roads.

tarn A small mountain lake or pond formed by the retreat of the glaciers or by glacial runoff.

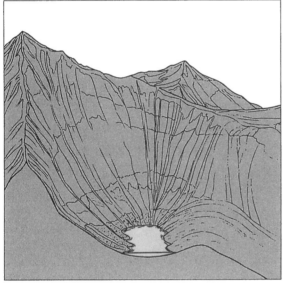

tarn

tarsus 1. In humans, the group of small bones that make up the ankle. 2. In most mammals and in some other animals, a similar joint found in the hind limb.

taste The sense by which the flavor of food and other substances is perceived by the taste buds on the tongue. There are four basic taste sensations: sweet, salt, sour, and bitter. Foods are often combinations of these tastes. Much of what we think of as taste, however, is actually smell or perception of odors.

taste bud A group of sensory taste cells found mostly on the upper surface of the tongue.

Taste buds that detect sweet sensations are concentrated at the tip of the tongue, those for salt and sour are along the sides, and those for bitter are mainly in the back.

taxonomy The science of classifying plants and animals. Animals or plants are grouped together according to their similarities and differences. Then each group, or taxon, is given a scientific name based on these relationships. Starting with the largest group and using conventional ways of printing, the taxa (plural of taxon) commonly used are: Kingdom, Phylum, Class, Order, Family, *Genus,* and *species.* Each kind of animal or plant is known scientifically by a dual name: both the *Genus* and the *species.* For example, a leopard's scientific name is *Panthera pardus.* A lion's scientific name is *Panthera leo.* The two big cats are different species but both belong to the same genus, showing that they have many things in common. [*Taxonomy* comes from Greek words meaning "arrangement" and "law."]

tear A drop of salty water secreted by a tear gland. Tears keep the surface of the eye and the inside of the eyelid moist. They also help to protect the eye by washing particles away. When excess tears are produced, they overflow the lower eyelid.

tear gland A gland that is located behind the upper eyelid at the outer corner of each eye and

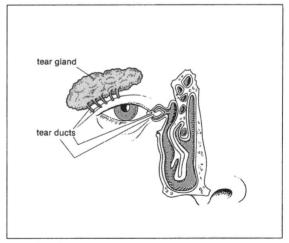

tear gland

produces tears. Each tear gland is about the size and shape of a large peanut. The tears pass across the eyes and then are drained into the nose through tear ducts located at the inner corners of the eyes. Also called the lachrymal gland.

technology An applied science, such as engineering, used to solve mechanical and industrial problems in many different fields. Technology produces machines such as video cameras, computers, automobiles, and spacecraft as well as simpler useful things such as hammers, rakes, and pots and pans.

tektite A small, rounded, glassy object of uncertain origin. Tektites have been found in Australia, West Africa, Texas, Georgia, and other parts of the world. Scientists think they may have come either from meteorite impacts that changed sedimentary rocks on Earth or simply from outer space as meteorites do. Tektites are thought to be from 5 million to over 30 million years old.

telecommunication The transmission of data or information by electrical, light, or electronic means such as the telegraph, telephone, radio, or television.

telephone An electrical, electromagnetic (including light waves), or electronic system of transmitting sound or speech from one place to another. The telephone works by changing sound waves into electrical signals, transmitting the electrical signals to a distant receiver over cable, using fiber optics, or by satellites, and then changing the electrical signals back into sound waves. The electromagnetic telephone was invented by Alexander Graham Bell in 1876. In 1878, the first commercial telephone system was opened in Connecticut. Local telephone networks soon appeared across the United States and elsewhere. Today, nearly the entire world is linked by telephone lines. [*Telephone* comes from Greek words meaning "distant" and "sound."]

telescope 1. An optical instrument that uses an arrangement of lenses and/or mirrors in a tube to make distant objects appear nearer or larger. 2. An electronic device, such as a radio telescope, that performs a similar function but uses a form of energy other than light, such as X-rays.

television A system that used electromagnetic energy to transmit moving pictures and sound from one place to another. A television camera is used to change pictures and sound into electrical signals. These are transmitted, either over the air, through cables, or via satellites, to a television receiver, which changes them back into pictures and sound.

temperate Describes a moderate climate what is neither very hot (tropical) nor very cold (polar or arctic). Most of the United States, and much of Europe, Asia, and South America, have temperate climates.

Temperate Zone In the Northern Hemisphere, the part of the earth that lies between the tropic of Cancer and the Arctic Circle. In the Southern Hemisphere, the part that lies between the Tropic of Capricorn and the Antarctic Circle.

temperature The degree of the average amount of warmth or coldness of an object. Temperature is measured by thermometers of various kinds using the Fahrenheit, Celsius (also called centigrade), or Kelvin scales. On the Fahrenheit scale the freezing and boiling points of water are 32° and 212° respectively. On the Celsius scale these values are 0° and 100°. Zero degrees Kelvin (0°K), or absolute zero, is–273.16°C; since the size of a Kelvin degree is the same as a Celsius degree, 0°C = 273.16°K, and 100°C = 373.16°K.

temperature-humidity index A measure of how uncomfortable warm-weather conditions are for people (abbreviated THI). The THI is used to predict the power demand for air conditioning. When the index is 70 or below, most people feel comfortable. When it is 80 or above, almost everyone is uncomfortable. Also called the discomfort index.

tendon A tough band of tissue found at the ends of most muscles. Tendons attach muscles to bones and transmit the force of the muscles that make bones move. [*Tendon* comes from a Greek word meaning "to stretch" or "to extend."]

tensile strength The resistance of a substance to being stretched or pulled. The maximum stretch that a material can withstand without breaking is measured in force per cross-sectional area (such as pounds per square inch). Steel wire or cable has great tensile strength.

tension A pulling or stretching force. The strings of a violin or a guitar or a stretched rubber band, are under tension.

tentacle 1. ZOOLOGY. A long, thin, muscular organ usually found around the head or the mouth of some kinds of invertebrate animals. The eight tentacles of an octopus are used for feeling, grasping and holding, and locomotion. 2. BOTANY. A hairlike growth in some kinds of plants such as a sundew. The surfaces of sundew leaves are covered by hundreds of tiny, sticky tentacles that trap and hold insects. [*Tentacle* comes from a Latin word meaning "to feel" or "to examine."]

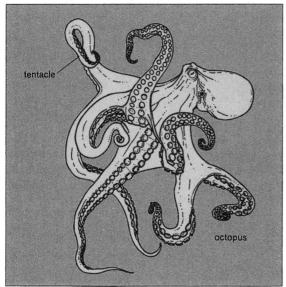

tentacle

terminal (adj.) In botany, growing at the end of a stem or branch, such as a terminal bud or flower.

terminal (n.) 1. ELECTRICITY, ELECTRONICS. A point in an electrical component to which a connection to wire cable can be made, such as the terminals of a battery. 2. COMPUTING. A device connected to a computer used to input or output data or information.

terminal moraine A heap of rocks and earth deposited at the end of a glacier.

terminator In astronomy, the line dividing the dark and sunlit parts of a moon or planet.

termite An insect with a soft, pale body that is sometimes called a "white ant" but is actually more closely related to a cockroach. Termites are social insects, living in large colonies made up of queens, workers, and soldiers. Most of the more than 2,000 different species of termites live in the tropics, but over 40 kinds live in the United States. Termites feed mainly upon wood fiber (cellulose) from dead trees, rotting plants, or houses, and furniture. Termites themselves cannot actually digest wood, but the workers have microscopic protozoans living in their intestines that turn cellulose into a substance that the termites can metabolize. Although some kinds of termites may damage buildings, they also play an important role in nature by recycling the chemicals in cellulose so that they can be used again by plants and bacteria. [*Termite* comes from a Latin word meaning "to wear something away."]

terrestrial 1. Having to do with the land or the ground rather than air or water. Terrestrial animals and plants live or grow on or in the ground. Continents are the terrestrial parts of the earth. 2. Having to do with the planet Earth. Humans are terrestrial beings. A terrestrial planet is a rocky planet similar to Earth.

territory In zoology, an area in which an animal lives and breeds and which it protects from other animals of its species. Mammals often mark the boundaries of their territories with scent; birds use song. The very strong behavioral drive in animals to set up territories is called territoriality.

Tertiary Period The first geological period of the Cenozoic Era just before the advent of humans. It lasted from about 65 million to about 2 million years ago. During the Tertiary, the great mountain chains of the Rockies, Alps, Himalayas, and Andes first appeared. Mammals developed into many different species and spread across the earth.

test An examination and analysis. A chemical test examines a substance to find out what it is, what it contains, or what its properties are. For example, litmus is used as a test for acidity or alkalinity: If litmus turns red, the substance is acidic; if blue, the substance is basic.

test tube A thin glass container used in performing chemical or biological tests. Test tubes can be used to hold small amounts of liquids or solids.

testis One of the two reproductive glands of male humans and other vertebrate animals. In most mammals, the two testes are enclosed in a sac of skin (the scrotum) behind the penis. A testis is a gonad that secretes sperm when the male is mature. Also called a testicle.

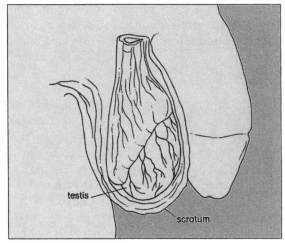
testis

tetanus An infectious disease of the nervous system, caused by a bacterium that produces a toxin. Tetanus may follow any type of wounding, including a cut or an animal bite. The toxin acts on the nerves and caused muscle spasms, most often in the jaw (lockjaw) and in the facial muscles. Tetanus is dangerous but it can be treated with an antitoxin or prevented by vaccination. [*Tetanus* comes from a Greek word meaning "muscle spasm.']

thalamus A large gray mass, located in the back of the upper brain stem, through which nerve pathways pass between the eyes and other sensory organs and the cerebral cortex. [*Thalamus* is the Greek word for "inner room."]

thaw (n.) Weather that is above the freezing point and warm enough to melt snow and ice.

thaw (v.) To raise the temperature of snow or ice above the freezing point so that they melt.

theodolite An instrument used in surveying to measure angles of the land or of buildings.

theodolite

theory An explanation, based on observations, experiments, and reasoning, of how or why something in the universe happens. Theories help to predict events or behavior and are usually supported by a great deal of evidence. A theory with not much evidence is sometimes called a hypothesis.

therm Any of the various units of heat, such as calories.

thermal (adj.) Having to do with heat or temperature.

thermal (n.) A rising column of warm air.

thermal pollution The discharge of warm water from a power plant or a factory into a river or lake. Such pollution can raise the natural water temperature enough to be harmful to the plant or animal life in it. Also, the discharge of heat into the surrounding air, which may affect the local weather.

thermodynamics A branch of physics that deals with heat and its relation to other forms of energy. Thermodynamics is based on two laws. The first law of thermodynamics says that energy can be neither created nor destroyed, only changed from one form into another. The second law says that heat always flows from a hot object toward a cooler object.

thermometer An instrument used for measuring temperature along a scale usually graduated in Fahrenheit or Celsius degrees. Most weather or fever thermometers are made of a sealed thin glass tube containing liquid

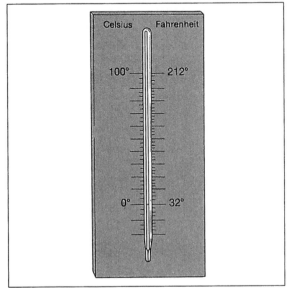

thermometer

mercury or colored alcohol. As the temperature changes, the liquid expands or contracts and the height of the liquid column rises or falls and can be read on the scale. An instrument consisting of a thermometer attached to a recording device, such as a mechanical pen or a computer, to record the temperature over a period of time is called a thermograph.

thermostat A device used to control temperature by automatically regulating the amount of heat. Thermostats are used in space heaters, ovens, the cooling systems of automobiles, and the heating and air-conditioning systems in houses.

Thomson, Sir Joseph John (1856–1940) An English physicist who received the 1906 Nobel Prize in physics for his study of the conduction of electricity through gases. In 1897 Thomson discovered the electron and studies its charge and mass. His model of the atom provided a good basis for later, more accurate, models.

Thomson, Sir Joseph John

thorax 1. ANATOMY. The region of the chest. The part of the body between the neck and the abdomen that contains the heart and the lungs. 2. ZOOLOGY. In insects, the middle section of the body between the head and the abdomen, from which project the legs and the wings.

throat A passage from the mouth and nose into the neck and then into either the gullet and stomach or the windpipe and lungs.

thrust 1. MECHANICS. The force of one thing pushing on another; for example, the thrust of a rocket engine on a spaceship. 2. GEOLOGY. The movement of one part of the earth's crust over another part. Also called a thrust fault.

thunder The sudden loud "clap" or longer rumble that follows a flash of lightning. Thunder is the sound of the shock wave caused by the sudden heating and expansion of air that results from a lightning discharge. Separate strokes and echoes can produce a rumble that lasts for several seconds and can be heard miles away.

thymus gland A gland located near the base of the neck in young persons that disappears or becomes smaller in adults. The thymus is important in the body's immune system and aids its ability to make antibodies to fight against disease. Also, a similar gland found in other young vertebrate animals.

thyroid gland A large gland located in the neck of humans. It secretes an important hormone called thyroxin that affects growth and regulates the rate at which the body uses energy. A large swelling of the thyroid called a goiter is sometimes caused by a diet containing too little iodine. Also, a similar gland found in other vertebrate animals.

tibia In humans, the shinbone; the longer and thicker of the two bones in the lower leg that stretch between the knee and the ankle. Also, a similar bone in the hind legs of other vertebrate animals.

tidal Having to do with tides.

tide The regular rise and fall of the oceans and seas. Most seacoasts have a high tide every 12 hours and 45 minutes. Tides are caused by the gravitational pulls of the moon and the sun on the waters and lands of the Earth. As the moon orbits the Earth, two tidal "bulges" travel around the Earth each day. The motion of the land is noticeable only with special instruments; the tides on the water are eas-

ily observed. Twice a month, during new and full moons, the moon, sun, and Earth are in line and the tides are much greater. These are called spring tides, though they have nothing to do with the season. During first-and last-quarter moons, the three bodies are at right angles to each other and we have weak tides, which are called neap tides.

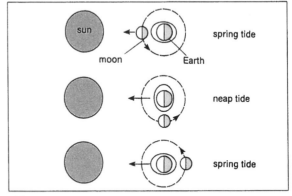
tide

timberline The natural boundary found on high mountains or in polar lands beyond which trees will not grow because of the cold. Also called the tree line.

timberline

time 1. A measurement of the continuous sequence of happenings in which one event follows another. 2. Any system of measuring the passage of these events based on the rotation or revolution of the Earth, or the frequency of some regularly vibrating or moving thing. 3. In geology, a unit such as an age, an epoch, or a period based on long changes in the rocks or in the crust of the earth.

tin A soft, silvery-white, metallic element. Tin can be easily molded and bent and has a low melting point. It is often used in plating steel to prevent corrosion and in making alloys such as solder, pewter, and bronze. Tin has an atomic number of 50 and an atomic weight of 118.69. Its chemical symbol is Sn.

tissue A group of similar cells working together to perform a particular function, such as muscle tissue and nerve tissue in animals or xylem and phloem tissue in plants. Tissues combine together to form the organs and systems of animals and plants. [*Tissue* comes from a Latin word meaning "to weave" or "to intertwine."]

tissue culture A method of growing cells or tissues in glass tubes, flasks, or other containers containing nutrient substances at a controlled temperature. Tissue culture allows scientists to grow cells outside the body of the animal from which they came and thus experiment upon them without harming the animal.

titanium A lightweight, silvery, metallic element. Titanium is strong and highly resistant to corrosion and is often used to make alloys for the aerospace industry. Titanium has an atomic number of 22 and an atomic weight of 47.90. Its chemical symbol is Ti.

Titius-Bode Law The Titius-Bode Law states that the distances of the planets from the sun follow a simple pattern. For the outer planets, each planet is predicted to be roughly twice as far away from the sun as the previous object.

tomography An X-ray technique that takes pictures of the internal anatomy of a body from various angles around an axis. A computer then assists to form a composite, readable image. CAT (computerized axial tomography) scanning has revolutionized medicine by aiding in the diagnosis of brain and spinal-cord illnesses, cancer, and many other conditions.

tongue 1. ANATOMY. The movable, muscular organ in the mouth of most vertebrate animals

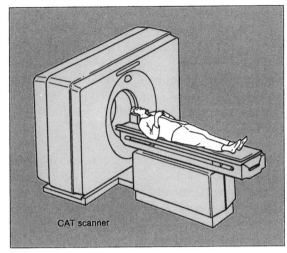

CAT scanner

tomography

including human beings. Taste buds on its surface are used to taste food. In humans, the tongue is also important in speech. In animals such as chameleons and frogs the long, sticky tongue also helps in taking in and swallowing food. 2. GEOGRAPHY, GEOLOGY. A narrow strip of land extending out into the water. Also, a long, narrow branch of a glacier or a lava flow.

tonsil Either of the two masses of tissue attached to the sides of the throat just in back of the tongue. Some scientists believe the tonsils aid in helping to prevent infections in children. Tonsilitis is an inflammation of the tonsils.

tooth In most vertebrate animals, one of a set of hard, bonelike parts attached along the edges of the upper and lower jaws. Teeth are used for biting, tearing, and chewing food. Many animals also use them to catch their prey and as weapons of attack or defense against other animals. Also, any tooth-shaped part on the edge of a leaf or other natural formation, or on a gear, saw, or other tool.

topaz A hard, transparent mineral used as a gemstone. Topaz is found as crystals of various colors such as yellow, pink, or golden brown.

topography 1. GEOGRAPHY. The description of, and drawing of, maps showing the surface features of a region, such as hills, mountains, lakes, roads, and bridges. Also the surface features themselves. 2. ANATOMY. A similar study or description of the body or its parts.

topsoil The upper, fertile part of soil, which contains materials plants need for growth. Topsoil is a thin layer usually only about 6 to 18 inches (15 to 45 centimeters) deep.

tornado A small but violent, funnel-shaped storm of strong winds whirling at speeds up to 320 miles per hour (480 kilometers per hour) that develops below a strong thunderstorm and extends toward the ground. The updraft at the center of a tornado may reach 200 miles per hour (320 kilometers per hour). A large tornado destroys houses, trees, bridges, boats, and almost anything else in its path. In the United States, most tornados occur during the summer in the Midwest or Southeast, because of the collision of warm, moist air at low levels in these regions with cooler, drier air coming from the north at higher altitudes. [*Tornado* comes from Spanish words meaning "thunderstorm" and "whirling."]

tornado

torque A twisting or turning force that tends to cause rotation of an object. For example, an automobile engine produces torque, which is transmitted to the drive shaft and finally to the wheels.

totality The time during a solar eclipse when the light of the sun is completely cut off by the moon. Also the time during a lunar eclipse when Earth's shadow completely covers the moon.

touch The body sense concerned with surface sensations, found in all parts of the skin. Touch feelings include heat, cold, pressure, and pain. Receptors for touch are particularly concentrated in the fingertips, the rest of the hand, and the face.

toxin A poison produced by a living organism. Some bacteria produce toxins that cause diseases such as tetanus or diphtheria. Poisonous snakes and spiders deliver toxins with their fangs or jaws. [*Toxin* comes from Greek words meaning "poison."]

trace element 1. An element such as zinc or iron needed in tiny amounts to provide suitable nutrition for humans and animals or for good growth in plants. 2. An element found in tiny amounts in another substance, such as uranium in pitchblende ore.

trachea 1. The windpipe. A hollow tube in humans and other vertebrates by which air passes to and from the lungs alongside the larynx. The trachea is ringed by cartilage so that it stays open. You can see the outlines of the trachea below the Adam's apple. 2. In insects and other arthropods, one of the tubes that carry air in the respiratory system.

trade wind A steady wind blowing toward the equator. North of the equator the trade winds blow from the northeast; south of the equator they blow from the southeast. In earlier times, trade winds were important for sailing ships.

transfusion A method of taking blood from one person and injecting it into the veins of another. The blood types of both persons must be compatible, or the blood may clot or otherwise harm the recipient.

transistor A small electronic device, made of a semiconductor such as silicon, used in

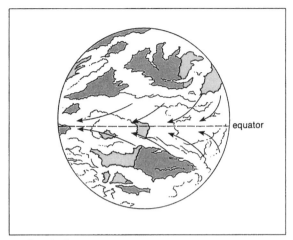

trade wind

a circuit as an amplifier or control switch. Transistors revolutionized the electronics and computer industries, but they have been replaced in many cases by integrated circuits, which can contain the equivalent of hundreds or even thousands of transistors. The transistor was invented by William Shockley, Walter H. Brattain, and John Bordeen in 1948. Transistor is a combination of *trans*fer and re*sistor*.

transit The passage of a star or other celestial body across an observer's meridian. Also, the passage of a smaller body across the disk of a larger one, such as Mercury or Venus passing across the disk of the sun.

transition element Any of the metallic elements with an incomplete inner shell of electrons. Transition elements belong to the short groups of the periodic table—groups IIIB to VIII, IB and IIB. They tend to be hard and have high melting points. Transition elements include many that are important in industry, such as iron, cobalt, copper, zinc, mercury, silver, and gold. Also called transition metals.

translucent Describing a substance that is not transparent but lets some light pass through. Tissue paper and thin clouds are translucent.

transmission 1. MECHANICS. A device for carrying power from its source to where it is needed. A transmission in a car carries power from the engine to the wheels. 2. ELECTRONICS. The broadcast or passage of a radio or television signal from a transmitter to a receiver.

transmission

transmit 1. ELECTRONICS. To broadcast radio or television signals. 2. MEDICINE. To carry a disease from one person to others.

transmitter 1. ELECTRONICS. A device used to send out radio, television, or other kinds of signals. 2. MEDICINE. A person or other living thing that carries a disease and can infect others. A person who has tuberculosis is a transmitter of the disease.

transparent Describing a substance that allows light to pass through it so that objects can be clearly seen through it. Clean air, clear water, and most window glasses are transparent.

transpiration The loss of water by evaporation from the surface of plant leaves. Transpiration takes place mainly through openings in the undersides of leaves, called stomata, as well as through the upper surfaces of the leaves. The stomata open and close, regulating the amount of water that the plant transpires. If too much water is lost, a plant wilts.

transplant (n.) A tissue or organ that has been or is being transplanted.

transplant (v.) 1. BOTANY. To take a plant from where it is growing and replant it somewhere else. 2. BIOLOGY, MEDICINE. To remove an organ or tissues from a person or an animal and transfer it into another person or animal. Eye corneas, hearts, and kidneys have all been successfully transplanted.

transuranium element Any of the thirteen known elements whose atomic numbers are greater than that of uranium (92). All transuranium elements are radioactive and none occur in nature. Plutonium, used in atomic bombs, is a transuranium element.

tree A large, woody, perennial plant with one main stem called a trunk, and branches and leaves several feet or more above the ground. Trees are classified as deciduous or evergreen. Deciduous trees, such as oaks and maples, periodically lose their leaves (usually in autumn) and are bare for part of the year. Evergreen trees, such as pines, spruces, and eucalyptus, keep most of their leaves or needles all year round.

tremor 1. GEOLOGY. A small quaking or vibrating of the land. Tremors are usually small quakes that often appear before or after a major earthquake. 2. MEDICINE. An involuntary shaking of a part of the body.

trench In geology, a long, narrow valley in the seabed. Some of the deepest trenches, such as the Marianas trench and the Tonga trench in the Pacific Ocean, lie tens of thousands of feet below the waves. [*Trench* comes from a French word meaning "to cut."]

Triassic Period The first or earliest geological period of the Mesozoic Era. The Triassic lasted from about 225 to 190 million years ago. The earliest dinosaurs and primitive mammals appeared during the Triassic. It was also a time of much volcanic activity, and the continents began to break apart. [*Triassic* comes from a Greek word meaning "three," the number of divisions of the Mesozoic Era.]

triceps The large muscles at the back of the upper arm, which extends the arm by straightening the elbow.

trilobite An extinct sea animal with jointed legs and a body divided into three parts. Small fossil trilobites are often found in rocks in many places around the world.

tropics The two parallels of latitude on Earth's surface that lie 23½° north (the Tropic of Cancer) or 23½° south (the Tropic of Capricorn) of the equator. These are the farthest north or south latitudes where the sun is directly overhead at noon at some time during the year. The tropics are the warmest regions of the world and, in tropical rain forests, often rich in plant and animal life. The regions between these lines are also called the tropics or sometimes the Torrid Zone.

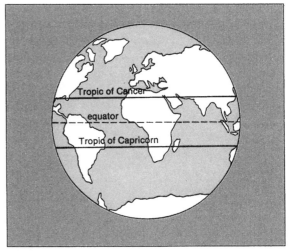

tropics

tropism The turning or growth of a plant toward a stimulus (positive) or away from a stimulus (negative), such as light (phototropism), gravity (geotropism), or water (hydrotropism). Plant leaves and stems often show positive phototropism and negative geotropism. Plant roots show positive hydrotropism and geotropism.

tropopause The boundary line of the atmosphere that lies between the troposphere and the atmosphere. The altitude of the tropopause is about 10 miles (16 kilometers) over the equator and gradually decreases toward the poles to about 4–5 miles (6–8 kilometers).

troposphere The lowest region of the atmosphere in which we live, extending to 10 miles (16 kilometers) above the surface of Earth. There is a steady fall of temperature as you go higher in the troposphere. At the top of the troposphere the temperature may be 100°F below zero (–74°C). Clouds, winds, storms, precipitation, and other weather changes all take place within the troposphere.

trough 1. GEOLOGY, OCEANOGRAPHY. A long, narrow valley or channel between hills on land or on the ocean floor. Also, the low part of an ocean wave between the crests. 2. METEOROLOGY. A long, narrow region of low air pressure usually associated with storms or cloudy weather.

trunk 1. BOTANY. The main stem of a tree that is neither the roots nor the branches. 2. ANATOMY. The body of a human or an animal, but not the legs, arms, neck, or head. 3. BIOLOGY. The main section of a blood vessel or nerve. [*Trunk* comes from a Latin word meaning "to chop off" or "to amputate."]

tsunami A large, fast-moving ocean wave that is caused by an underwater earthquake or volcano. On the open ocean, tsunamis are only a few feet high and are barely noticeable. But when a tsunami approaches a shore, waves build up to heights of 90 feet (27 meters) or more and hit with the force of an explosion. In coastal areas a tsunami can result in many deaths and large amounts of property damage. [*Tsunami* is a Japanese word meaning "harbor" and "waves."]

tuber A swollen underground part of a stem or root that contains stored food and from which new plants may grow. Potatoes are stem tubers. [*Tuber* is a Latin word meaning "a swelling" or "a tumor."]

tufa A kind of rock formed of powdery material, especially limestone, deposited in underground springs and lakes.

tumor A swelling on or in the body; usually, an abnormal growth of tissue.

tundra A vast, level, treeless plain found generally in northern North America and Siberia. For most of the year air temperatures on the tundra are below freezing and the ground remains frozen even during the brief summer. The soil is a thin covering over the frozen ground. Tundra plants include lichens, mosses, and small shrubs. [*Tundra* comes from the Lapp word for these plains.]

tungsten A hard, silvery-gray metallic element. Tungsten has a higher melting point than any other metal and is used in making the filaments in electric light bulbs and in tungsten-steel alloys for high-temperature uses. Tungsten has an atomic number of 74 and an atomic weight of 183.85. Its chemical symbol is W. Also called wolfram. [*Tungsten* is a Swedish word meaning "heavy stone."]

turbine A machine used to change the energy of a continuous stream of fluid into rotational energy that turns a shaft that can

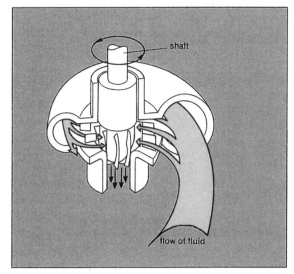

turbine

drive machinery. The fluid may be air, hot gas, steam, or water. For example, in a hydraulic turbine in a hydroelectric power station, water falls on a series of blades around a shaft, causing it to rotate, and this motion is used to drive the rotor of an electric generator.

turbulence An irregular or swirling motion of a fluid, such as an interruption of a wind in the atmosphere or a swiftly flowing current in a river or ocean. Turbulence is the usual condition of most fluid motion found in nature.

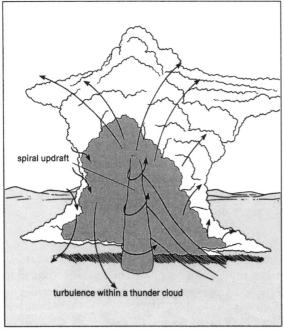

spiral updraft

turbulence within a thunder cloud

turbulence

tusk A very long pointed tooth, usually one of two, that projects from the jaw of elephants, walruses, wild boars, and some other animals.

twin One of two children born at the same time to the same mother. There are two types of twins: Identical twins are genetically the same and are the result of the splitting of a single fertilized egg. Fraternal twins develop from separate fertilized eggs and are no more similar than ordinary brothers or sisters coming from the same parents.

tympanic membrane A thin tissue layer that separates the outer ear from the middle ear. Also called the tympanum or eardrum.

typhoid fever An infectious disease caused by a kind of bacterium found in contaminated water or milk or carried by food handlers, who may not be aware that they have the bacterium. Symptoms include high fever and digestive-system problems. The disease is treated with antibiotics and can be prevented by a vaccine. [*Typhoid* comes from a Greek word meaning "to smolder or burn."]

typhoon A violent tropical storm that forms over the western Pacific Ocean or the Indian Ocean, most often during the summer or early autumn. Typhoons are similar to the hurricanes that form over the Atlantic Ocean. [*Typhoon* comes from Chinese words meaning "big" and "wind."]

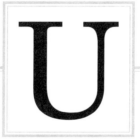

U

ulcer An inflamed sore on the skin or on an internal organ. Ulcers may develop as the result of an injury, a loss of blood supply to a tissue, or cancer, or for unknown reasons. A peptic ulcer occurs in the walls of the stomach or the intestines. Too much acid secretion in the stomach, often a result of emotional disturbance or stress, is believed to play a part in the formation of peptic ulcers. Stopping smoking, rest, antacids, and drugs that block gastric-acid secretions may help ulcerated areas to recover, but surgery to repair organs may also be attempted.

ulna The thin, longer bone of the forearm on the side opposite the thumb. Also, a similar bone in the front limb of other vertebrate animals.

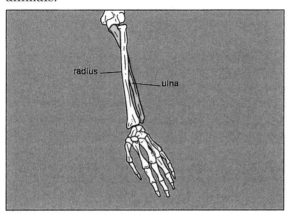

ulna

ultrasonic Having to do with sound waves whose frequencies are above 20,000 hertz, or cycles per second (human hearing range is 20 to 20,000 hertz). Ultrasonic waves are used in industry in many ways, from sonar devices to cleaning machine parts. Whistles used to summon dogs are ultrasonic. The science that studies these things is called ultrasonics. In medicine, ultrasonic sound waves (also known as ultrasound) are used to study the fetus, to detect heart damage, and in most branches of medicine to picture internal organs without surgery and the attendant risks of radiation, infection, or reactions.

ultraviolet Having to do with an invisible part of the electromagnetic spectrum whose rays have frequencies between that of visible violet rays and X-rays. Ultraviolet (UV) light can be detected by photographic methods or fluorescent screens. While UV rays make up a part of incoming sunlight, most of the UV is absorbed by the atmosphere, particularly by the ozone layer. UV radiation can also be produced artificially in sun lamps. Direct exposure of the skin to a very small amount of UV from the sun or other sources is beneficial and produces vitamin D in the body. Too much UV can be dangerous to humans and other forms of life.

umbilical cord A long, flexible, tubelike structure that connects the developing embryo or fetus with the placenta of a mammal mother during pregnancy. It contains blood vessels that carry blood, containing oxygen and food, to the fetus and waste products from the fetus to the placenta. At birth the placenta and umbilical cord are expelled from the mother after the baby, and the cord is cut close to the newborn's body; what remains becomes the navel (umbilicus or belly button).

umbra The darkest part of a shadow, especially the shadow cast by Earth or the moon during an eclipse. Also, the darkest or central part of a sunspot.

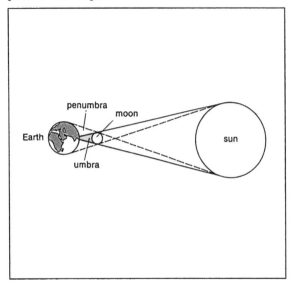

umbra

uncertainty principle A part of the quantum theory first put forth by Werner Heisenberg in 1927. It states that there is an absolute limit to the accuracy of determining simultaneously both the position and the velocity of an object. This applies to the movement of electrons and other phenomena at the atomic level.

undertow A strong water current flowing beneath the surface in a direction different from the surface current.

ungulate Any of a group of mammals that have hoofs, such as horses, cattle, sheep, pigs, deer, and elephants.

unicellular Having to do with single-celled living things such as bacteria, algae, yeast, and protozoa.

unified field theory A theory that tries to link electromagnetic force, nuclear forces, and gravity together in some mathematical or physical way. Scientists are still working on this.

universe All the matter and energy in space now and in the past, including the Milky Way, all the other galaxies, the stars, and everything else that exists.

uplift A rise, or upthrust, of a section of the surface of the earth, such as a mountain formed by the raising of part of the seafloor.

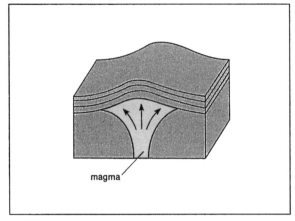

uplift

uranium A very heavy, silvery-white, radioactive, and highly reactive metallic element, discovered in 1789 by Martin Klaproth, a German chemist. It occurs in nature as a mixture of three isotopes with different atomic weights. The rare uranium-235 (U-235) isotope is the only kind that can be used as natural fission fuel in atomic power plants. But a kind of atomic reactor called a breeder is used to convert the more common uranium-238 (U-238) into fissionable plutonium-239, which can be used in atomic reactions—for both atomic power and nuclear weapons. Uranium has an atomic number of 92 and an atomic weight (its most common isotope) of 238. Its chemical symbol is U.

Uranus The seventh planet from the sun and the third largest. Uranus was discovered by William Herschel in 1781. The planet is about 1,783 million miles (2,871 kilometers) from the sun—19 times farther away than Earth—and it takes 84 years to make one orbit. Like Jupiter and Saturn, Uranus is a giant planet made up mostly of gases. About 31,763 miles (51,138 kilometers) across, Uranus is about halfway in size between Jupiter and Earth. Astronomers have discovered 27 moons and a system of faint rings circling Uranus. Oberon and Titania are the largest Uranian moons.

urea A crystalline substance rich in nitrogen excreted by mammals in their urine. Synthetic urea is manufactured for use in fertilizers and medicine, and in making plastics.

urine A waste product of vertebrates that is excreted by the kidneys. Urine contains salts, urea, and other substances. In humans and other mammals, urine is an amber-colored liquid that passes through tubes called ureters into the bladder and is then discharged from the body through a tube called the urethra. In birds and reptiles, urine is a watery paste.

URL In computing, URL stands for *U*niform *R*esource *L*ocator. The best known example of a URL is the address of a web page on the World Wide Web, for example http://www.seymoursimon.com.

USB In computing, USB stands for *U*niversal *S*erial *B*us. USB can be used to connect keyboards, printers, digital cameras, and many other computer devices. USB is on most personal computers and is now often used on cellular phones and computing tablets.

uterus A body organ in most female mammals that protects and nourishes the developing baby through the embryo and fetus stages until birth. Also called the womb.

vaccination   A method of introducing a substance, called a vaccine, into a human or other animal in order to induce immunity against an infectious disease caused by bacteria or viruses. The vaccine is usually a weakened or killed culture of the microorganisms causing the disease. The body develops antibodies against the disease and the ability to produce them rapidly in the future. In earlier times, the method used was deliberate vaccination from a mild case. In the 1790s Sir William Jenner invented the procedure: He induced immunity against smallpox by vaccinating patients with a version of a milder similar disease called cowpox. Louis Pasteur continued this work by developing vaccines against anthrax and rabies. Today, vaccinations are used to prevent diseases such as influenza, (flu), diphtheria, polio, measles, and chicken pox. [*Vaccination* comes from a Latin word meaning "cow."]

vacuum   A region of space without any matter, even atoms or molecules. Also, an enclosed space from which almost all the air or gas has been removed by a device called a vacuum pump. [*Vacuum* is from a Latin word meaning "empty" or "hollow."]

vacuum tube   A sealed enclosure from which most of the air has been removed.

vagina   In female mammals, the passage between the uterus and the external genital organs. [*Vagina* is a Latin word meaning "a sword's sheath" or "a scabbard."]

valence   The chemical combining tendency of an atom of an element, or of a group of atoms called a radical. The valence is determined by the number of electrons the atom or radical tends to add, lose, or share with other atoms in chemical reactions. Elements such as the nonmetals whose atoms gain electrons in reactions are said to have a negative valence. Elements such as the metals whose atoms lose electrons are said to have a positive valence. [*Valence* comes from a Latin word meaning "strength" or "power."]

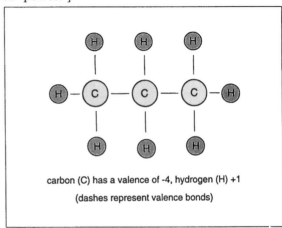

carbon (C) has a valence of -4, hydrogen (H) +1

(dashes represent valence bonds)

valence

valley 1. A long, narrow area of lower land lying between hills or mountains. Valleys are usually formed when the land is eroded by the action of rivers or glaciers. Valleys that have formed recently, called young valleys, are narrow, steep-sided, and V-shaped. Older valleys are broader, with more gentle slopes. 2. A large region of flat land formed by a major river and its branches, such as the Hudson Valley or the Valley of the Nile.

valve 1. ENGINEERING. A mechanical device that controls the flow of fluid in a pipe or other container by opening or closing. A sink faucet is a valve that is opened or closed manually. Safety valves on car or home radiators are designed to open automatically if the pressure reaches a dangerous level. 2. ANATOMY. One of the flaps of tissue that control the flow of blood into and out of the heart and prevent blood from flowing backward in the veins. Also, other structures in the body that open and close to control the flow of some substance. 3. ZOOLOGY. One of the hinged parts of the shells of clams, mussels, and certain other mollusks. 4. BOTANY. One of the parts into which some kinds of seeds split. [*Valve* comes from a Latin word meaning "a folding door."]

Van Allen radiation belts Belts of high-energy charged particles surrounding Earth outside the atmosphere. The charged particles are captured from the incoming solar wind by Earth's magnetic field. They extend about 400 to 40,000 miles (650 to 65,000 kilometers) above Earth's surface. The belts are probably responsible for the auroras seen above polar regions and sometimes in the higher latitudes in temperate regions. They were discovered by American physicist James Van Allen from information sent back by magnetic detectors aboard *Explorer 1,* the first satellite sent into orbit by the United States (1958).

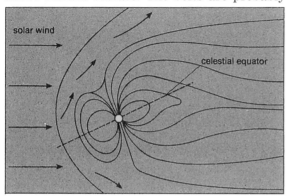

Van Allen radiation belts

vapor A gas formed from a substance that is usually a solid or liquid at room temperature. Water vapor is water in its gaseous state.

variable star A star that changes regularly or irregularly in brightness. Variable stars include pulsars, novas, and double stars, one of which may eclipse the other as they revolve around each other.

variation 1. BIOLOGY. The difference of an animal or plant from a normal or standard type. Variation results from the fact that each living thing has its own unique genetic makeup. This is important in the evolution of a species, because variation assures a range of characteristics, some of which may be better adapted for survival that others in a changing environment. 2. ASTRONOMY. The deviation of a celestial body, such as a planet or a comet, from its average orbit or motion.

variety A subspecies. A group of similar animals or plants in a species that differ from others in the species in some minor but permanent ways. For example, domestic dog breeds, such as the collie and the springer spaniel, are varieties of the dog. *Floribunda* and *grandiflora* are varieties of the rose.

vascular Having to do with the vessels that carry nutrient body liquids in a living thing. The vascular system in an animal is the circulatory system; in a plant it is the xylem and phloem that carry sap. A vas is a vessel or a duct in a living thing.

VCR *Video Cassette Recorder.* A machine that can record and play back pictures and sound on a cassette of magnetic tape.

vegetable (adj.) In botany, describing a substance obtained from a plant, such as vegetable oil.

vegetable (n.) Commonly, the term for an edible plant eaten during the main course of a meal, while the term "fruit" refers to an edible plant eaten by hand or as dessert. Tomatoes, corn, and string beans, which are commonly called vegetables, are really fruits—they are the ripened ovaries of plants.

vegetation Plant life; also, the kinds of plant life living in a particular area or region such as a desert or a grassland.

vegetative reproduction A type of reproduction in plants in which new plants develop from the leaves, stems, or runners of one parent without fertilization or the formation of seeds. Also called vegetative propagation.

vein 1. ANATOMY. One of the many tubes or vessels in the circulatory system that carry blood from all parts of the body back to the heart. Veins have thinner walls than arteries and one-way valves that prevent the blood from flowing backward. 2. BOTANY. One of the fine tubes or strands that form the frame of a leaf and carry nutrients to it. 3. ZOOLOGY. One of the fine ribs that form the framework of an insect's wings. 4. GEOLOGY. In a rock, a crack or deposit filled with a mineral—usually a desirable kind such as gold or copper—that is different from the surrounding rock.

velocity The rate at which a body moves in a given direction, expressed in units of distance and time, such as miles per hour in a straight line. Speed is not exactly the same as velocity, because it is the rate of motion regardless of direction. [*Velocity* comes from a Latin word meaning "swift" or "rapid."]

vena cava Either of two large veins (the upper or the lower) that carry blood from the upper and lower body back into the right atrium of the heart. [*Vena cava* is a Latin term meaning "hollow blood vessel."]

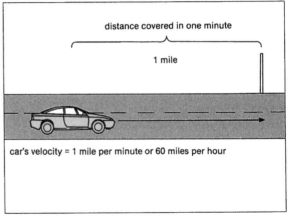

distance covered in one minute

1 mile

car's velocity = 1 mile per minute or 60 miles per hour

velocity

venom A poisonous substance that is secreted, and can be injected, by any of several kinds of snakes, spiders, scorpions, fishes, and other animals into the body of another animal by biting or stinging.

vent 1. GEOLOGY. The opening on the surface of a volcano through which lava, gases, and other volcanic materials flow. 2. ZOOLOGY. An excretory opening at the end of the digestive tract of birds, reptiles, and other vertebrate animals (but not mammals). [*Vent* comes from a Latin word meaning "wind."]

ventricle 1. In mammals of birds, either of the two lower chambers of the heart that pump blood through the body. Reptiles, amphibians, and fish usually have only one ventricle. 2. Any of the four connected chambers in the brain

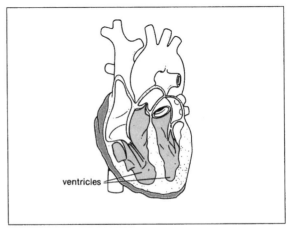

ventricles

ventricle

that contains a liquid that nourishes and helps protect it from injury. 3. Any hollow cavity or space in the body.

Venus The second planet from the sun. Venus orbits the sun every 225 days at an average distance of 67 million miles (108 million kilometers). Venus comes closer to Earth than any other planet. Venus rotates slowly on its axis in a clockwise direction, which astronomers call a "retrograde" rotation because it is the opposite of the way the seven other planets rotate. A rotation takes about 243 Earth days, so a Venusian day is longer than a Venusian year. Even though Venus has been called Earth's "sister planet," conditions on Venus are quite different from those on Earth. The dense atmosphere is composed of carbon dioxide and sulfuric acid, which acts as a greenhouse and traps the heat. Venus is an enormously hot desert with day and night temperatures over 900 degrees Fahrenheit (484 degrees Celsius). The temperature on Venus is so hot it could melt lead. Life as we know it could not exist on Venus.

vertebra Any of the many small bones (vertebrae) that make up the spinal column or backbone.

vertebrate Any animal that has a backbone or spinal column, including mammals, birds, reptiles, amphibians, and fishes.

Vesalius, Andreas (1514–1564) A Flemish physician whose discoveries were based on the dissection of human bodies. His most important work, *On the Structure of the Human Body* (1543) described several internal organs for the first time. He is regarded as one of the founders of modern anatomy.

veterinary medicine The medical care and treatment of animals. A doctor who practices this kind of medicine is called a veterinarian.

vibrate To move quickly back and forth or up and down at a steady rate. When a tuning fork is struck, it vibrates back and forth and sets the air in motion, which we hear as sound.

villus One of the many tiny, hairlike projections growing out of the lining of the small intestine. Villi (plural of villus) increase the surface area of the small intestine, causing food substances to be absorbed more quickly and easily, [*Villus* is a Latin word meaning "a tuft of hair" or "a patch of mossy growth on a tree."]

virus 1. BIOLOGY. Any of a large group of very tiny infectious agents shaped like rods or spheres. Viruses are smaller than bacteria and can be seen only with an electron microscope. They are composed of a core of DNA or RNA surrounded by a coat of protein. When viruses enter a living plant, animal, or bacteria, they begin to multiply and may cause diseases. In humans, viruses can cause such diseases as measles, mumps, chicken pox, rabies, polio, AIDS, influenza, or the common cold. Some viruses are known to cause cancer in animals and are thought to cause some kinds of cancer in humans. Vaccination is used to immunize people and animals against many kinds of viral diseases. 2. COMPUTERS. A program that is secretly attached to another program and causes something unexpected to happen. [*Virus* is a Latin word meaning "venom" or "poison."]

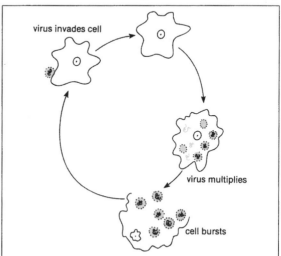

virus

viscosity A property of a fluid that prevents it from flowing easily as a result of internal friction between the molecules when they move against each other. All fluids have some degree of viscosity.

viscous   Describes a fluid that does not flow easily, such as heavy oil or molasses.

visible spectrum   The part of the electromagnetic spectrum that is visible to the human eye, as contrasted with ultraviolet, infrared, radio, and other waves that are invisible.

vision   The sense of sight; the ability to receive and interpret light waves reaching the eye.

vitamin   Any of a group of organic substances needed in the diet of humans and other animals for normal growth and maintenance of life processes (metabolism). Vitamins are found in small amounts in various foods and are also manufactured artificially for use by injection or in the form of pills. Several, such as vitamins D and K, are produced by the body itself. Vitamins are often grouped together as fat soluble or water soluble; they are also listed alphabetically. Fat-soluble vitamins include A, D, E, and K; the B-complex vitamins and vitamin C are water soluble. A well-balanced diet usually supplies the minimum vitamin needs of most people. A poor diet can lead to vitamin deficiency diseases such as rickets or scurvy and generally poor health.

vitreous humor   The clear, colorless, jelly-like substance that fills the space in the eye behind the lens. Light is transmitted from the lens through the vitreous humor to the retina. The vitreous humor gives shape to the eyeball. *Vitreous humor* comes from Latin words meaning "glass" and "fluid.]

vocal cord   Either of two pairs of muscle bands in the throat of humans, other mammals, and some other animals, that stretch across the opening of the larynx or voice box. The lower pair of cords can be stretched tight and be made to vibrate when air is forced past them. The vibrating cords produce sounds that in humans can become speech or song.

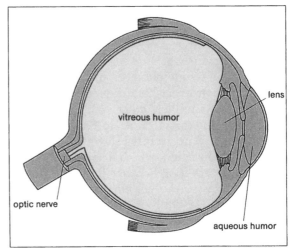

vitreous humor

voice   The sound of speech or song.

void   An empty space or vacuum, as in the void of outer space.

volatile   Describing a liquid that evaporates quickly at room temperature, such as alcohol or gasoline. [*Volatile* comes from a Latin word meaning "to fly."]

volcanism   The events associated with volcanos and volcanic activity, such as when magma is forced to the surface and becomes lava. Also spelled vulcanism.

volcano   1. An opening or vent in Earth's crust, through which hot gases, lava, and

volcano

ash are discharged during the time the volcano is active (an eruption). A volcano may be described as active, dormant, or extinct. About 500 volcanoes around the world are known to be active. 2. A cone-shaped hill or mountain built up around a volcanic vent by lava and ashes. 3. A similar structure found on other planets such as Mars, or found on moons such as Io, a satellite of Jupiter that has at least eight active volcanoes. [*Volcano* honors Vulcan, the Roman god of fire and metalworking.]

volt A unit of measurement of electrical pressure needed to drive a current of one ampere when the power lost is equal to one watt.

Volta, Alessandro (1745–1827) An Italian physicist who invented the Volta's pile (or voltaic pile,) the first electric battery. The volt is named after him.

Volta, Alessandro

voltage The strength of an electromotive force or electric pressure measured in volts. The voltage of the electric current used in households is generally 110 to 220 volts.

voltmeter An instrument used to measure the voltage between different points in a circuit.

volume 1. The amount of space occupied by a three-dimensional object. 2. The strength

of loudness of a sound or the electric current transmitting the sound.

vomit Food or other substance from the stomach forcibly ejected through the mouth. Also called vomitus.

vortex A spiraling, inward motion of a liquid or gas such as water or air. A vortex of water is often called a whirlpool; a vortex of air is a whirlwind or tornado.

Voyager Either of two U.S. space probes launched in 1977, named *Voyager 1* and *Voyager 2*. The probes passed by Jupiter and Saturn in 1979 and 1981, sending back detailed photographs of the planets, their moons, and their ring systems. *Voyager 2* next encountered Uranus and Neptune in 1986 and 1989, sending back equally revealing photographs of these distant planets. Both *Voyager*s carry gold-plated record disks containing the sound of thunder, the songs of whales and birds, human laughter, and other sounds of life on Earth. By now both *Voyager*s are beyond human contact and on their way out of the solar system into interstellar space.

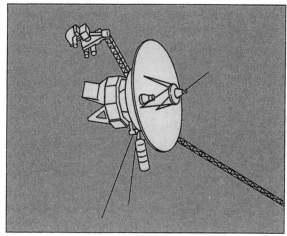

Voyager

vulva The external female reproductive organs. [*Vulva* is a Latin word meaning "womb."]

Waksman, Selman Abraham (1888–1973) An American biochemist who developed streptomycin, the first antibiotic against a specific disease (tuberculosis). He won the Nobel Prize for medicine in 1952.

Wallace, Alfred Russel (1823–1913) A British naturalist whose theory of natural selection as a blueprint for the origin of species was developed independently of Charles Darwin's. Wallace and Darwin presented their similar theories in a joint paper in 1858.

Wallace, Alfred Russel

warm-blooded Describing an animal whose body temperature stays about the same regardless of the temperature of its surroundings. Birds and mammals, including humans, are warm-blooded. Endothermic is another word for warm-blooded.

waste 1. BIOLOGY. In living things, unused material left over from digestion, respiration, or other functions. Urea and carbon dioxide are animal waste products. 2. ECOLOGY. Unwanted products of manufacturing, machinery, or home, such as cans, empty containers, and old rubber tires. 3. GEOGRAPHY. Lands that are not able to be farmed or not livable. Wastelands may have been caused naturally by erosion or weather, or by human activities such as chemical dumping, overfarming, or diversion of natural resources.

water A colorless, odorless, tasteless liquid. (Sea water tastes salty because of the minerals dissolved in it.) Water covers nearly three fourths of Earth's surface in the form of oceans, lakes, and rivers and frozen icecaps and glaciers. At normal atmospheric pressure, water freezes at a temperature of 32°F (0°C) and boils at a temperature of 212°F (100°C). It has the rare property of being denser as a liquid than as a solid, which is the reason that ice floats on water. It is a good solvent for many substances and is both a weak acid and a weak base. Life began in the oceans and water is essential for life as we know it to continue to exist. Chemically water is a compound whose molecule is made up of two atoms of hydrogen and one atom of oxygen: H_2O.

water cycle 1. GEOLOGY. The natural series of changes in which water from oceans, lakes, and soil evaporates, condenses to form clouds, falls back to earth in the form of rain or snow, and returns to the oceans, lakes, and soil. 2. BIOLOGY. The process by which animals and plants take in water from their surroundings and then return it to the atmosphere by respiration, transpiration, or some other method.

waterfall A sudden fall of water from a river or stream flowing on a high ground level to a much lower level. Often called a falls, as in Niagara Falls on the border between the United States and Canada or Angel Falls in Venezuela.

water pollution The presence of sewage, industrial waste products, oil, or other harmful or objectionable material in rivers, lakes, harbors, or other bodies of water. In large quantities, theses substances can harm or kill plants and animals, upset the balance of nature, and degrade the quality of water used by people.

waterproof Describing a material, such as rubber, that will not let water pass through.

watershed An area of land drained by a river or river system.

water table The upper level of water that collects in the ground. Below the water table, the ground is saturated with water. After a heavy rain, the water table may rise so high that the ground is flooded and water collects on the surface. Also called the water level.

water vapor Water in its gaseous state. Water vapor in the air is called humidity.

Watson, James Dewey (1928–) An American biologist who with Francis Crick shared the 1962 Nobel Prize in physiology and medicine with Maurice Wilkins for their work in establishing the molecular structure of DNA.

Watson, James Dewey

watt A unit of the measurement of electrical power. A watt is equal to the current in amperes multiplied by the voltage. In large electrical systems, the terms kilowatt (one thousand watts) and megawatt (one million watts) are commonly used. Named after James Watt.

Watt, James (1736–1819) A Scottish engineer and inventor. Repairing an early kind of steam engine, he made changes that resulted in a new type of engine (patented 1769) with a separate condensing chamber that made it much more efficient. Watt also was the first to use the term "horsepower."

Watt, James

wave 1. OCEANOGRAPHY. A raised ridge of water that moves across the surface of an ocean or a lake. Waves are caused by the winds, currents or tidal forces, or combinations of these. 2. PHYSICS. A vibrating motion or a rapidly changing electromagnetic field that passes through a medium such as air or water or through space without causing any permanent change in the medium. Sound waves can travel through gases, liquids, or solids. Light, other electromagnetic radiation, and heat can travel through these and through a vacuum. 3. GEOLOGY. Shaking movements of the ground, called seismic waves, are caused by earthquakes or explosions.

wavelength The distance between two successive waves of energy, usually measured from one peak, or crest, to the next peak. The wavelength of radio waves is measured in meters; the wavelength of light is in angstrom units (one meter is equal to 10 billion angstroms).

wax Any of various compounds or mixtures of compounds secreted by certain plants and animals or made from petroleum. Wax is similar to fats: It is a solid at room temperature, has a glossy look, and is insoluble in water. Lanolin (extracted from wool fibers), carnauba wax (extracted from the leaves of a palm tree), and paraffin (extracted from petroleum) are examples of waxes.

weather The constantly changing state of the atmosphere in a particular location with respect to temperature, humidity, clouds, wind speed and direction, precipitation, and barometric pressure. Also, the state of the atmosphere at a particular time.

weathering The processes by which rock and other material at the earth's surface is broken down and decomposed by the actions of rain, running water, oxidation, wind, and other natural mechanical and chemical means. Weathering contributes to the formation of soil from rock and organic materials.

weather map A map or chart showing weather conditions such as temperature, winds, and precipitation over an area at a given time. A daily weather map is often printed in a newspaper or shown on television.

Weather maps used by forecasters to predict the weather include locations of fronts and air masses and the distribution of air pressure and temperature.

weather satellite An artificial Earth satellite used to gather cloud, storm, and other atmospheric information on a worldwide basis in order to improve weather forecasting. The first weather satellite was *Tiros 1,* launched by the United States in 1960.

web 1. The structure of fine silk threads spun by a spider. Webs are used to trap insects and other prey and as nests and shelters. 2. The skin or membrane that joins the toes of ducks, geese, frogs, and certain other water animals to make swimming more efficient.

weed An unwanted plant growing in a garden or on a farm, especially a plant that may crowd out crops or is poisonous to animals.

Wegener, Alfred Lothar (1880–1930) A German geologist, meteorologist, and explorer. He is best known for his theory of continental drift, set forth in his book *The Origin of Continents and Oceans* (1915).

weight 1. The force with which an object attracted to Earth or another massive body by gravity. Technically, the weight of an object is its mass multiplied by the local pull of gravity and is expressed in units of force called newtons. More simply, the weight of an object on Earth is the force by which it is pulled vertically downward toward Earth, using standard weight units of measure such as ounces and pounds or grams and kilograms. 2. A system of standard weight units, or a unit of that system such as an ounce or gram.

weightlessness The sensation of not experiencing the effects of gravity and having no weight. Astronauts feel weightless when in orbit or in outer space, so they anchor themselves down to keep from floating around their ship. Actually, astronauts are still attracted to Earth's gravitational field, but the pull on them is counterbalanced by the centrifugal force on them, their orbiting spacecraft, and other objects in their spacecraft.

well A hole drilled or dug in the ground used to tap fluids such as water, petroleum, or gas from inside the earth.

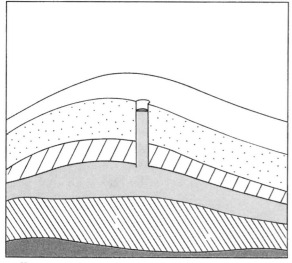

well

wetland An area of land that is often flooded and where the water level stands at or above the surface for at least part of the year.

whale Any of several kinds of large mammals that live in oceans all over the world. Whales have a fishlike shape but are not fish. Whales have tails that are flattened horizontally and moved up and down to propel the whale through the water. Although they can dive for long periods of time, whales have lungs and must surface to breathe. The young develop in the mother's uterus, are born rather than hatched, and live on mother's milk during infancy. Whales vary greatly in size and include the largest animal that has ever lived, the blue whale, up to 100 feet (30 meters) long and weighing 150 tons.

wheel A disk or round frame that turns on a central hub called an axle. Wheels are used to transmit power, move heavy loads, store energy (flywheels), and steer vehicles on land and water. Wheels are used in all kinds of machinery, including clocks and watches, mechanical toys, automobiles, and many other vehicles.

whirlpool A current of whirling water that carries things into its center and then pulls them down. Whirlpools arise in the ocean from the interaction of tides or in rivers or other waters where two currents meet.

whirlwind A whirling current of air caused by an area of low pressure near the ground. Whirlwinds are small windstorms, far less violent than tornadoes. Whirlwinds that pass over dry land are sometimes called dust devils.

white blood cell A colorless blood cell with a nucleus, found in the blood of vertebrates and some other animals. White blood cells are active in defense against body infections and poisons. There are several types of white blood: Phagocytes move like amoebas to engulf and destroy bacteria and other cells at the point of infection. Lymphocytes are involved in immune reactions and produce antibodies against disease. Also called white corpuscle or leucocyte.

white dwarf star A dim, white star near the end of its life cycle. A white dwarf is small but very heavy and dense; a teaspoonful would weigh over a ton.

Whitney, Eli (1765–1825) An American inventor of the cotton gin (1793), a machine that rapidly separated the fiber of cotton from the seed.

Wiener, Norbert (1894–1964) An American mathematician known for his theory of cybernetics (which makes analogies between computers and animal intelligence) and for his contributions to the development of computers and calculators.

wild Describes an animal or plant growing in a natural environment without being domesticated or cultivated. Most animals and plants are wild.

Wilkins, Maurice Hugh Frederick (1916–2004) An Irish biophysicist who shared the 1962 Nobel Prize in physiology and medicine with James Watson and Francis Crick, who together used Wilkins's research to build a model of the DNA molecule. Wilkins made X-ray studies of fibers of DNA, which showed a molecular structure in the shape of a helix.

wilt In plants, to have the leaves droop and wither because of disease or a lack of water.

wind A stream or flow of air moving over Earth's surface. Winds are caused by the unequal heating of Earth's surface by the sun and are affected by Earth's rotation. Warmed by contact with the surface, air expands, becomes lighter, and rises. Cooler air rushes in from surrounding areas to fill the empty space, creating winds. Winds are named according to the direction in which they blow; for example, a wind blowing from the west is a west wind. Winds influence climate by transferring heat from hotter to cooler places and carrying moisture from oceans to land areas.

windchill The combined effect on the human body of air temperature and wind speed. Wind makes a person feel colder than the actual temperature because the wind carries away body heat faster than still air does.

windmill A simple mechanical device that uses wind power to turn vanes, or armlike

windmill

structures, in order to pump water, grind grain, or drive an electric generator. Modern windmills are made of lightweight materials, turn even in light winds, and are used to generate electricity.

windpipe The trachea; the tube that connects the nose and throat to the lungs. Air passes into and out of the body through the windpipe.

wing 1. ZOOLOGY. One of the moveable parts used for flying in a bird, bat, insect, or other animal. Also, a similar part of a bird or insect that does not fly (such as the wing of an ostrich). 2. AERONAUTICS. One of the structures that support an airplane in flight. 3. BOTANY. A stiffened structure on the seeds of some plants that enables them to be blown about by the wind.

winter The coldest season of the year. Winter comes between autumn and spring.

wire Metal that has been drawn into a thread of even thickness. Copper, steel, iron, and aluminum are widely used for wires. Copper and aluminum, are used in electrical wiring, while iron and steel are used in construction. [*Wire* comes from a Latin word meaning "to weave" or "to twist."]

wisdom tooth The third molar in humans on each side of either jaw. Wisdom teeth are so called because they usually appear when a person reaches his late teens or early twenties.

woman An adult female human.

womb The uterus. The female reproductive organ in most mammals, in which the embryo and fetus develop before birth.

wood The hard, fibrous part of the trunk or branches of a tree or shrub located between the bark and the soft inner pith. Wood is made up of cellulose fibers bound together by a substance called lignin.

wood pulp Wood fibers that are chemically and mechanically broken down to be used in paper manufacturing.

wool The animal fiber that forms the fleecy protective coat on sheep and other animals such as goats, camels, and alpacas. Wool is the soft, curly hair of these animals that is spun into thread and used to make cloth. Also, a manufactured fiber such as steel wool or glass wool.

word processor A computerlike machine, or a program used in a computer, for writing. Word processing usually includes the use of a particular program, a keyboard, a computer, a video display, and a printer.

work The transfer of energy that occurs when a force causes a body to move. Work is equal to the force multiplied by the distance through which the body moves in the direction of the force. It is measured in units such as foot-pounds, ergs, or joules. For example, if 10 pounds of force makes an object move 2 feet, 20-foot pounds of work is done.

worm Any one of many kinds of long, thin, soft-bodied, legless invertebrates that live in the soil, in freshwater lakes or ponds, in the oceans, or as parasites in other animals.

Wright, Orville and Wilbur (1871–1948) (1867–1912) American engineers who invented and built the first successful powered heavier-than-air aircraft. The Wright bothers used their Dayton, Ohio, bicycle shop to construct their early aircraft. On December 17, 1903, near Kitty Hawk, North Carolina, they made the first controlled flights in a power-driven airplane.

Wright, Orville and Wilbur

WWW The World Wide Web, often just called the Web. A computer network that consists of interlinked files and Internet sites. The web is connect by hypertext and hyperlinks so that a user can immediately go from one site or file to another by a mouse click or keyboard input.

X and Y chromosomes The two chromosomes that determine sex in humans and many other animals. A fertilized egg that contains two X chromosomes, one from each parent, develops into a female. A fertilized egg that contains an X chromosome from the mother and a Y chromosome from the father develops into a male.

xanthin The yellow coloring matter of flowers.

xenon A heavy, colorless, odorless, tasteless, rare gaseous element, discovered in 1898. Xenon is an inert gas used in electric arc lamps, in photographic flash lamps, and in radiation-detection instruments. Xenon is four times denser than air. It has an atomic number of 54 and an atomic weight of 131.3. Its chemical symbol is Xe. [*Xenon* comes from Greek words meaning "strange" or "foreign."]

xerophyte A plant that loses very little water in transpiration and is adapted to living in dry conditions such as deserts Cactuses are xerophytes. [*Xerophyte* comes from Greek words meaning "dry" and "plant."]

X-ray An invisible, highly penetrating kind of electromagnetic radiation. X-rays were discovered by William Roentgen in 1895. They are artificially produced by bombarding a metal target with high-energy electrons in a highly evacuated glass tube. X-rays occur naturally in stars. They can penetrate body tissue and other substances and make an image on photographic film. X-rays are used in diagnostic medicine to locate breaks in bones and to find and treat diseases. They are also used to study the structure of materials.

X-ray astronomy A branch of astronomy that studies the X-rays coming from space. This can be done only from satellites or space probes, because X-rays are absorbed by the atmosphere and do not strike Earth.

xylem The strong, water-conducting tissue in trees and woody shrubs. Water and dissolved minerals pass upward through the xylem from the root to the leaves. The long fibers in xylem give wood its toughness. Xylem is formed, during the growing season, by the cambium. [*Xylem* comes from a Greek word meaning "wood."]

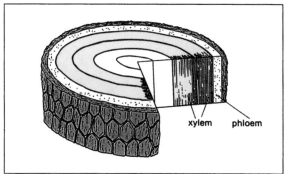

xylem

Y

year 1. A solar year: the time it takes for Earth to make one revolution around the sun. A solar year is 365 days, 5 hours, 48 minutes and 45.5 seconds. 2. The time it takes any planet to make one revolution around the sun. 3. A sidereal year: the time it takes Earth to make one revolution around the sun measured against the background of any particular star in space. A sidereal year is 20 minutes, 23 seconds longer that the solar year.

yeast Any of the microscopic, single-celled fungi that produce alcohol when they decompose sugar. Yeasts are oval cells that reproduce by fission (as do bacteria), by budding (a small bud forms and grows into a new cell), and by means of spores. Some yeasts are used in baking, brewing beer, and in making wine. Brewer's yeast is high in B-complex vitamins and is sometimes used as a dietary supplement.

yellow fever An infectious disease caused by a virus carried by the female aëdes mosquito. Yellow fever causes fever, chills, vomiting, yellow jaundice, and, in severe cases, death. A disease of tropical and subtropical areas, yellow fever was once prevalent in Panama and all over the Caribbean. In 1900, a medical team headed by Walter Reed in Panama proved that mosquitoes transmitted the disease. Mosquito eradication measures were used to control the disease before construction of the Panama Canal could begin. Today, vaccination is also used to control the disease.

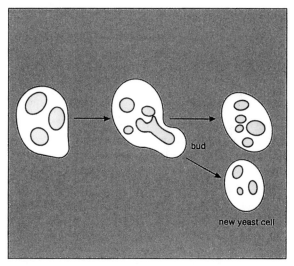

yeast

yolk The yellow substance in a bird or reptile egg. A yolk is rich in fat and protein and provides food for a developing embryo. [*Yolk* comes from an Old English word meaning "yellow."]

217

zenith 1. In astronomy, the point is the sky that is directly overhead. If you stood at the North Pole, the North Star would be almost at the zenith. 2. The point of highest altitude in the sky for a star or other celestial body. [*Zenith* comes from an Arabic word meaning "path" or "way."]

zero 1. The temperature that corresponds to 0 on a thermometer scale. For example, 0°Celsius is equal to the freezing point of pure water at sea level. 2. Absolute zero, or 0° on the Kelvin temperature scale (273.15°C or −459.67°F), the temperature at which, theoretically, all molecular motion ceases. [*Zero* comes from an Arabic word meaning "empty."]

zero gravity In an orbiting spacecraft, a condition in which gravity cannot be felt and objects float about. Also called free-fall.

zero gravity

zinc A shiny, bluish-white, metallic element that is ductile and malleable when heated. Zinc is used in galvanizing iron; in some alloys, such as brass; for the negative plates in electric batteries; in paint; and for roofing and gutters. Zinc in trace amounts is needed for the growth of plants and animals. Zinc has an atomic number of 30 and an atomic weight of 65.37. Its chemical symbol is Zn.

zircon A hard mineral that occurs in various colors. Transparent crystals of zircon are used as gemstones.

zirconium A grayish-white metallic element. Zirconium is a very strong, malleable, ductile, shiny metal that is very resistant to heat and corrosion. It is used in atomic reactors to protect uranium fuel from water that is being heated. Zirconium compounds are also used in furnaces, crucibles, and ceramic glazes. Zirconium has an atomic number of 40 and an atomic weight of 91.22. Its chemical symbol is Zr.

zodiac The pathway of the sun through the sky over the year. The zodiac is divided into 12 parts named after 12 constellations: the bull, twins, crab, lion, virgin, scales, scorpion, archer, goat, water carrier, fishes, and ram. The moon and the planets (except Pluto) pass through the zodiac constellations as they travel around the sun.

zone 1. GEOGRAPHY. One of the five major climate divisions of the earth. These are the Torrid Zone (nearest the equator), the North and South Temperate zones (on either side of the Torrid Zone), and the North and South Frigid zones (at the poles). They are bounded by the Tropics of Capricorn and Cancer and the Arctic and Antarctic circles. 2. BIOLOGY, ECOLOGY. A region or an area, similar to an ecosystem, that has certain kinds of animals and plants and a particular set of environmental conditions; for example, the tidal zone along an ocean shore. [*Zone* comes from a Greek word meaning "a belt."]

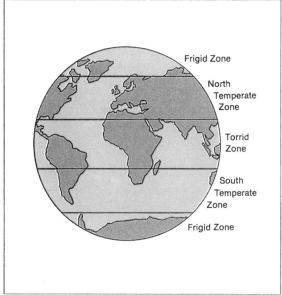

zone

zoo A place where wild animals are kept for scientific research, public viewing and education, and the breeding of endangered species. Modern zoos try to exhibit animals in areas that simulate the animals' natural habitats. Large zoos include those in the Bronx, New York; San Diego; Chicago; Washington D.C.; London; Paris; and Berlin. [*Zoo* comes from a Greek word meaning "an animal" or "a living thing."]

zoogeography The study of the geographical distribution of animals around the world. Also, the relationships between geographical areas and the animals that inhabit them; ecology.

zoology The branch of biology that deals with the scientific study of animal life. Once mostly concerned with the classification of animals into different species, zoology now includes the study of animal behavior, genetics, evolution, ecology, and biochemistry.

zooplankton The tiny animals that float through the waters of the oceans. Zooplankton includes the larval stages of larger sea animals such as crabs and clams, jellyfishes, and coral, as well as protozoa.

zygote The cell formed by the union of mature sperm and ovum, with each of these two bearing half the normal number of chromosomes. The zygote that results has a full number of chromosomes. A fertilized egg is a zygote. The zygote eventually develops into a mature individual. [*Zygote* comes from a Greek word meaning "to join things together."]

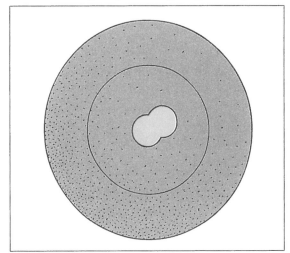

zygote

Charts and Tables

Classification of Living Things

Kingdom	Phylum	Class
Monerans	Bacteria	
	Blue–green algae	
Protists	Amoebas	
	Diatoms	
	Euglenas	
Fungi	Slime molds	
	True fungi	
Plants	Green algae	
	Red algae	
	Brown algae	
	Mosses and Liverworts	
	Club mosses	
	Horsetails	
	Ferns	
	Conifers	
	Flowering plants	Monocotyledons; Dicotyledons
Animals	Cnidarians	Corals; Jellyfish; Sea anemones; Hydras
	Sponges	
	Bryozoans	
	Flatworms	Free-living flatworms; Flukes; Tapeworms
	Nematode worms	
	Annelid worms	Earthworms and bloodworms; Leeches; Lungworms and other marine worms
	Arthropods	Millipedes; Centipedes; Insects; Arachnids; Crustaceans
	Mollusks	Chitons; Snails; Clams and scallops; Tooth shells; Octopuses, squids and cuttlefish
	Echinoderms	Sea stars; Sea urchins; Brittle stars; Sea cucumbers; Sea lilies and feather stars
	Chordates	Jawless fish; Cartilaginous fish (sharks and rays); Bony fish; Amphibians; Reptiles; Birds; Mammals

Complete Classification of White Clover

Species • Trifoleum repens
White clover

Genus • Trifoleum
All clovers

Family • Legumes
Peas   Clovers   Beans

Order • Rosales
Roses   Peas   Clovers   Beans   Apples etc.

Class • Dicotyledons
All plants with two seed leaves

Phylum • All Flowering Plants

Kingdom • All Plants

Complete Classification of Modern Humans

Species • Homo sapiens
Modern humans

Genus • Homo
Neanderthals   Modern humans

Family • Hominids
Peking Man   Modern humans   Neanderthals

Order • Primates
Monkeys   Lemurs   Modern humans   Neanderthals   Peking Man

Class • All Mammals

Phylum • Chordates
All animals with notochords or backbones

Kingdom • All Animals

The Nine Planets

Planet	Mercury	Venus	Earth	Mars
Average distance from sun, in millions of miles (km)	36 (58)	67 (108)	93 (150)	141 (228)
Revolution, in Earth days or Earth years	87.97 days	224.7 days	365.26 days	686.98 days
Rotation, in Earth days or Earth hours	58 days, 15 hrs., 30 min.	243 days, 14 min.	23 hrs., 56 min., 4 sec.	24 hrs., 37 min.
Orbital velocity, in miles per second (km/s)	27.9 (47.9)	21.8 (35)	18.5 (29.8)	15 (24.1)
Diameter at equator, in miles (km)	3,033 (4,883)	7,503 (12,080)	7,927 (12,762)	4,221 (6,796)
Mass (Earth = 1)	0.056	0.82	1	0.107
Volume (Earth = 1)	0.056	0.86	1	0.15
Density (water = 1)	5.4	5.25	5.52	3.9
Surface temperature °F (°C)	−356 to +800 (−180 to +430)	+896 (+480)	−158 to +133 (−70 to +55)	−248 to +77 (−120 to +25)
Atmosphere (main gases)	almost none	carbon dioxide	nitrogen, oxygen	carbon dioxide
Surface gravity (Earth = 1)	0.38	0.91	1	0.38
Number of known satellites (moons)	0	0	1	2
Number of rings	0	0	0	0

Jupiter	Saturn	Uranus	Neptune	Pluto
483 (778)	887 (1,428)	1,783 (2,871)	2,794 (4,498)	3,666 (5,902)
11.86 years	29.46 years	84.01 years	164.8 years	248.5 years
9 hrs., 55 min.	10 hrs., 39 min.	17 hrs., 14 min.	16 hrs., 7 min.	6.375 days
8.1 (13.1)	6 (9.6)	4.2 (6.8)	3.4 (5.4)	2.9 (4.7)
88,734 (142,861)	74,977 (120,712)	31,763 (51,138)	30,540 (49,169)	1,430 (2,302)
318	95	14.5	17	0.002
1,319	744	67	57	0.01
1.3	0.69	1.18	1.64	<1
−238 (−150)	−292 (−180)	−353 (−214)	−364 (−220)	−382 (−230)
hydrogen, helium	hydrogen, helium	helium, hydrogen, methane	hydrogen, helium, methane	methane (?)
2.64	1.13	1.17	1.19	.08 (?)
16	21	15	8	1
1	1,000(?)	13(?)	2	0

The Solar System

Stars Visible from the U.S.

(in order of apparent brightness)

Common Name	Constellation in Which Star Can Be Found	Color	Month When Visible on the Meridian at 9:00 P.M.
Sirius	Canis Major	bluish	February
Vega	Lyra	blue-white	August
Capella	Auriga	yellow	January
Arcturus	Boötes	orange-yellow	June
Rigel	Orion	blue-white	January
Procyon	Canis Minor	yellow-white	March
Altair	Aquila	yellow-white	September
Betelgeuse	Orion	reddish	February
Aldebaran	Taurus	orange	January
Pollux	Gemini	yellow	March
Spica	Virgo	bluish	May
Antares	Scorpius	reddish	July
Fomalhaut	Southern Fish	white	October
Deneb	Cygnus	white	September
Regulus	Leo	blue-white	April
Castor	Gemini	green-white	February
Polaris	Ursa Minor	yellowish	visible all year
Mizar	Ursa Major	green-white	visible all year

Constellations: The Northern Sky

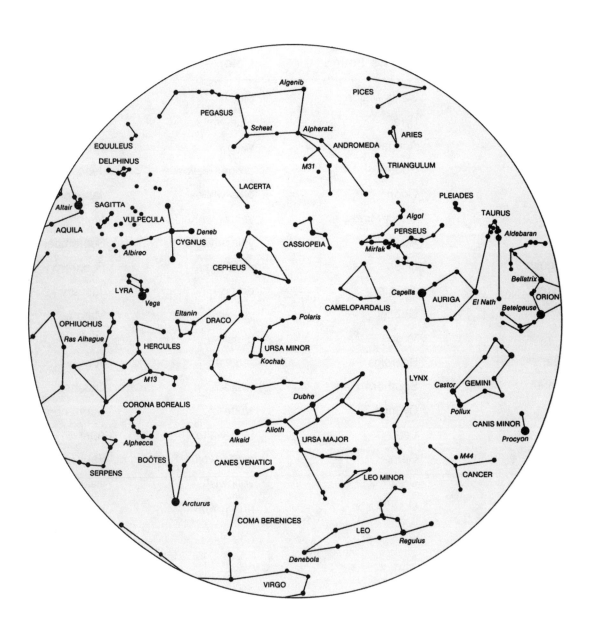

Common Weights and Measures

U.S. Unit	Equivalent
Length	*Length*
1 foot	12 inches
1 yard	3 feet
1 mile	1,760 yards
Area	*Area*
1 square foot	144 square inches
1 square yard	9 square feet
1 acre	4,840 square yards
1 square mile	640 acres
Volume	*Volume*
1 pint	16 fluid ounces
1 quart	2 pints
1 gallon	4 quarts
Mass	*Mass*
1 pound	16 ounces
1 ton	2,000 pounds

Metric Unit	Equivalent
Length	*Length*
1 centimeter	10 millimeters
1 meter	100 centimeters
1 kilometer	1,000 meters
Area	*Area*
1 square centimeter	100 square millimeters
1 square meter	10,000 square centimeters
1 hectare	1,000 square meters
1 square kilometer	1 million square meters
Volume	*Volume*
1 cubic centimeter	1 milliliter
1 liter	1,000 milliliters
1 cubic meter	1,000 liters
Mass	*Mass*
1 kilogram	1,000 grams
1 tonne	1,000 kilograms

Converting Units

(approximate)

To Convert U.S. Units	Into Metric Units	Multiply By
Length	*Length*	
inches	centimeters	2.54
feet	meters	0.30
miles	kilometers	1.61
Area	*Area*	
square inches	square centimeters	6.45
square feet	square meters	0.09
acres	hectares	0.40
square miles	square kilometers	2.59
Volume	*Volume*	
cubic inches	cubic centimeters	16.39
pints	liters	0.57
gallons	liters	4.55
Mass	*Mass*	
ounces	grams	28.35
pounds	kilograms	0.45
tons	tonnes	.907

To Convert Metric Units	Into U.S. Units	Multiply By
Length	*Length*	
centimeters	inches	0.39
meters	feet	3.28
kilometers	miles	0.62
Area	*Area*	
square centimeters	square inches	0.16
square meters	square feet	10.76
hectares	acres	2.47
square kilometers	square miles	0.39
Volume	*Volume*	
cubic centimeters	cubic inches	0.061
liters	pints	1.76
liters	gallons	0.22
Mass	*Mass*	
grams	ounces	0.04
kilograms	pounds	2.20
tonnes	tons	1.102

Symbols for Scientific Terms

Symbol	Meaning
α	alpha particle
β; β^-	beta particle
$\beta+$	positron
γ	gamma radiation
Δ	a small change; heat
λ	wavelength; radioactive-decay constant
μ	micron; micro-
μc	microcurie
ν	frequency; neutrino
π	pi (3.14159); osmotic pressure
Σ	the sum of
σ	nuclear cross section (barns); area
Ω	electrical resistance (ohms)
ω	angular speed; angular velocity
♂	male
♀	female
$>$	is greater than
$<$	is less than
$\propto$	is proportional to
∞	infinity
$\sqrt{}$	square root of
⬡	ring of six carbon atoms
°	degrees; temperature; angle measurement (e.g., 30°)
[]	molar concentration
$+$	positive electric charge; mixed with
$-$	negative electric charge; single covalent bond
$=$	equals; double covalent bond; produces
$\equiv$	triple covalent bond
$\rightarrow$	produces; forms; chemical reaction
$\rightleftarrows$	reversible chemical reaction
$\uparrow$	gas produced by a chemical reaction
$\downarrow$	precipitate produced by a chemical reaction
✿	radioactive substance (follows symbol of element; e.g., Cl✿)

Common Physics Equations

$$\text{Average speed} = \frac{\text{distance moved}}{\text{time taken}}$$

$$\text{Force} = \text{mass} \times \text{acceleration}$$

$$\text{Acceleration} = \frac{\text{change in velocity}}{\text{time taken for this change}}$$

$$\text{Momentum} = \text{mass} \times \text{velocity}$$

$$\text{Impulse} = \text{force} \times \text{time}$$

$$\text{Work done} = \text{force} \times \text{distance moved in the direction of the force}$$

$$\text{Average power} = \frac{\text{work done}}{\text{time taken}} \quad \text{or} \quad \frac{\text{energy change}}{\text{time taken}}$$

$$\text{Efficiency} = \frac{\text{work output}}{\text{work input}} \times 100\%$$

$$\text{Pressure} = \frac{\text{force}}{\text{area}}$$

$$\text{Density} = \frac{\text{mass}}{\text{volume}}$$

Weather Map Symbols

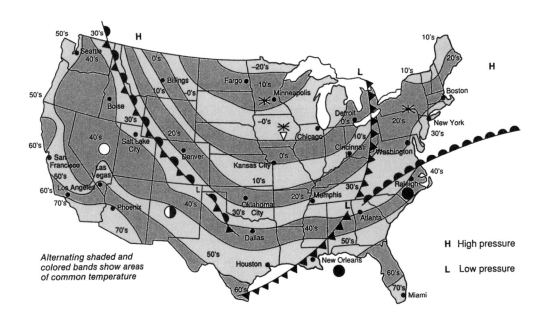

Alternating shaded and
colored bands show areas
of common temperature

H High pressure

L Low pressure

KEY			WIND SCALE			
			Symbol	Miles per hour (km)	Description	Beaufort scale
▲▲▲	cold front	◗ drizzle	○	0	calm	0
●●●	warm front	● rain		1–3 (1–5)	light air	1
▲▼▲	stationary front	✳ snow		4–7 (6–11)	light breeze	2
▲▲▲	occluded front	▽̇ rain shower		8–12 (12–19)	gentle breeze	3
○	clear	✳̽ snow shower		13–18 (20–28)	moderate breeze	4
◗	partly cloudy	△̽ hail shower		19–24 (29–38)	fresh breeze	5
●	cloudy	⟆ thunderstorm		25–31 (39–49)	strong breeze	6
═	mist			32–38 (50–61)	moderate gale	7
═	fog	◗ hurricane		39–46 (62–74)	fresh gale	8
				47–54 (75–88)	strong gale	9
		direction of wind ○⎯ east wind		55–63 (89–102)	whole gale	10
		⎯○ west wind		64–73 (103–117)	storm	11
				74–above (118–above)	hurricane	12–17

Layers of the Earth

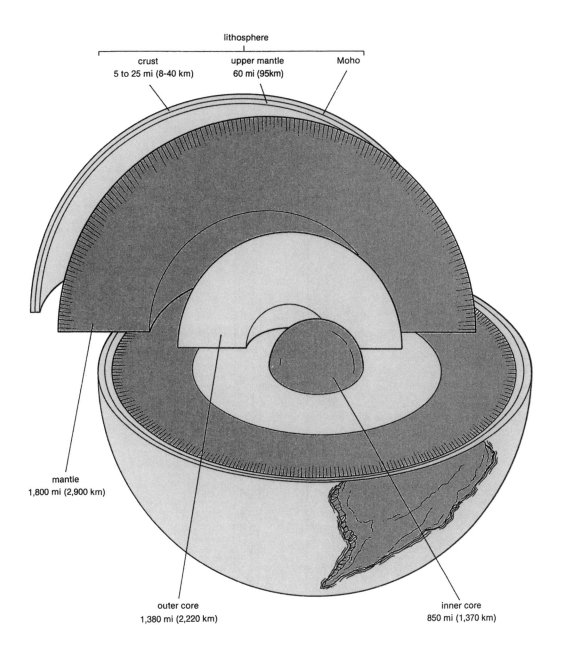

lithosphere

crust
5 to 25 mi (8-40 km)

upper mantle
60 mi (95km)

Moho

mantle
1,800 mi (2,900 km)

outer core
1,380 mi (2,220 km)

inner core
850 mi (1,370 km)

Layers of the Earth's Atmosphere

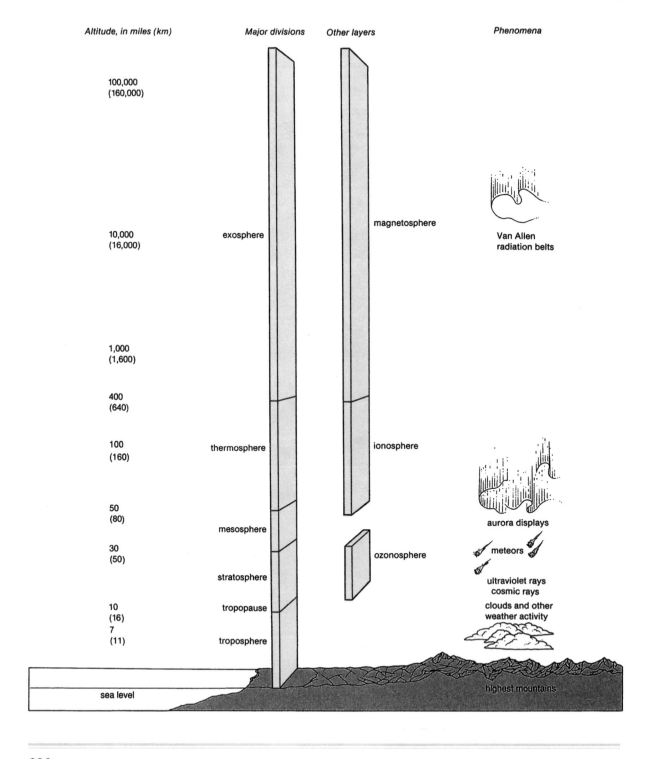

Altitude, in miles (km)	Major divisions	Other layers	Phenomena
100,000 (160,000)			
10,000 (16,000)	exosphere	magnetosphere	Van Allen radiation belts
1,000 (1,600)			
400 (640)			
100 (160)	thermosphere	ionosphere	
50 (80)			aurora displays
	mesosphere		
30 (50)		ozonosphere	meteors
	stratosphere		ultraviolet rays cosmic rays
10 (16)	tropopause		clouds and other weather activity
7 (11)	troposphere		
sea level			highest mountains

Geological Time Scale

ERA	DURATION (In millions of years)	PERIOD	EPOCH	DURATION (In millions of years)	TIME AT WHICH INTERVAL BEGAN (In millions of years ago)	DOMINANT LIFE FORMS, AS REVEALED IN FOSSIL RECORDS
CENOZOIC	65	Quaternary	Holocene (or Recent)	.01	.01	First humans
			Pleistocene	2.5	2.5	
		Tertiary	Pliocene	4.5	7	Mammals Flowering plants
			Miocene	19	26	
			Oligocene	12	38	
			Eocene	16	54	
			Paleocene	11	65	
MESOZOIC	160	Cretaceous		70	135	Last dinosaurs / First flowering plants
		Jurassic		55	190	First birds / Reptiles / Conifers
		Triassic		35	225	First dinosaurs / First mammals / Wide extinctions
PALEOZOIC	309	Permian		55	280	Mammal-like reptiles
		Carboniferous — Pennsylvanian		35	315	First reptiles
		Carboniferous — Mississippian		20	345	Amphibians, Ferns / First seed plants
		Devonian		55	400	First amphibians / Air-breathing fishes
		Silurian		40	440	First jawed fishes / First vascular plants / First land-dwelling invertebrates
		Ordovician		80	520	Jawless fishes
		Cambrian		24	544	First vertebrates / Invertebrates widely established / Appearance of numerous invertebrate fossils
PRECAMBRIAN				3,456	4,000	Fossils rare / Algae

The Periodic Table

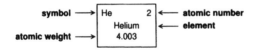

symbol →	He 2	← atomic number
	Helium	← element
atomic weight →	4.003	

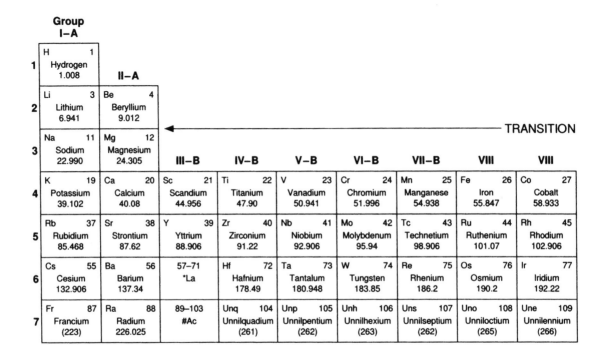

Group
I–A

	I–A	II–A	III–B	IV–B	V–B	VI–B	VII–B	VIII	VIII
1	H 1 Hydrogen 1.008								
2	Li 3 Lithium 6.941	Be 4 Beryllium 9.012							
3	Na 11 Sodium 22.990	Mg 12 Magnesium 24.305							
4	K 19 Potassium 39.102	Ca 20 Calcium 40.08	Sc 21 Scandium 44.956	Ti 22 Titanium 47.90	V 23 Vanadium 50.941	Cr 24 Chromium 51.996	Mn 25 Manganese 54.938	Fe 26 Iron 55.847	Co 27 Cobalt 58.933
5	Rb 37 Rubidium 85.468	Sr 38 Strontium 87.62	Y 39 Yttrium 88.906	Zr 40 Zirconium 91.22	Nb 41 Niobium 92.906	Mo 42 Molybdenum 95.94	Tc 43 Technetium 98.906	Ru 44 Ruthenium 101.07	Rh 45 Rhodium 102.906
6	Cs 55 Cesium 132.906	Ba 56 Barium 137.34	57–71 *La	Hf 72 Hafnium 178.49	Ta 73 Tantalum 180.948	W 74 Tungsten 183.85	Re 75 Rhenium 186.2	Os 76 Osmium 190.2	Ir 77 Iridium 192.22
7	Fr 87 Francium (223)	Ra 88 Radium 226.025	89–103 #Ac	Unq 104 Unnilquadium (261)	Unp 105 Unnilpentium (262)	Unh 106 Unnilhexium (263)	Uns 107 Unnilseptium (262)	Uno 108 Unniloctium (265)	Une 109 Unnilennium (266)

TRANSITION →

Rare Earth Elements

} * Lanthanides

} # Actinides

La 57 Lanthanum 138.905	Ce 58 Cerium 140.12	Pr 59 Praseodymium 140.908	Nd 60 Neodymium 144.24	Pm 61 Promethium 147	Sm 62 Samarium 150.4
Ac 89 Actinium (227)	Th 90 Thorium 232.038	Pa 91 Protactinium 231.036	U 92 Uranium 238.029	Np 93 Neptunium 237.048	Pu 94 Plutonium (244)

Groups in columns under Roman numerals indicate
elements with similar properties.
Periods in rows opposite Arabic numerals indicate
elements with similar structures.

ELEMENTS ─────────────►

			III–A	IV–A	V–A	VI–A	VII–A	0
								He 2 Helium 4.003
			B 5 Boron 10.81	C 6 Carbon 12.011	N 7 Nitrogen 14.007	O 8 Oxygen 16.0	F 9 Fluorine 18.998	Ne 10 Neon 20.179
VII	I–B	II–B	Al 13 Aluminum 26.982	Si 14 Silicon 28.086	P 15 Phosphorus 30.974	S 16 Sulfur 32.06	Cl 17 Chlorine 35.453	Ar 18 Argon 39.948
Ni 28 Nickel 58.71	Cu 29 Copper 63.546	Zn 30 Zinc 65.37	Ga 31 Gallium 69.72	Ge 32 Germanium 72.59	As 33 Arsenic 74.922	Se 34 Selenium 78.96	Br 35 Bromine 79.904	Kr 36 Krypton 83.80
Pd 46 Palladium 106.4	Ag 47 Silver 107.868	Cd 48 Cadmium 112.40	In 49 Indium 114.82	Sn 50 Tin 118.69	Sb 51 Antimony 121.75	Te 52 Tellurium 127.60	I 53 Iodine 126.905	Xe 54 Xenon 131.30
Pt 78 Platinum 195.09	Au 79 Gold 196.967	Hg 80 Mercury 200.59	Tl 81 Thallium 204.37	Pb 82 Lead 207.2	Bi 83 Bismuth 208.981	Po 84 Polonium (210)	At 85 Astatine (210)	Rn 86 Radon (222)

Eu 63 Europium 151.96	Gd 64 Gadolinium 157.25	Tb 65 Terbium 158.925	Dy 66 Dysprosium 162.50	Ho 67 Holmium 164.930	Er 68 Erbium 167.26	Tm 69 Thulium 168.934	Yb 70 Ytterbium 173.04	Lu 71 Lutetium 174.97
Am 95 Americium (243)	Cm 96 Curium (247)	Bk 97 Berkelium (247)	Cf 98 Californium (251)	Es 99 Einsteinium (254)	Fm 100 Fermium (257)	Md 101 Mendelevium (258)	No 102 Nobelium (255)	Lr 103 Lawrencium (257)

A number in parentheses is the atomic weight of the most stable isotope.

Scientific Prefixes and Suffixes

Prefix	Meaning	Example
aero–	air	aerodynamics
an-	absence of, without	anaerobic
ante-	before	anterior
anthropo-	man	anthropology
anti-	against	antibody
astro-	star	astronomy
audio-	hear	audiometer
bi-	two	binary system
bio-	life	biology
calori-	heat	calorimeter
cardio-	heart	cardiograph
chrom-	color	chromatography
cycl-	circle	cyclotron
denti-	tooth	dentine
dextr-	right	dextrose
di-	two	dicotyledon
dyna-	force, power	dynamo
epi-	upon, over	epicenter
equi-	equal	equilibrium
ex-	out of, away from	exhale
gastro-	stomach	gastrointestinal
geo-	earth	geomagnetism
gyro-	turn	gyroscope
halo-	salt	halogen
helio-	sun	heliocentric
hemo-	blood	hemoglobin
hydro-	water	hydrosphere
hyper-	above, excessive	hyperon
hypo-	under	hypothalamus
infra-	below, beneath	infrared
inter-	between	intergalactic
iso-	equal, same	isotope
kin-	motion, moving	kinetic
macro-	large, great	macromolecule

Prefix	Meaning	Example
meso-	middle, intermediate	Mesozoic
meta-	after, beyond	metamorphosis
micro-	small, one millionth	microscope
mono-	one	monocotyledon
multi-	many	multicellular
neuro-	nerve	neuron
ovi-	egg	oviparous
paleo-	old, ancient	paleontology
para-	beside, almost	parasite
per-	intensified, increased	perennial
peri-	around	periscope
petro-	rock	petroleum
photo-	light	photosynthesis
pneuma-	air, lung	pneumatic
poly-	many	polymer
proto-	first, original	protozoan
pyr-	fire	pyrite
radio	radiant energy, radium	radioactivity
semi-	half, imperfectly	semiconductor
sol-	sun	solar
strati-	layer	stratify
strato-	horizontal	stratosphere
sub-	under, below	submarine
super-	above, beyond	supernova
sym-	with, together	symmetry
syn-	with, together	synthetic
tele-	distant, far off	telescope
therm-	heat	thermodynamics
trans-	across, through	transmission
tri-	three	trilobite
ultra-	more than, excessive	ultrasonic
uni-	one	unicellular
zoo-	animal	zooplankton

Suffix	Meaning	Example
-cardium	heart	pericardium
-chrome	color	monochrome
-cide	kill	insecticide
-cision	cut	incision
-coccus	spherical cell	streptococcus
-cyte	cell	leucocyte
-derm	skin	blastoderm
-duct	guide, tube	viaduct
-gen	produced	hydrogen
-graph	drawn, recorded	seismograph
-ic	of, pertaining to	organic
-ide	chemical compound	oxide
-itis	inflammatory disease	tonsilitis
-ium	element, group	radium
-lith	stone	laccolith
-logist	specialist	biologist
-logy	study of	geology
-lysis	loosen	electrolysis
-mer	part	polymer
-meter	measure	thermometer
-morph	form	metamorphic
-oid	resembling	asteroid
-ose	denoting a sugar	glucose
-ped	foot	quadruped
-phore	bearer, carrier	chromatophore
-phyte	possessed by a plant	saprophyte
-plasm	growth material	protoplasm
-pod	foot	arthropod
-saur	lizard	ichthyosaur
-scope	examine, see	microscope
-septic	infection	antiseptic
-sphere	round	lithosphere
-stat	stationary	thermostat
-therapy	treatment	chemotherapy
-tomy	cut	anatomy
-zyme	ferment	enzyme